INTERDISCIPLINARY PLANNING

Interdisciplinary Planning

*A Perspective
for the Future*

Edited by
Milan J. Dluhy and Kan Chen

Published in the United States of America
by the Center for Urban Policy Research
Building 4051—Kilmer Campus
New Brunswick, New Jersey 08903

Library of Congress Cataloging-in-Publication Data

Interdisciplinary planning.

  Bibliography: p. 199
  Includes index.
  1. Planning.   I. Dluhy, Milan J., 1942–
II. Chen, Kan, 1928–
HD87.5.I58   1986   361.6   86–6854
ISBN 0–88285–116–0

Contents

Part IV. Interdisciplinary Planning

Appendices

Foreword

There is much rhetoric in universities about the need for interdisciplinary approaches to planning but few instances where these have succeeded over time. Of course, this is not a unique failure of planning programs because universities have considerable difficulty in implementing interdisciplinary programs of any kind. Therefore, it should be observed that the Urban, Technological, and Environmental Planning (UTEP) program which has produced this book, and its predecessor, the Urban and Regional Planning program, have been notable exceptions to this general rule. They have attracted their share of excellent faculty members and students in a variety of fields, and have been productive of interesting ideas and research over a period of at least 15 years.

The reasons for the continued success of this program are worth considering, not just for the sake of planners but because other developing disciplines may benefit from this experience. Forces outside the program as well as those inside must converge to assure that an interdisciplinary program is established in the first place and that it remains viable thereafter. Clearly, there must be a core of excellent faculty members who perceive the need for a new alliance among fields and they must persuade administrators at appropriate levels to endorse the idea. This was accomplished by the originators of this program who found hospitality to an experiment among their colleagues and others.

Once this was accomplished, the major reason for its success has been a clear view of the intellectual terrain it should encompass and the vision to keep abreast of necessary changes as the program matured. Although the faculty has been responsible for this attitude, they have benefited by strong leadership to maintain a coherent program of high quality. These needs are greater in interdisciplinary programs than in departments because of the vulnerability of any extra-departmental group within a university. Such dependence stems from the usual lack of appointive power for tenure-tract faculty members and for promotions. Therefore, if an interdisciplinary program is to succeed, some means of ameliorating this vulnerability is essential if the best faculty are to be attracted to it. Indeed, participation by high-quality faculty members is the best guarantee of continued departmental interest and support.

The UTEP Program has indeed succeeded in attracting the best faculty as it has evolved and changed. In addition, it has increased its self-sufficiency through its own grants and gifts efforts, which have improved its visibility nationally as well. Rigorous periodic scrutiny has assured the maintenance of high quality and standards for the program.

This book is an important piece of evidence to corroborate my positive view of this program. This is so not only because of the central place occupied by the publication of research in a university like ours, but because it is further proof of the productive synergism that must exist if an interdisciplinary program is to work. Therefore, I am pleased to introduce this volume and to recognize a program that works well.

Alfred S. Sussman
Dean, Rackham School of Graduate Studies
University of Michigan

Preface

In 1982, the Ph.D. program in Urban, Technological, and Environmental Planning (UTEP) at the University of Michigan was restructured. As the final chapter in this volume indicates, the program was organized around an interdisciplinary theme with faculty participation from nine different schools and colleges within the University—Architecture and Urban Planning, Business Administration, Education, Engineering, Medicine, Natural Resources, Public Health, Social Work, and the College of Literature, Science, and the Arts, which contains the traditional disciplines. The challenge within the UTEP program for the past three years has been to continue to question the intellectual rationale for this interdisciplinary Ph.D. program, while also moving ahead with a tentative structure which emphasizes academic rigor and a balanced educational experience. In 1984, Kan Chen, the current director of the program, and Milan Dluhy, a faculty associate in the program, decided to solicit working papers from faculty and former graduates of the program that illustrated the kinds of issues and concerns that were present within the field of interdisciplinary planning. On January 12, 1985 all the authors who contributed chapters now included in this volume, plus Professors Allan Feldt, Ron Inglehart, Mitch Rycus, James Snyder, and Kate Warner, met for a daylong conference to discuss these emerging planning issues and concerns. This informal conference was taped and all the participants were asked to respond to a set of questions generated at the conference within a week. The Introduction to this book includes some of these more formal responses. The goal of the conference was therefore to move beyond the working papers and identify key issues and concerns that cut across the various disciplines represented at the conference. All found the conference intellectually stimulating and urged that future events of this kind be held.

This edited book tries to incorporate the thinking of various faculty and former graduates of the program about the planning enterprise. As the Introduction points out, there are "common threads" in planning regardless of background and training. What emerges in this volume is an interdisciplinary perspective on planning for the future.

Milan J. Dluhy and Kan Chen
Ann Arbor, Michigan
Summer, 1985

Acknowledgments

Several people have supported our efforts in producing this book. Without them, we would not have been able to collectively produce our ideas so efficiently and quickly. Ms. Jan Fisk was instrumental in making sure we had faithful copy and reproductions. Mr. Robert Vernon coordinated all publishing activities and, as our thoughts and ideas evolved, carefully incorporated them into his work for us on the appendices. Both of these people have made our efforts much easier.

In the end, Alfred Sussman provided both the intellectual and moral support to allow us to see that interdisciplinary planning continues to have a role to play in graduate education. We thank him for reminding us that we all have something to share with the larger community.

Introduction: Planning Perspectives

Milan J. Dluhy

Critiques of traditional urban planning abound (Bolan, 1980; Checkoway, 1983; Forester, 1980; Klosterman, 1981; and Krueckeberg, 1984). And as Warner said at the conference, "In the field of urban planning there are few heroes, people with fuzzy skills, and an uncertain mission." The debate about direction within the urban planning profession as well as why urban planning seems to be in a state of atrophy was of minimal interest to the members of the conference. It was agreed early in the conference that the more critical issue to discuss was the future direction of planning, particularly interdisciplinary planning. The narrow focus on urban planning was dropped and planning was viewed, as Mathes suggested, "as a societal problem solving process which is process-oriented, not subject or topic oriented," for the duration of the conference. A review of the conference proceedings revealed that five major areas of concern were discussed at length. Amazingly, among such a diverse group of participants (see "Preface"), there was considerable support for the five propositions (below) based on these principal areas of concern.

1. *Planning is action research.* It is research to provide knowledge for meaningful intervention. Planners then focus on facilitating the provision of information to decision makers.

2. *Planning is knowledge driven.* Planners are constantly seeking to keep up with the changes in information technology. As computer-based information technology expands, planners will be capable of providing more sophisticated information than ever before.

3. *Planning is both process and technique oriented.* Planners pay attention to the realities of the problem-solving process while also utilizing the most effective analytical techniques available.

4. *Planning is interdisciplinary.* A single discipline is unable to pro-

vide sufficient insight into complex planning problems. Only interdisciplinary perspectives can provide both the theoretical and practical insights into real planning problems.

5. *Planning is adaptive to emerging concerns.* While public sector planning is downsizing and refocusing, private sector planning is expanding and innovating. Also, planning in third world countries, planning in high-technology fields, and planning in the non-profit sector have all received renewed attention. The theme is that planning skills and perspectives are capable of responding to a broad and ever-changing set of circumstances.

As Hemmens (1980) points out, the planning literature emphasizes that planning is still both a technical as well as a moral activity. Herein lies a dilemma. Can planners be both advocates for a particular solution or concern as well as technicians providing knowledge in a value-free way? This dilemma of role conflict is discussed in Chapter 1 by Rothman and Hugento-bler. Reviewing the literature and empirical studies on planning roles and attitudes, the authors conclude that planners, for the most part, seem committed to symbols and expressions of both advocacy as well as traditional planning doctrine which emphasizes rational planning and neutral policy roles for practitioners. Without a guiding theory to give a unified approach to practice, planners remain free to select the role most compatible with their personal background and training. The broader question raised in this chapter is the reason for the continued fragmentation and theoretical diversity within the field. This volume asserts that diversity need not be a drawback as long as careful analysis and open planning processes are used.

While Part I illustrates many of the critical dilemmas in planning, Part II focuses on planning skills and orientations. Kochen and Barr point out that within the constraints of rational planning, knowledge-intensive planning will continue to flourish. Concepts from artificial intelligence and the widespread use of computers to support planning will make it essential for planners to keep up with the new information technology. Bulkley persuasively argues that planners need powerful analytic techniques in order to inform decision makers about alternatives and the consequences of their choices. Drawing from the water resources area, he describes a rational planning process that can be used to both minimize the risk of damage to a water system as well as keep the costs of constructing safeguards for this system down. The larger point is that both process and technique are central to successful planning. Bitondo stresses process even more than Bulkley. Using technology planning in industry, he shows why it is critical for scientists and engineers to be involved in every step of the planning process in industry. Bitondo further argues that successful technological planning means that planners are more than just technical advisors—they are equal partners with top management. Finally, Chen and Mathes stress the importance of communication in planning. The assumption these authors make is that many public policy issues are inherently conflictual and therefore planners can facilitate decision making by helping decision makers to clarify problems, issues, and choices. Using the procedure VOSDA (Value Oriented Social Decision Analysis) as an aid to achieving optimum social decisions, these authors illustrate the kind of role a good planner can play. They can enhance the quality of information, they can educate parties as to value differences, and finally, they can point out the relevant trade-offs between choices.

Part III focuses more sharply on planning roles. Hart points out that traditional decision tools and techniques (i.e., operations research, quantitative modeling, and formal planning) don't always work. Unless the planner can transcend the exclusive use of analysis and adapt to the larger social processes in which planning takes place, the planner can become the isolated technician having little practical impact. Hart carefully cautions us, however, to think of planning as being informed by analysis but not totally dependent on it. Dluhy, using the public budgeting process as an example, shows why quantitative and analytical skills are not enough to guarantee an impact on decision making. He argues for more communication skills, but mainly his argument is that adroit planners should gain more knowledge and skills on the socio-political context of planning environments. Checkoway reinforces this last point and illustrates why planners must go beyond rational models and apply socio-political methods to build support for planning at the community level. In total, the chapters in this section stress that effective planners need to think both analytically and politically. While others (for example, Baum, 1983 and Bolan, 1983) have made this point, these chapters illustrate through examples the consequences of not adopting this "hybrid" planning role.

The final section, Part IV, raises perhaps the most fundamental question in this volume: Can interdisciplinary planning offer a more useful perspective than others on how to achieve more successful planning outcomes? Jarboe, drawing upon industrial policy in this country, argues for a structural approach to planning that takes a system-wide view and accepts multiple goals and complex decision environments. His approach is truly interdisciplinary, and he suggests that system wide intervention that is goal driven rather than problem driven is what constitutes effective planning. Chen shows through example the importance of considering human resources in technology planning. Without taking into account the human element, scientists, engineers, and top management may overlook serious obstacles to the implementation of their proposals. Only an interdisciplinary perspective in the case of the auto industry allowed automation to proceed without serious setbacks. Finally, Chen, in the concluding chapter, articulates the rationale and design for the interdisciplinary Ph.D. program at the University of Michigan. In the end, planners need better technical skills than ever before, but they also need to become better problem solvers so they can connect effectively with decision makers and decision-making bodies. And somewhere along the line, they need to recast or gain a value orientation from which to practice. As Mathes so clearly pointed out at our January 1985 conference, planners must also be process oriented because:

> A process oriented planner will explore rather than assume a problem, define rather than accept a problem, engage rather than respond to the various interested parties, expand rather than narrow the context of the problem and therefore the ranges of possible actions and solutions. The process oriented planner allows the societal context to be open ended rather than circumscribe it in terms of a particular discipline, subject area, or accepted category of social problems.

While historically planning has been clustered with history and the social sciences, the perspective of this volume is that law, business, engineering, and the professions are just as relevant to planning. What is of central importance is that planning education should respond to the changing demands of society. The planner of today and perhaps tomorrow needs to respond to these challenges. At our conference, Kochen succinctly identified some of these challenges.

> *Providing security.* This includes physical, economic, psychological, and other aspects of security. Individuals, social groups, firms, cities, nation-states and other forms of community need both to be and to feel secure. Technological fixes by themselves are no more adequate than insurance. We need to explicate the "security" concept and investigate in greater depth what it takes to provide security, and how to plan in practical ways to attain reasonable goals in that direction.
>
> *Strategic management of aids for self-servicing.* We are likely to shift from being a service society to a self-servicing society, with new forms of productive activity to support that.
>
> *Selected new technologies,* such as computers-communications, biotechnology, flexible manufacturing, etc. are "high" in the sense that they bring about a major modification in the nature of the tasks they are called on to help us cope with, in that they change the very meaning of what a problem is, and in that they require knowledge-intensive skills and amplify higher mental functions. Such technologies often develop according to a momentum of their own; they must be managed and planned.

To cope with crises, advance planning is necessary. Increasingly, crises tend to occur in multiples. The greatest challenge to coping with crises occurs when several of these occur simultaneously, straining our coping capacities beyond their limits. Such situations require new forms of flexible planning, with considerable recommittable resources.

The problems people need to cope with are becoming more complex. Two examples are how to deal with information overload and time management. We need to plan ways to help such people increase their coping power.

This volume provides a perspective on these planning challenges. While each chapter stands alone and is worth reading, the central message is that dilemmas do exist, and probably always will, but a clear understanding of planning at a minimum means the acquisition of analytic and technical skills, knowledge of planning practice, a balanced role orientation, and an interdisciplinary perspective. As Forester (1980) suggests, the practice of planning is enhanced by combining pragmatics and vision.

References

Baum, H. "Politics and Ambivalence in Planners' Practice," *Journal of Planning Education and Research*, 3:13–22, 1983.

Bolan, R. "The Practitioner as Theorist: The Phenomenology of the Professional Episode," *Journal of the American Planning Association,* 46:261–274, 1980.

Bolan, R. "The Structure of Ethical Choice in Planning Practice," *Journal of Planning Education and Research,* 3:23–35, 1983.

Checkoway, B. (ed.). "Special Issues: New Perspectives on Planning Practice," *Journal of Planning Education and Research,* 3:3–67, 1983.

Forester, J. "Critical Theory and Planning Practice," *Journal of the American Planning Association,* 46:275–286, 1980.

Hemmens, G. "Introduction," *Journal of the American Planning Association,* 46:259–260, 1980.

Klosterman, R. "The Evolution of Planning Theory," *Journal of Planning Education and Research,* 1:1–11, 1981.

Krueckeberg, D. "Planning and the New Depression in the Social Sciences," *Journal of Planning Education and Research,* 3:78–86, 1984

Part I

Dilemmas in Planning

1

Planning Theory and Planning Practice: Roles and Attitudes of Planners

A Synthesis of Empirical Research and Formulation of Derived Applications

Jack Rothman and Margrit Hugentobler

Introduction

It has been asserted that the planner enters the planning process with a "set of values and procedures" which constitutes the planner's heritage (Ranney, 1969). This heritage—rooted in the history of the planning profession—presumably exerts an influence on the way planners perceive and interpret their work, and is an important influence on the roles and attitudes they exhibit. In this discussion we will examine planners' roles and attitudes with a particular emphasis on determining whether planners exhibit a relatively homogeneous set of behavioral and cognitive characteristics or whether there are variations and of what types. We will also draw policy or application implications from our observations.

The Rise and Fall of Classic Planning Theory

Planning theory was marked initially by a rationalistic model of decision making, crystalized, perhaps, in the writings of Simon (1957). Planning was viewed as a process whereby through use of proper rules of logic an optimal solution to a problem is determined. Persons were seen as utility-maximizing beings whose relations to others were defined in instrumental terms. Classic decision-making theory involved following a task-oriented set of basic steps, including ordinarily: setting a goal; identifying all the alternative means of

3

attaining the goal; evaluating means in order to arrive at the single best solution; and implementing the decision. Hudson (1979) characterizes this approach in modern form as examining "problems from a systems viewpoint, using conceptual or mathematical models relating ends (objectives) to means (resources and constraints), with heavy reliance on numbers and quantitative analysis." This may entail use of forecasting and analysis techniques such as multiple regression analysis, Markov chains, econometric modeling, or Bayesian methods.

Historically, planning concentrated on physical land-use elements of the community, rather than stressing larger social concerns. This is related to the profession's association with the housing reform movement of the late 19th and early 20th centuries. This movement was characterized by an environmental-deterministic philosophy, suggesting that social conditions could be altered by changing the situation of the urban poor through the manipulation of housing designs and thus improving the deteriorating physical environment found in crowded slums. Most of the early planners were architects and engineers by professional training and thus quite predictably focused on the physical and locational aspects of urban development.

Another major feature of traditional planning theory was the association of the planning field with that of the municipal reform movement. It was characterized by an emphasis on the service function of municipal governments over the political function, expressed in a distinct ideology of commitment to a public interest that should prevail over competing private interests. The belief in the existence of such a solitary public interest reflected a strong anti-political bias, neglecting to see the city as a pluralistic political entity. Suggestions for two major structural changes resulted, namely the replacement of the mayor-dominated city by a council–manager form of government and the substitution of non-partisan for partisan elections.

The concept of city government as a non-political body in pursuit of governmental efficiency was instrumental in shaping the traditional planning doctrine. It adopted the concept of a solitary public interest, providing planners with the legitimation based on their objectivity and technical expertise. They were to intervene as neutral judges in the private-market system by allocating land uses to benefit the public as a whole, mainly through the development of comprehensive master plans. As Altshuler (1965) points out, the assumption underlying the concept of master planning is that of a common interest of society's members that constitutes an aggregate of all interests. Additionally, conflicts in society are illusory and about minor matters. They can be foreseen and resolved by just arbiters, planners who understand the total interests of all parties. This traditional planning outlook, imbued with a disdain of politics, was characterized also by elements of scientific management, expressed in the suggested role of the rationalistic, presumably value-free technician.

Despite or perhaps because of its elegance and simplicity, the rationalistic, comprehensive concept has been subjected to criticism from various quarters. A variety of limitations have been attributed to the model, including limits to rationality, limits to analytic methodology, limits to environmental control, limits to professional expertise, and limits of value uniformity. (See Rothman and Zald, in press.)

This classical model of planning apparently no longer commands consensus within the planning profession. In the early sixties, various issues were raised about the viability of the comprehensive planning model, given the characteristics of local political systems. Among the most influential was Banfield's (1967) critique in which he questioned many of the essential assumptions of this planning ideal, suggesting that the decentralized nature of American community politics mitigates against the ideal of comprehensiveness, and pointing to the enormous complexity in predicting change in the environment.

The contradictions between decision-making styles and the time frames of politics versus the development of comprehensive plans have been extensively discussed by both Altshuler (1965) and Lowi (1969). Lindblom's (1969) critique of planning as a rational approach to societal guidance focused on the inability of decision-makers to truly consider all values because of incomplete information and the dynamic of the political system, reflecting a continuous adjustment process. Davidoff (1965), one of the major proponents of advocacy planning, rejects outright the existence of a solitary public interest in which all societal groups share equally. He questioned the notion that planners can resolve conflicts among different competing goals in expert fashion. Unlike traditional planning theory, advocacy planning is explicitly partisan, suggesting that there are no neutral, value-free criteria for evaluating plans, thus rejecting the role of the neutral expert-technician planner. Catanese (1974) notes that there will always be a need for planners to fulfill the requirements of an apolitical, technical-expert role, but that this role should not be confused with additional roles necessary for meeting the greater potential of professional planning, which he sees in a planning approach committed to social change.

Rather than a single model of planning and community intervention with its precise set of roles and attitudes, planning has increasingly been defined in multi-model terms (Friedmann and Hudson 1974; Hudson, 1979; Rothman, 1974).

A Kuhnian Analysis

The breakdown of the rationalistic, comprehensive decision-making model in mainstream planning theory can be understood in part through the work of Kuhn (1970) on the structure of scientific revolutions. Kuhn rejects the conventional notion that scientific breakthroughs occur through the orderly, progressive aggregation of knowledge by means of a linear chain of related studies. Rather, he posits random activities and contributions as the pattern associated with significant scientific leaps. This process is blurred, he states, by textbooks which attempt to depict a more orderly, cumulative process than actually takes place. Critical changes in scientific thought, according to Kuhn, come about when established paradigms no longer work and are not capable of explaining anomalies that present themselves within the scientific community. These anomalies are the driving force for radical departures in thinking.

In a useful discussion, Galloway and Mahayni (1977) apply the Kuhnian framework to analyze changes that have taken place with respect to developments in the urban planning field. Although Kuhn applied his theory to the sciences, especially natural science, one can use it heuristically to explore changes in other fields of thought. The authors use the five-phase process formulation of Kuhn as a basic framework, illustrating each step with relevant developments in planning.

1. *Preparadigm Period.* In this period there is no consensus concerning a basic paradigm. Competing schools of thought vie with one another for legitimacy and dominance. Taking as a starting point the turn of the century and going up to the early 1920s, the authors illustrate a variety of different urban planning developments: city beautiful, master planning, the park movement, housing reform, social reform-settlement houses, and municipal reform. Diversity and ferment characterize the preparadigm state.

2. *Paradigm Development.* A formalized community of adherents appears. This period extends roughly from the 1920s through the mid-1940s. Consensus forms regarding a particular orientation. In urban planning the comprehensive land-use concept took hold. Planning and zoning power were established and land-use planning became legitimized as a function of local government.

3. *Paradigm Articulation.* Problem-solving research and theory development are stimulated and guided by the paradigm. The paradigm is extended during this time. This period covers the mid-1940s through the 1950s. The rationalist theory is better articulated by

Simon, Lindblom and others. Social scientists contribute to developments.

4. *Paradigm Anomaly.* In this period, one is faced with paradoxical phenomena. The paradigm falters as anomalies appear. Here we are talking of the 1960s and the early 1970s. There is inability to predict or successfully address critical social and racial problems and inability to deal with the political environment. Widespread criticism of planning activities is expressed. Social action and advocacy formulations employing conflict tactics begin to appear.

5. *Paradigm Crisis.* Attempts are made to resolve anomalies within existing paradigms as well as to formulate alternative ones. Again, there is the emergence of competing schools of thought. This period involves the late 1970s and 1980s. Fragmentation is extensive. Different constituencies form within the profession. Professional boundaries become less clear. Notions of endemic turbulence guide and disturb theory formulation. Concepts of societal planning come to the fore through the policy analysis school.

The development described here, however, is not unique to the planning field. The rationalistic planning model was influenced by the classical scientific method based on the Cartesian-Newtonian paradigm which has inspired the natural sciences and was adopted by the social sciences and related professional disciplines. The essence of this world view was the definition of the universe as a mechanical system composed of elementary building blocks which, taken apart, could be analyzed in order to find cause-effect relationships, reflecting the fundamental laws of interaction. This reductionist model of static structures was translated to theories of social phenomena, suggesting that there were laws of nature governing society similar to those determining the physical universe. Planning then, similar to other professions in the field of applied social science (i.e., clinical psychology, social work, etc.) attempted to gain acceptance and legitimacy through the application of strategies and techniques closely modeled after the traditional scientific method of inquiry, i.e., increased use of modeling, forecasting, and other quantitative techniques of various kinds.

The appropriateness of the mechanistic world view has been questioned increasingly in recent years, initiating a process of reflection affecting many disciplines. For Capra (1982) this is the expression of a broad paradigm shift, initiated by developments in physics, such as quantum theory, which has made it impossible to continue to analyze the world into independently existing separate parts which are connected by causal laws. Rather, it must be recognized that there are no static structures in nature but only patterns of dynamic balance with all parts being interdependent and interrelated. The inability to successfully address large-scale societal problems such as air pollution, poverty, hunger, disease, economic instability, etc., has led to growing criticism of reductionist approaches in other academic disciplines. An example is the biomedical model in health care which has created exorbitant costs to society without being able to address the major diseases of our time. The emphasis on scientific rigor in economics, to take another example— where cost/benefit analyses convert social and moral choices into pseudo-technical ones—is a reflection of the widespread belief that all problems have technical solutions. Kenneth Boulding has called this issue of unstated values "a monumentally unsuccessful exercise . . . which has preoccupied a whole generation of economists (indeed, several generations) with a dead end, to the almost total neglect of the major problems of our age" (quoted by Myrdal, 1973, p. 149).

Based on this discussion, the analysis by Galloway and Mahayni, and the previously mentioned criticism of the limitations of the classical planning model, we would expect that planners reflect divergent roles and attitudes concerning the theory and practice of planning. The field may be characterized as centrifugal rather than centripetal in its value stance. In order to assess this assumption from an empirical standpoint, we engaged in a comprehensive retrieval and synthesis of research studies concerning the roles and attitudes of planners. Hence, in this further discussion, we will restrict our conclusions to derivations from empirical research findings on the subject, drawing specifically on eighteen data-based studies that we have been able to locate in the literature (Appendix B). Utilizing a research and development methodology formulated by one of the authors (Rothman, 1980), studies were systematically evaluated and synthesized. When a set of studies yielded consensus findings which converged on a given topic, these are presented in italicized form in the text as generalizations. The implications of findings for professional planning policy are given prominence and treated at appropriate points throughout the analysis.

Results of Empirical Review and Synthesis

The findings have been categorized into four major areas. The first two refer to planners' roles in practice, and the impact of planning education. The third and fourth areas include organizational and community-linkage aspects of the planners' structural environment. A note of caution is in order here, relating to the fact that most findings are based on information gathered by survey questionnaires, reflecting self-reported statements which may not necessarily coincide with behavior or observed phenomena in all cases.

Planners' Role Orientations

This group of generalizations relates to roles planners adopt and variables such as political attitudes, values, and ethics related to role performance.

> Planners working on the local level vary considerably with regard to the kinds of role orientations they choose for themselves. Three major roles can be identified: a) a political role, defining planners as participants in the planning process as advocates of particular positions wherein they organize and actively lobby for acceptance or defeat of particular plans; b) a technical role, defining planners as "objective" in the sense of keeping their policy views to themselves and obtaining effectiveness through expertise; and c) a political/technical role combining elements of both of the above-mentioned roles, embracing expertise for effectiveness, yet at the same time acknowledging the need for active political behavior when striving for the implementation of certain plans.

Two major studies (Howe, 1980 and Vasu, 1979), including samples of between 500 and over 1,000 members of the American Institute of Planners, found an amazing overlap, in both cases classifying 18 percent of the respondents as politicians or advocates, respectively.

Both studies also clearly identified the technically oriented role as well as a combined political/technical role, which Howe (*op. cit.*) called hybrids and Vasu (*op. cit.*) classified as moderates. The proportion of the respondents classified in these groups varies in the two studies, probably based on the somewhat different definitions of the hybrids versus the moderates. Howe (*op. cit.*) found half the planners interviewed to belong to the hybrid group, whereas Vasu (*op. cit.*) classified only 32 percent as moderates.

A third study of roles in community planning (Needleman and Needleman, 1974) also identified three different types of roles. The predominant group among those planners were the politicians, with only a minority of the planners interviewed belonging to what can be called a combined or technical role. The large number of politically oriented planners found in this study seems related to the particular situation of community planners, which seems to favor a political role orientation over a moderate or technician perspective.

Planners with a more politicized role orientation tend to be significantly more liberal in their political perspective than technicians, with hybrids/ moderates being somewhere in between.

The liberal-politician and moderate/conservative-technician trends were found in all of the three studies mentioned before.

Vasu (*op. cit.*) indicates that planners as a group, however, tend to be significantly more liberal than the general American public. Forty-three percent of the planners in his study identified themselves as Democrats, only 12 percent as Republicans, with 44 percent being independents, of which the majority were closer to Democrats. The same study has found planners to be a politically active group, with 98.7 percent of them saying that they are voting regularly.

Attitudes about planning issues and views held about ethical professional behavior vary considerably with differences in political perspectives and role orientations. Politician planners tend to be more strongly committed to social issues and client groups, while technician-type planners were found to be more agency oriented. Age, sex, as well as the possession of a planning degree, are not found to be determining factors in this respect.

These findings are supported by several studies. Howe and Kaufman (1979) found politician planners to be more committed to transit and environmental protection with a rather strong anti-developer bias, compared to technicians. Hybrids were found to be between those two groups, yet leaning more toward the politician planners' attitudes.

Needleman and Needleman (*op. cit.*) found a strong anti-developer bias among the predominantly politically oriented community planners, indicating a commitment to the needs of citizens groups.

With regard to ethical professional behavior, planners as a group consider the use of threats, distortion of information, and leaking of information as unethical behavior. Actions to dramatize problems to overcome apathy and the use of expendables as trade-offs were generally considered rather acceptable tactics. Politicians, as would be expected, had a less restrictive view on the use of the first set of tactics (Howe and Kaufman, *op. cit.*)

The community planners in the Needleman and Needleman (*op. cit.*) study use a range of tactics such as those mentioned above, going as far as mobilizing citizens "behind the scenes" to put pressure on the local government or planning department. Many of those planners consider the use of such strategies necessary to effectively promote their clients' interests.

Planners' attitudes toward citizen participation in general are favorable, but within limits. Most planners see citizen input as valuable in the policy exploration stage; when it comes to citizen impact on the decision-making process or veto power, most planners indicate a critical or even negative attitude.

Several studies explored this question. Vasu (*op. cit.*) found that half of the planners interviewed considered citizens groups as not representative, suggesting limited legitimacy. Howe and Kaufman (*op. cit.*) found the mean response of their planners on this issue slightly favorable toward involving citizens in all planning. A majority of planners thought, however, that citizens should not have veto power over plans. Politician planners were found to have a more positive attitude on this score.

Even the community planners (Needleman and Needleman, *op. cit.*), although committed to community group interests, suggest limitations to citizen participation. Many of them consider citizens groups as an important resource for putting pressure on city hall for the implementation of plans. But a majority of them question the value of citizens' input with regard to final decision making. They point to the diversity of interests among different groups, which they see as problematic for the development and implementation of broader, more comprehensive plans.

Planners as a group seem to be committed to symbols and expression of both advocacy planning and traditional planning doctrine, pointing to potentially conflicting perspectives.

Vasu (*op. cit.*) found that a majority of planners do not believe in the existence of a solitary public interest anymore. Planners indicate by a majority that no plan can be neutral. At the same time, however, most of them still believe in the possibility of comprehensive planning, albeit admitting that the planning process cannot be strictly technical, but necessarily includes value judgments.

Howe and Kaufman (*op. cit.*) found this attitude to be specifically typical for hybrids, the category to which half of their sample belonged.

It is interesting to note that even the community planners with an explicit advocacy perspective felt frustrated by the obligation experienced to the still deeply rooted planning ideal of a technical, rational process. The reality they experience, however, suggested an almost exclusively political role, emphasizing bargaining, mobilizing, and communicating skills as the key to goal attainment (Needleman and Needleman, *op. cit.*).

Implications Regarding Role Orientations. Since there is no unified professional value system, planners can adopt different roles and legitimize their position based on the variety of roles performed in planning practice. It seems important, however, that planners assess the potential as well as the restrictions a specific role choice may present in relationship to different objectives. A unidimensional role definition may lead to unnecessary limitations and may be dysfunctional, if based only on ideological concerns and value orientations. This seems to be particularly true for the "pure" technical approach, a role choice which may often be based more on ideological concerns about what planners should do, rather than on a rational assessment of role performance which proves effective in practice.

More client/advocacy-oriented planners can communicate the lack of a crystallized, uniform value system within the profession to legitimate political roles among their professional peers.

Planners should become aware of the existing contradictions and seek ways of dealing with contradictory value pulls. This seems important in order to reduce frustration and possible cynicism that may result from ignoring conflicting demands. The hybrid role seems to be one way for planners to deal with this dilemma, attempting to gain effectiveness through the use of political skills, while at the same time also relying on the use of the profession's major resource, its reputation for expertise.

For citizens groups trying to influence the planning process, this suggests an analysis of the planners' role orientation, values, and attitudes to assess the potential for effective cooperation. More politically oriented, liberal planners would be more responsive to client groups' input and less agency oriented. They should be the target group for citizens wishing to communicate their concerns and influence planning processes. Technicians, although open to some degree to citizens' input, would probably have to be considered less reachable. Citizens groups may want to emphasize different value orientations, depending on whom they are dealing with. For example, with traditional planners the emphasis may be on their gathering as much information as possible to make an optimally rational decision; with politically oriented planners the focus may be on obtaining the views of normally disenfranchised groups.

Planning departments or local governments hiring planners should assess the appropriateness of different tasks for different kinds of planners, i.e., if the focus of the task to be performed is designing and developing plans, technicians may be more appropriate. For planning tasks involving a more active role in plan implementation, including interaction with different community groups, politician planners would seem to be the choice.

Planning organizations with a mixed planning staff may have to anticipate internal conflicts, possibly arising due to the staff's different perspectives on what planning should be and do. Assigning different tasks to different planners may be one solution. In-service clarification of roles may ease tension and might contribute to conflicts being dealt with more productively.

Planning Education

These generalizations address the role of planning education related to planning practice and role performance, skills needed, and the question of general versus substantive knowledge.

Education, although in general thought to be a powerful socialization force for professionals, does not differentiate planners very well with regard to role or professional values held.

None of the studies comparing degree versus non-degree holders found a significant difference between these two groups (Howe and Kaufman, Vasu, Needleman and Needleman, *op. cit.*). The findings suggest that differences found in role orientations between more technically and more politically oriented planners seem to be based much more on the major shifts found in planning theory which affected planning education over the past 20 years (from an almost exclusively technical/expert-oriented focus before the 1960s to a more politically oriented, advocacy perspective in the later 1960s and early 1970s).

Support for this notion is found in Howe and Kaufman's study (*op. cit*) which indicates that planners who graduated in earlier periods tend to emphasize a more technical role, while planners graduated between the late 1960s and mid-1970s tend to be politically oriented. Hybrids were found in earlier as well as later periods.

Needleman and Needleman (*op. cit.*) also point to the differences found between "old style" and "new style" planners, finding that the mean age for community advocacy-oriented planners was considerably lower than that of comparable groups of planners with the more traditional role.

The possession of a formal planning degree does not provide unique access to planning jobs.

Hemmens, Bergman and Maroney (1975) found that planners with different educational backgrounds move relatively easily between different types of planning jobs, i.e. social planning, policy analysis, etc.

Beauregard (1976), in an analysis of census data, indicates that approximately 60 percent of the population classified as urban and regional planners hold a Master's degree, and that 25 percent of this population have less than four years of college education.

Similar to the above are Vasu's (*op. cit.*) findings that 19 percent of his sample had no graduate training whatsoever, and only 48 percent of his sample had a Master's degree in planning. (The differences among those studies seem to be related to the fact that Vasu's study did not differentiate between private and public planners, at least with respect to this question.)

Planners use a variety of skills in their daily practice. The skills suggested to be most important in the following order are: a) writing skills—including presenting synthesizing analyzed information; b) reasoning skills—for consultation, advising, negotiating and bargaining; c) designing and development skills—for drafting and changing plans; and d) mathematical and statistical skills (ranking low).

Different studies found that the highly appreciated generic skills of reasoning and communicating are considered of increasing importance for the planning function.

Schön, Cremer, Osterman and Perry (1976) found in a survey of MIT graduates that appreciation of these generic skills has increased from only 6 percent valuing them highly among graduates leaving school between 1960 and 1963, to over 50 percent among planners graduating after 1964. This indicates that changes in planning styles occurred over the past 20 years.

Bryson and Delbecq (1979), in a case study analyzing how planning teams deal with a given project, found that as planners were presented with political difficulties they increasingly focused on communication, group process, and political skills.

Hemmens's et al. (*op. cit.*) study of planners' evaluation of their education found similar preferences for representation and communication skills.

Planners tend to emphasize knowledge of generic competencies and the belief that their expertise is mainly based on transsubstantive skills, while at the same time indicating the importance of knowledge in a substantive area. The latter is considered a vital prerequisite for being able to hold and move on to new jobs.

The findings here offer some explanation for this seeming contradiction. Hemmens et al. (*op. cit.*) found that the notion of the importance of transsubstantive skills is often set forth by planning schools. The still-important notion of comprehensive analysis seems to be one factor supporting this idea in planners' minds, although their practice experience indicates a strong need for knowledge in at least one substantive area. Nutt and Susskind (1970) and Denbow and Nutt (1973), exploring goals and programs of a variety of planning schools, indicate that most of the schools aim at training generalists (20). A smaller group (10) focuses on training planners for a special role/field. Three schools indicate that they are training social-change agents. Common to all these goal statements were vagueness and lack of clarity with regard to the skills planners were supposed to learn in these schools. Curriculum descriptions were found to be very general in most cases, lacking the definition of a coherent, well thought-out program.

Implications for Planning Education.   Since planning education in itself does not seem to have a significant impact on planners' values, there should be encouragement in the field for clarification of underlying values in adopting different role orientations and carrying out different tasks. These generalizations also suggest that planning practice, moving away from the traditional technical expert focus, may become more open to other professionals, such as community organizers, community psychologists, or applied sociologists, etc. For the planning profession and for planning education this means reconsidering the specific contribution planners can and should make in relation to others involved in community intervention and "change agentry."

Planning schools should emphasize training in generic skills related to representing and synthesizing information as well as communication (including consultation, bargaining, and negotiating, which reflect a political role orientation). More emphasis on such skills would facilitate the adoption of a broader role set for planners, adding to the traditional technical analysis and design perspective.

At the same time it seems important for planning schools to realize the need for knowledge in at least one substantive area. Stressing both generic skills and their possible application in a substantive area may alleviate some of the contradictions mentioned by planners and would facilitate a better start in the practice setting. The development of a coherent curriculum, reflecting choices open to planners, and clearly defining relevant skills and substantive knowledge areas, would be a first step away from the questionable assumption that training planners to become generalists serves them best in practice.

Planning and the Organizational Environment

This group of generalizations is related to organizational aspects of planning such as the kind of governmental structure planners work with, characteristics of important local political actors, and considerations of the large setting in which local government and planning operate.

Planners with a more political role orientation tend to work in larger cities more often than technician planners. A larger number of hybrids compared to technicians is also found in big cities.

Howe and Kaufman (*op. cit.*), supported by earlier studies, found that almost three times as many politician planners and more than twice as many hybrids (combined role) than technicians are found to be working in large cities. Whether the politically oriented planners and the hybrids seek out those jobs or whether the work setting shapes their role in such a way remains unclear.

Needleman and Needleman (*op. cit.*) similarly found a disproportionately large number of politician planners working in community projects in big cities.

Reformed local governments, characterized by a council-manager structure and nonpartisan elections, tend to be more conservative (focus on municipal spending which largely benefits the middle class), compared to cities with a mayor-council structure and partisan elections.

Dye and Garcia (1978) in their study of structure, function, and policy in 243 American cities, concluded that reformed local governments tend to be less responsive to the social and ethnic character of the community with regard to municipal spending, thus neglecting the needs of smaller, less powerful groups in the community.

Almy (1977) found that council-manager cities tend to have a predominant middle-class composition, which may be related to the middle-class orientation of city managers.

Vasu (*op. cit.*), supporting the tendency of reformed governments to be more conservative, found strong preference among the planners interviewed in his study for employment within reformed governmental structures. This somewhat surprising discovery—given the statements above—seems to be related to the planning profession's traditional heritage characterized by the public interest doctrine and an anti-political bias. These are also two of the major characteristics of the reformist movement.

Major local political actors—mayors and city council managers—vary in their attitudes toward planning and in their policy preferences, depending on such factors as community structure and perception of community problems.

Almy (1975) found that more politically active city managers, interested in policy change and innovation, are found in larger numbers in big cities. These city managers seem to be more independent from local community pressures and have a more professional management perspective than locally oriented city managers. These were often found to be strongly limited in their decision making by influential groups among the local political cliques. The former more-cosmopolitan-type managers are found predominantly in cities of high complexity and are more inclined to perceive and deal with community controversies than their more locally oriented colleagues in smaller cities.

In agreement with another study done by the same author (Almy, *op. cit.*), Almy found that this type of more independent, cosmopolitan city manager tends to be less interested in and responsive to citizens' input.

Sacco and Pearle (1977), in conducting a study of mayors' preferences and attitudes in 46 cities, found that government efficiency seems to be mayors' top-priority item, followed by community attractiveness and economic development. Citizen participation and aid to the disadvantaged were items of rather low priority, except in situations where strong indicators for pressing social problems existed. The study suggests, on the other hand, that mayors' preferences for ranking economic development high is not necessarily related to objective need in this area. A majority of mayors were found to operate more independently from local economic pressure groups than could be anticipated, suggesting a highly politicized, rather cosmopolitan and independent perspective.

Implications of the Organizational Environment. Looking at organizational context, work setting and planners' roles, the planners might increase their effectiveness and at the same time experience less tension and conflict when choosing a work setting compatible with their role orientation. Planners working in smaller cities should consider the possibility of a hybrid role (jack-of-all-trades) or a more traditional technical role. Politician planners, on the other hand, may find such a narrow local setting difficult and rather limiting. Planners working with more locally oriented city managers should take the relatively high sensitivity of these managers toward local group pressures into account, and make use of this characteristic by strengthening the influence and visibility of client groups whose influence they want to support.

Politically oriented planners may find a more conducive setting for the acceptance of a politicized planning function in larger cities with cosmopolitan city managers or mayors. Planners looking for a more innovative policy climate and committed to social issues would seem to be more effective in cities with non-reformed governments. At the same time, planners working in such settings should be aware that top political actors may not be very responsive to or interested in citizens' input and representation regarding policy decisions. Planners attempting to increase the influence of citizens groups and politicians' awareness of social problems in the city may have to develop tactics for making such problems more visible and for increasing pressures from citizens groups if they want these issues to be on the agenda.

It seems important for planners to realize the contradiction between their preference for reformed governments and the limitations which this governmental structure seems to impose on planners with a role orientation directed toward social change and support of disadvantaged groups. It would be appropriate for planners to make their peers aware of such contradictory perspectives and for planning schools to provide such information to students.

Planning as the Linking Role Between Community and Local Government Structures

This last group of generalizations refers to the situation of planners when playing linking-agent roles between the community and the local government. Specific dilemmas and conflicts are discussed, along with solution strategies employed by planners for dealing with such conflicts.

Planners playing a linking-agent role between local governments and citizen groups often find themselves in a very difficult situation, based on: a) the function and structure of planning departments within the local government; b) competing demands from different community groups; and c) the planners' own often-controversial values and loyalty conflicts.

Various studies explored the dilemmas planners confront when trying to play a mediating role between local government expectations and citizen demands. Plant and White (1981) studied different means of planners attempting to play a mediating and coordinating role regarding the distribution of HUD Community Block Grant funds in seven cities. They found that a major dilemma resulted from the variety of incompatible particularistic demands of neighborhood groups, and the pressure from city hall to develop a general plan for equal distribution.

Another rather typical conflict is described by Cohen (1979) in analyzing planning approaches to neighborhood development. Planners found it difficult to adopt a more comprehensive perspective of the situation, focusing mainly on physical aspects of development, while residents increasingly demanded that broader social concerns needed to be addressed. Frustration was experienced by both sides.

In a similar vein, Johnston (1977), studying approaches to new-town planning, confirmed that planners tended to focus on physical aspects, reflecting their own middle-class values and desired patterns of behavior and association. As a result, developed plans eliminated many of the facilities, land uses, and institutions of working-class people and ethnic groups.

The Needleman study (*op. cit.*) explores extensively the dilemmas community planners are faced with in mediating between citizen groups and local government planning. In order to be trusted by community groups they feel pressured to produce results and to disassociate themselves from the planning department, which is suspect to citizens. This leads to varying degrees of agency betrayal, putting planners in a double-agent role. The pressure to produce presents additional problems, since planners often have little influence upon other operating agencies in the local government which would need to address the problems raised by citizens. Planners thus find themselves torn between their commitment to community groups and their professional commitment to an orderly, rational approach to problem solving.

Planners in such problematic linking roles use a variety of strategies to deal with the role conflicts experienced. Some of the major strategies adopted seem to be: a) trying to balance conflicting expectations; b) emphasizing the traditional professional aspects of role performance; c) playing a double role; and d) withdrawal from role performance.

It is interesting to note here that Rothman (1974) found community organizers working for social change to develop similar patterns of dealing with role conflicts.

Plant and White (*op. cit.*) found that planners attempting to coordinate the distribution of HUD funds use different strategies. In two cities, the planners developed a general plan, outlining the budget for each neighborhood and letting citizens groups indicate their demands within these limits. Given such a framework, planners seemed to be able to fulfill the expectations of the planning department without at the same time alienating the citizens groups too much. Another strategy used in this situation was to multiply channels for citizens' input by involving other local operating agencies in the process, which took some of the pressure away from the planning department.

A third approach was to establish a citywide advisory board with representatives from various community groups and local government agencies. This approach, although workable, led to co-optation of citizens' representatives in some cases.

As indicated by Cohen (*op. cit.*) as well as Johnston (*op. cit.*), another way of dealing with seemingly unmanageable demands from community groups is to focus on the traditional planning role (responsibility for physical aspects of development only), thus ignoring demands for addressing other social problems. Based on their findings, Howe and Kaufman (*op. cit.*) suggest that the development of the hybrid role may be a way through which planners attempt to deal with conflicting demands—playing a more politicized role when it seems appropriate and retreating to the more technical role orientation when called for.

Needleman and Needleman (*op. cit.*) found a considerable group of their sample of community planners to experience severe role conflicts. They adopted a guerilla role by developing what they call a "double underground" and an elaborate information system to various groups and agencies. These planners, themselves relatively powerless, often mobilized groups to put pressure on city hall without it being known that they were "agitators" behind the scene. Although in some cases very effective, the role of taking a strong advocacy position forced planners into disloyalty to the planning department or to citizens' interests (at least this seems to be the way many planners saw it). This put heavy psychological pressure on these planners. The average tenure among such community planners was only two to three years. At this point, withdrawal from role performance was the strategy used to deal with the burnout and high frustration level experienced in this kind of conflict-laden role.

An interesting aspect to be mentioned here is the fact that when community planners became too successful in building up community pressures the programs almost without exception were cut back or completely eliminated by local governments, which were unwilling and unable to deal with the increased pressures.

Implications of Linking Roles.   Planners should realistically assess the potential kind of role conflict they are likely to face when considering different work assignments. This may help anticipate tensions, thus encouraging an early development of strategies for reducing unproductive role disparities. Recognizing the often structural determination of such conflicts may help to prevent feelings of personal failure and inadequacy, frequently leading to burnout and withdrawal from role performance. Planners focusing on a technical role orientation when having to perform tasks involving cooperation with citizens groups and mediating roles, should realize the contradiction in this situation early. They should also appreciate the limited potential for success.

The various solution strategies adopted by planners for dealing with role conflicts may be problematic. Focusing on an almost exclusive client orientation and advocacy function seems to lead to a burdening role. Though increasing citizens' input and power, this role is hard to play for an extended period of time due to the many pressures put on the planner. Planners who choose this role consciously should be aware that they may need to set a time limit for themselves and possibly change jobs before burnout symptoms and cynicism take over.

A useful approach may be to involve other agencies, thus spreading the pressures and demands from community groups and increasing awareness in other agencies about existing problems. This would allow planners to play a truly mediating role between various interests, with potential for dealing more productively with competing expectations from city hall and citizens.

It seems difficult to assess the type of solution strategies most effective for different situations, since the kind of conflict, the specific structural arrangement, planners' role orientations, and personality are all factors that may call for variations in dealing with such conflicts. Planners may have to realize that certain roles, although effective in the short run, cannot be performed on a long-term basis in a given organizational setting. This seems true particularly for community planners who may find their programs cut if they become too effective, thus jeopardizing long-term desired outcomes. It can be said, on the other hand, that planners performing a purely technical role may set unwarranted boundaries on their effectiveness when aiming for social change.

For organizations hiring planners this implies that roles and expected functions should be clearly formulated in order to achieve mutual agreement about the planning task. Organizations or planning departments may have to anticipate conflict among staff when different roles are performed. Different expectations should be clarified, and the difficulty of linking roles should be anticipated by planning departments.

For citizens trying to have an impact on planning decisions, this raises the question of expectations that are reasonable in cooperating with planners. Recognizing the limitations in the planner's double loyalties (hired by the local government, yet subject to citizens' concerns), community groups should recognize the danger of early burnout which may lead to the loss of a carefully built relationship to city hall. This suggests that citizens groups should seek to diversify their links with local government by not exclusively burdening specific planners with their demands, but by building a network of contacts.

Summary and Conclusions

What emerges from our review of the empirical literature is that the field of planning has not managed to escape the contemporary tendency toward fragmentation and theoretical diversity. The same is true for other professions in the social arena, where longstanding theoretical foundations are being questioned and shattered. The pervasive imprint of Freud had faded in clinical psychology; Parsonian dominance has receded in sociology. Kroeber's influence in the field of anthropology has declined, as the many diverse currents described by anthropologist Eric Wolf (1980) indicate:

> Social-cultural anthropologists have also split into sub-divisions, turning themselves into applied, cognitive, economic, ecological, legal, political, psychological, urban, or even psycho-pharmacological anthropologists. Area specialization

has grouped anthropologists working in a particular geographical area with, say, Latin Americanists or Middle Easternists from other disciplines. Such lines of tension were deepened by opposition between older and younger members of the institutions, and between those teaching within academe and those working outside (p. E9).

Comprehensive, rationalistic planning theory that once held sway is now only one of multiple contending perspectives, and not enjoying very high repute at that. Several observers have made note of the prevailing theoretical condition. Burchell and Hughes (1979) indicate that "Planning has simply become a very broad and sometimes leaky umbrella. It shelters many different kinds of skills and approaches" (p. xvii). And Branch (1978) adds, "only bits and pieces of a general theory of planning exist today" (p. 48).

It can certainly be said that planning practice has been found to reflect the diversity of approaches to planning that is also suggested in planning theory. The traditional ideology of comprehensive planning for the broad public interest—although hardly defended anymore in its classical form—still seems to have a considerable and problematic impact on planners' roles and attitudes, even for planners who want to see themselves in an advocacy role. Although the two different approaches to planning are reflected in different roles planners emphasize—the politician planner and the technician planner—planners for the most part seem to be committed to symbols and expressions of both advocacy as well as traditional planning doctrine, which creates a considerable potential for experiencing tension and frustration. Contradictions and uncertainty are reflected in planning education, too. The schools in many cases seem to have maintained a focus on the training of generalists capable of comprehensive analysis. This seems to present problems for planners moving into practice, finding that substantive knowledge in one area is important. Generic skills as they relate to a more politically active role are needed but do not seem to be provided adequately in planning education. Other findings indicate variations in practice settings that seem to favor one planning role over another. The more politically oriented planner may want to work in larger cities with non-reformed governments which promise more potential for a politicized planning function.

Highly politicized roles, such as mediating between local government and citizens groups, almost inevitably seem to create dilemmas. The data show that such roles frequently lead to conflicts which seem to be based on the competing and often incompatible expectations of citizens' groups on one hand, and local government on the other.

The fragmentation found in planning theory and practice undoubtedly creates problems for the planners involved but also raises some basic questions about the future, identity, and legitimacy of planning as a profession. Schwab (1972/64) considers the following aspects as crucial to the definition of a profession:

- a specific question/topic and a related problem situation (subject)
- a specific way of perceiving the problem situation itself, its determinants, and consequences
- a specific methodology operationalized in prescribed procedures of analysis and intervention which indicate how the problem situation is to be described, explained, and acted upon—followed by more or less precisely defined strategies and action guidelines
- a view of the problem solution which indicates what goals should be aimed for by what kind of professional actors

If we apply these criteria to the reality of planning practice today, problems seem to emerge in various areas:

- The subject planning is to address on the local level has become blurred. Clearly, confining themselves to narrowly defined questions of land use, physical planning, and economic development seems increasingly inadequate for planners—in their own perspective, and in view of the complexity of urban problems and the interdependence of social issues.
- With shifting problem definitions, moving from the notion of the common good to be achieved by an "objective" determination of means and ends to advocacy planning requiring explicit value statements and the analysis of broader social issues, technical skills and sophisticated analytical mathematical models no longer suffice to address these problems, thus raising questions as to the content of planning education curricula. With a shift in this direction, the profession furthermore becomes open to competition from other professionals in this field such as community organization, community psychologist, etc., creating problems as to legitimacy, professional identity and boundaries.

Planning finds itself increasingly faced with the absence of a guiding theory that would allow for a more unified approach to practice. If planning is indeed to give up the value-free technician's approach to social problem solving, a more comprehensive theory about social problems will have to be developed, capable of providing a framework in which different professions in the social arena are able to define and locate themselves.

Staub (1983), in attempting to develop such a comprehensive theoretical approach, suggests a process-oriented systemic problem paradigm (going beyond a static view of social structures and processes). "It is insufficient to define in a dualistic manner 'what is,' and 'what should be' in the social arena without contemplating the genesis and structures of such discrepancies and without reflecting on the emerging interdependencies and interactions—which means that every form of social reductionism can be questioned" (p. 51). Planning thus cannot be neutral but is value-infused, whether this is perceived and acknowledged by the profession or not. For planners to continue to emphasize a social harmony world view perpetuates an incongruous gap between theory and practice, and makes planning ineffective as a force for positive societal developments, aimed at such basic values as freedom, equality and justice.

Appendix A

Bibliography—General Background Literature

Altshuler, A. *The City Planning Process: A Political Analysis.* Ithaca, New York: Cornell University Press, 1965.

Banfield, E.C. "The Uses and Limitations of Comprehensive Planning in Massachusetts," in *Taming Megalopolis.* H.W. Eldridge, ed., New York, NY: Doubleday, 1967.

Beckman, N. "The New PPBS: Planning, Politics, Bureaucracy and Salvation," in *Planning and Politics: Uneasy Partnership.* T.L. Beyle and G. Lathrop, eds. New York, NY, 1970.

Baer, W.C. "Urban Planners: Doctors or Midwives," *Public Administration Review,* November/December, 1977.

Branch, Melville. "Critical Unresolved Problems of Urban Planning Analysis," *Journal of The American Institute of Planners,* 44:1, January 1978, pp. 47–59.

Burchell, Robert and James Hughes, "Planning Theory in The 1980's—A Search for Future Directions," in Robert Burchell and George Sternlieb, eds., *Planning Theory in The 1980's.* New Brunswick, NJ: Center for Urban Policy Research, 1979, pp. xvii–liii.

Capra, F. *The Turning Point: Science, Society and the Raising Culture.* Simon and Schuster, 1982.

Catanese, A.J. *Planners and Local Politics.* Beverly Hills, CA: Sage Publications, 1974.

Davidoff, P. "Advocacy and Pluralism in Planning," *Journal of the American Institute of Planners,* Vol. 31, 1965.

Friedmann, John and Barclay Hudson. "Knowledge and Action: A Guide to Planning Theory," *Journal of The American Institute of Planners,* January 1974, pp. 2-16.

Galloway, Thomas D., and Riad G. Mahayni. "Planning Theory in Retrospect: The Process of Paradigm Change," *Journal of the American Institute of Planners,* January 1978, pp. 62-71.

Hudson, Barclay. "Comparison of Current Planning Theories: Counterparts and Contradictions," *Journal of The American Institute of Planners,* 45:4, October 1979, pp. 387-398.

Kuhn, Thomas. *The Structure of Scientific Revolutions,* Second Edition. The University of Chicago Press, 1970.

Lindblom, C. "The Science of Muddling Through," *Public Administration Review,* Vol. 19, 1969.

Lowi, T.J. *The End of Liberalism.* New York, NY: W.W. Norton, 1969.

Myrdal, G. *Against the Stream.* New York, NY: Pantheon, 1973.

Ranney, D.C. *Planning and Politics in the Metropolis.* Columbus, Ohio: C.F. Merrill Publishers, 1969.

Rothman, J. *Planning and Organizing for Social Change: Action Principles from Social Science Research.* Columbia University Press, New York, NY, 1974.

_____. *Social R & D: Research and Development in the Human Services.* Englewood Cliffs, NJ: Prentice Hall, Inc., 1980.

_____, and Mayer Zald. "Planning Theory and Social Welfare," in Robert Roberts and Samuel H. Taylor, *Theory and Practice of Community Social Work.* New York, NY: Columbia University Press. In press.

Schwab, J.J. "Die Struktur der Wissenschaften: Sinn und Bedeutung" in Ford, G.W. and L. Puguo, *Wissenschaftsstruktur and Curriculum.* Düsseldorf, Germany, 1972/64, p. 27; 37-38.

Simon, Herbert A. *Administrative Behavior: A Study of Decision Making Processes in Administrative Organization.* New York, NY: MacMillan, 1957.

Staub-Bernasconi, S. *Soziale Probleme-Dimensionen ihrer Artikulation.* Diessenhofen, Switzerland: Verlag Rüegger, 1983.

Vasu, M.L. *Politics and Planning.* Chapel Hill, NC: The University of North Carolina Press, 1979.

Wolf, Eric. "They Divide and Sub-Divide, and Call It Anthropology," *The New York Times,* November 30, 1980.

Appendix B

Bibliography—Empirical Research Data Pool for Generalizations

Almy, T.A. "Local Cosmopolitanism and U.S. City Managers," *Urban Affairs Quarterly,* March 1975.

_____ . "City Managers, Public Avoidance and Revenue Sharing," *Public Administration Review,* January/February 1977.

Beauregard, R. "The Occupation of Planning: A View from the Census," *Journal of the American Institute of Planners,* April 1976.

Bryson, J.M. and A.L. Delbecq. "A Contingent Approach to Strategies and Tactics in Planning," *Journal of the American Institute of Planners,* April 1979.

Cohen, R. "Neighborhood Planning and Political Capacity," *Urban Affairs Quarterly,* March 1979.

Denbow, S. and T.E. Nutt. "The Current State of Planning Education," *Journal of the American Institute of Planners,* May 1973.

Dye, T.R. and J.A. Garcis. "Structure, Function and Policy in American Cities," *Urban Affairs Quarterly,* September 1978.

Hemmens, G.C., E.M. Bergman, and Maroney, R.M. "The Practitioner's View of Social Planning," *Journal of the American Institute of Planners,* April 1975.

Howe, E. "Role Choices of Urban Planners," *Journal of the American Institute of Planners,* October 1980.

Howe, E. and J. Kaufman. "The Ethics of Contemporary American Planners," *Journal of the American Institute of Planners,* July 1979.

_____ . "The Values of Contemporary American Planners," *Journal of the American Institute of Planners,* July 1981.

Johnston, M. "Public Policies, Private Choices: New Town Planning in Three Nations," *Urban Affairs Quarterly,* September 1977.

Needleman, M.L. and C.E. Needleman. "Guerillas in the Bureaucracy: The Community. Planning Experience in the U.S." New York, NY: John Wiley and Sons, 1974.

Nutt, T.E. and L.E. Susskind. "Prospects for Urban Planning Education," *Journal of the American Institute of Planners,* July 1970.

Plant, J.F. and L.G. White. "Planning Under New Federalism," *Journal of the American Institute of Planners,* April 1981.

Sacco, J.F. and W.M. Pearle. "Policy Preferences Among Urban Mayors," *Urban Affairs Quarterly,* September 1977.

Schon, D.A., N.S. Cremer, P. Osterman, and C. Perry. "Planners in Transition," *Journal of the American Institute of Planners,* April 1976.

Vasu, M.L. *Politics and Planning.* Chapel Hill, NC: The University of North Carolina Press, 1979.

Part II

Planning Skills and Orientations

2

How Rational Can Planning Be: Toward an Information Processing Model of Planning

Manfred Kochen and Charles Barr

Mach'mal einen Plan
Sei nur ein grosses Licht
Mach dann noch 'nen zweiten Plan
Gehn tun sie beide nicht
        B. Brecht

Introduction

To plan is to try shaping the future. We plan by saving for a rainy day. The bride plans a wedding. The navigator plans a course. The student plans his education, perhaps for a career. An architect or builder plans construction of a structure. A businessman plans a meeting or a new product. Many of us plan our next meal, our weekends, and all of us plan numerous small activities in our daily lives.

Too often, the best-laid plans are not followed, and when they are, they don't work. A plan works if the planned actions lead to predicted consequences. When they do not, it may be because (1) the assumptions about which actions lead to what consequences under given conditions are wrong; or (2) not acted on; or (3) the given conditions do not hold; or (4) are not accurately known; or (5) the actions are not taken on time.

We who plan usually fail to make explicit our starting assumptions. Nor are we willing to formulate them clearly, either because of lack of knowledge or unwillingness to confront the uncertainty or risk. Planning requires *boldness, imagination, ambition* and *commitment.* Successful planning requires, in addition, knowledge of all kinds, understanding and wisdom.

Quite often, the attainment of goals or conditions that are highly valued by a person is the result of his power. Skeptics about the role of rationality in planning would argue that it is that person's *power* that accounts primarily for his success, and that he or others can attribute his success to a rational plan only in retrospect, and in complete candor not even then. They argue that "planning" is merely a term *describing* maneuvers for position, the skillful use of resources to get results and enforcement of sanctions for coercing others to comply with their will, if necessary. The rational aspects of planning, in their view, are an appearance and a cover for the deeper emotional and social forces at work; regarding planning as a rational process is idealistic, utopian and non-descriptive of reality. Even if genuinely rational planning overcomes its tendency to provide a theatre for power plays, it will generate intensive demands for detailed, timely information. Decentralized markets may summarize the highly individualistic circumstances of time and place for decision making better (Benjamin, 1976).

Nature abounds with instances of success in what resembles planning. Spiders plan webs. Ants plan elaborate tunnels. Bees plan hives and supply routes. Beavers plan dams, and the nucleotide sequences in cells seem to embody the plans for the development of daughter cells. We do not call complex molecules or even insects knowledgeable, ambitious, imaginative or bold. And we do not see people with those qualities succeed in their planning of seemingly simpler activities nearly as well. The resemblance between planning in nonhuman systems and human systems may be superficial. Nonhuman living systems have evolved behavior patterns whose success is concomitant with natural selection. In many cases genetic mechanisms play a central role.

If modern sociobiologists (Wilson, 1975) are on the right track in the neo-social Darwinism of their postulates, then human planning systems may also have evolved through natural selection. But cultural rather than genetic information transfer mechanisms are involved (Lumsden & Wilson, 1981). This makes our actions essentially more flexible and iterative, though baggage in the form of obsolete administrative overhead and traditions encumbers and constrains adaptiveness. Moreover, human planning is conscious and deliberate. The idea that we can shape our future is relatively new in history, and makes man unique among species in the play of evolution.

The issue of how much of this evolution is preprogrammed versus epigenetic arises when we try to explicate planning as if it could be programmed. It is possible to simulate evolution by a computer program, including the possibility that flexible planning programs could generate results that are themselves the output of a program-generating program. What we call planning in nonhuman natural systems may be a programmed behavior evolved through natural selection; it is not iterative or flexible. Nor does it usually take as its working material the built or social environment of its community.

Between this notion of programmed planning and the normative ideal of rational planning lies a descriptive view of planning in the practice of human affairs. This is a political process driven by imagination, ambition and commitment, as well as by power. But it does and should have a rational component. There is an upper limit to the influence of that component on the planning process. To explore this limit—to estimate how rational planning could be—we focus this analysis on the cognitive, rational aspects of planning. We try first to clarify what we mean by rational planning.

In what follows, we explore the value of concepts from artificial intelligence for an explication of "planning" that could help organize research and teaching, and perhaps stimulate development of new planning practices, even in the face of the problems noted by Alexander (1965), Lee (1973), Friedman (1973), and Schon (1977). Of all the various aspects of what a professional planner does—political, social, fiscal, economic, emotional, etc.—we focus in this chapter on the cognitive aspects, and particularly the objective, knowledge-based, problem-solving aspects. This is not to deny that the other aspects are often, in practice, more important. The cognitive aspect is selected because of progress in information technologies (especially in artificial intelligence) that can support problem solving.

We start with the proposition that the thinking used in "artificial intelligence," particularly about information and control in animals, machines, and persons, may help in explicating "rational planning." Computer programs, algorithms and mathematical proofs, constructions, or derivations must be planned in advance. An intelligent machine that is to solve a new problem, such as making an inference, steering a robot around an obstacle, playing a game, or solving a puzzle must plan the solution. So must a program that can paraphrase simple stories about a given topic for which it has a script, such as going to restaurants (Schank & Abelson, 1977).

Planning for problem solving was discussed in one of the first review articles on artificial intelligence (Minsky, 1961). Planning was viewed as equivalent to analyzing a problem: dividing it into parts, each of which can be solved with less effort or further divided. One way to do that is to find another, essentially similar, problem that is easier to solve, so that the solution of the simpler problem can be used as a "plan" or "model" of the harder one. Another way is to find an interpretation of the given problem in another system that is more familiar and in which there are more powerful methods.

Both these methods are used when a child is asked to subtract two three-digit numbers, say 123 and 117, by using "Dienes Blocks," such as those in Figure 2.1, which represent 123. Procedures from the simpler concrete problem are analogous to procedures in the abstract problem. These procedures become meaningful with use, and this requires knowledge about the parts of the procedure and how they fit together. Such knowledge has been formally represented in a more recent contribution to artificial intelligence by means of a "planning net."

We discuss the cognitive elements of planning, the knowledge needed for planning, what can and cannot be planned, and finally, planning procedures.

Cognitive Elements of Planning

The *Cognitive Paradigm* (De Mey, 1982) stresses the integration of what we know about the world into a model to use for selection of goals and procedures to attain them. Values, feelings, and social constraints must, of course, be integrated as well. The cognitive approach calls on planners to make their values and interests explicit, or bring them to the surface, to ensure that everyone concerned is aware of them at the appropriate times. It also suggests the use of an issue map that makes a planner aware of issues, their relative importance, and the relations among issues, so as to provide him with the perspective necessary for sound judgment. Such a map should also make him aware of major opportunities, traps, and, above all, constraints.

Once values, interests, and constraints are explicit, selection of goals, targets, time, and scope horizons can become more objective. Analytic reasoning and a scientific foundation could be brought to bear to a greater

FIGURE 2.1

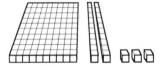

extent. Inevitable conflicts can be managed by principled rather than by positional negotiations (Fisher and Ury, 1981). This is not to say that planning can be automated. It is probably not possible to evaluate many plans prior to their implementation. Perhaps a plan cannot even be evaluated by hindsight, even after enough time has elapsed for historical perspectives to emerge. To be sure, the success of product or production plans in a firm can be readily measured. But complex urban, social, or environmental plans can perhaps only be *justified*, and their quality measured, by the degree to which the justification is "appropriately" persuasive to all those who are affected by the plan and who must implement it.

What are the relations among strategic management, highest-level decision making, and planning? These distinctions are often blurred. This ought to be remedied, because the kinds of needed support tools, the kinds of persons to be placed in appropriate positions, and the knowledge they should have turns on those distinctions. Is a plan a way to implement the solution to a problem formulated by a decision maker? Is it a network of decisions? The artificial intelligence community has traditionally defined planning as the process of creating a procedure from a set of constraints. It stressed the design of procedures. It has not concerned itself with the *formulation* of constraints. In this view, a plan is a sequence of steps that apply a constraint, starting with a goal and progressively refining goals into subgoals. The goal and the constraints are given. The result of these steps is a "planning net." This is a directed graph. Its nodes represent plans in the form of a flow chart. One node is linked by results from a second by applying constraints to the second. The top node is the general goal statement to be expanded. But that could be a subgoal of an even larger plan. The bottom node is a "final" plan, but that could be detailed even further.

Strategic management thus refers to the larger plans, at higher levels of aggregation. Decision making refers to selection of procedures at every level. Planning appears to be the more comprehensive concept.

The example below of proposal planning and processing may clarify this conceptualization of plans and planning. The proposal must be written, typed, approved by the authorized sender, and then mailed and received by the funding agency. At any time the proposal is in one of a set of possible states, as are the various participants in the process. Suppose there is only a *W*riter and an *A*dministrator who must approve it, each being in only one of two states: *b*usy or *f*ree (~b). The *P*roposal is in one of the following states: *u*nstarted, *c*onceived, *d*rafted, *r*evised, *f*inalized, *a*pproved for submission, in the *m*ail, arri*v*ed, ac*k*nowledged. The recipient or *F*unding agency is in one of two states: in *p*ossession of the proposal or not, ~p. The following is a minimal repertoire of actions: _CON_ceptualize, _WRI_te, _APP_rove, _DIS_approve, _SEND_. "_A_," the administrator, can take actions: _APP_rove or _DIS_approve or _URG_e for progress. "_F_," the funding agency, can: _ACK_nowledge receipt, or _URG_e for progress. We represent a state as: (_W:b_, _A:b_, _F:b_, _P:v_), interpreted that at a certain time _W_, _A_, and _F_ are all busy and the proposal has arrived at _F_. Actions effect transitions from one state to another, as in the acknowledgment by the funder below:

$$F.ACK$$
$$(W{:}b,\ A{:}b,\ F{:}b,\ P{:}v)\ \rightarrow\ (W{:}x,\ A{:}x,\ F{:}x,\ P{:}k).$$

The _x_'s on the right-hand side denote either _b_ or ~_b_, and thus this represents eight possible states, the set of goal states. A possible initial state is (_W:b_, _A:b_, _F:b_, _P:u_); again, seven others are possible.

The following illustrate some constraints.

1. Goal: _P:k_ (since the states of _W_, _A_, and _F_ don't matter, we need not write them out).
2. Action _F.ACK_ requires state _F_: ~_b_, that _F_ not be busy. Similarly for _F.URG_, _A.APP_, _A.DIS_, _A.URG_, etc. _F.ACK._ can be applied only to _P:v_ and results in _P:k._
3. Any action by _F_, _A_, and _W_ implies that the actor is not busy afterward.
4. _W.SEN_ can be applied only if _P:a_, and results in _P:m._
5. _A.URG_ and _F.URG_ can be applied any time.
6. _W.CON_ can be applied only to _P:u_, _P:d_, _P:r_.
7. _W.WRI_ can be applied only to _P:c_, _P:d_, _P:r_.
8. _W.APP_, _W.DIS_, _A.APP_ and _A.DIS_ can be applied only to _P:f_.
9. We assume that _P:v_ follows automatically from _P:m_ without actions.
10. If both of two actions are to be performed and neither has to precede the other, then select one arbitrarily (by any rule, or at random), do it first and then do the other. (This is a commonsense heuristic.)

These rules are not a complete set. A state-action transition table will certainly be needed as well.

A node in a planning net is a plan in the form of a flow diagram, at some level, such as:

Scanning the above constraints/heuristic rules, we find that only rule 2 will help. This leads us to replace the above plan by:

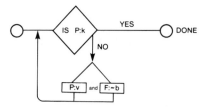

By rule 10, this can be made sequential:

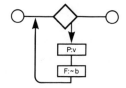

Continuing, we replace

by

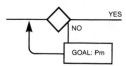

by rule 9. To reach this subgoal, rule 4 applies. The process is repeated to produce a network of figures in which the bottom node is a plan with detail corresponding to the specified actions.

We have used the terms "objective," "justified," "appropriately persuasive," and "principled" to characterize the cognitive or rational aspects of planning. We have also made a distinction between planning, decision making and strategic management, in which planning, regarded as successive goal refinement, comprises the other two as special cases. The view of planning as goal refinement may capture an essential feature of any planning process, whether genetically programmed, rational, or in-between. What it clearly implies is that planning is knowledge-based, particularly the knowledge about realistic constraints that drive goal refinement. What makes planning "rational" is the requirement that such knowledge be consensually valid, that it is used in ways that help those concerned with the problem that stimulated planning to adequately cope, and that basic values and principles shared by planning actors are consistently applied.

Knowledge for Planning

The above text, despite its detailed description of planning as if it were meant for automated task planning, is not intended to suggest that planning can or should be automated. But computers can be used to *support* planning (Goldsteen, 1981).

First, the planner must specify the various participants or stakeholders in the planning process for a given planning task. (These were W, A, F in the above example.) Often he will not think of including at an early-enough stage persons who he in retrospect feels he should have included, with costly consequences in loss of political goodwill, needed support, and good ideas. He may also err in including too many, including persons who should not have been included, with resulting costs in loss of confidentiality, efficiency, and time. Experienced or expert professional planners are less likely to make these errors than are novices. The experience of such experts can be captured by a knowledge engineer who interviews them to determine their specific choices in given situations. The experts usually cannot articulate any general rules they use in making their choices, but may, in dialogue with the knowledge engineer, come to agree on the formulation of heuristics governing their choices. These heuristics comprise a knowledge base that a novice planner can consult, or can arrange to have advise him without his prompting. The essence of this assistance is to have recognized in the planning task a pattern, or a character that describes a class of essentially similar planning tasks so that transfer can occur whenever possible. The possibility of such transfer—that not all planning tasks are essentially unique even if no two are *precisely* identical—is required for a scientific approach to planning.

Secondly, the planner must specify the area(s) in which planning occurs. In the above example, it may have been the construction of a multilevel garage in some downtown area, with many competitive bidders, many potential collaborators, supporters, etc. Both knowledge bases containing statements about the issues and relations among them, as well as database management systems, can help more. Large-scale systems to sustain such knowledge bases for land information have been proposed (National Research Council, 1983).

Thirdly, the planner must specify the things, instruments, materials, and funding that are to be procured or produced. In our earlier example these were the proposal (and its budget). Knowledge bases, inference aids, databases and model bases—in other words, an expert system integrated into a package of "decision-support," word processing, and computer conferences—can help in the proposal preparation process (Dandekar, 1982).

Within the constraints on rational planning we argue for more knowledge-intensive planning, especially at this third level of planning support. Up-to-date, machine-readable knowledge can perform the tasks of clarification and specification of planning contexts and impacts. Sometimes this "enrichment" of information processing in planning constitutes an overload. This is sometimes deliberate. There are parallels to legal proceedings in which, for example, the discovery stage in antitrust proceedings builds up massive amounts of documentation requiring an adjunct information retrieval and management project employing dozens of lawyers, assistants, and specialists. Information management costs become burdensome because of human information processing limits, which may be an objective of one party to such proceedings as one strategy for pressuring a favorable settlement without full consideration by a court.

There are, however, many channels for effective and efficient impacts on planning. "Worst options" can be ruled out, popular options can be legitimized by clarifying their implications, costs can be better estimated, time frames and trends quantified and bounded, and risks reduced or better profiled.

We have plans within plans. We may plan proposal writing; working out the content of the proposal is yet another plan. If the proposal is accepted, then a plan of execution is formed and activities are monitored to check if they are proceeding according to plan. This, too, is information processing and could be computer-supported.

Elsewhere (Kochen, 1983), one author pointed to a paradox or dilemma: we do not know enough to plan, yet we cannot afford not to plan. We need to distinguish between challenges to planners about which we *cannot* know enough, and challenges about which we do not *at the moment* know enough. The former issue will be discussed in the section on limits, which focuses on the possibility of planning even when we cannot substantiate adequate claims about the effects of planned interventions. At the end of that section, we offer the example of a hypothetical sociotechnological system to control incompetent driving, which is fraught with dangerous side effects. In the next section, we consider challenges that cannot be planned for, even in principle.

We conclude this section with a proposed traffic information and control system that illustrates the dual role of information processing in planning: the use of knowledge as an input for planning, and knowledge as a critical part of what is being planned as an output. Imagine a driver seeking to get from a certain point in a congested city to another during a rush hour. He is willing to take an indirect route if and when he learns that such a route is less congested at just that time. If this information is widely broadcast, other drivers may choose that same indirect, route and by the time he gets under way on that route, it too is congested. To be adequately planned, a system should be capable of anticipating its own emergent systemic properties. This means that it cannot be designed or planned in such detail as would make such systemic effects inevitable. It must leave a great deal of freedom of choice to individual drivers, in a statistical sense. It could select a random sample of given size of drivers entering the most-congested area to inform them about alternative routes. Accurate, up-to-the-minute knowledge about traffic conditions at various points in the city must thus be maintained and made available in real time to selected drivers in certain locations whose destinations are also known. At the lowest level, the system helps each selected driver plan an optimal routing (or re-routing) from his present location. It monitors information at a higher level of aggregation. At the highest level, the system uses such information to balance idleness and congestion of the city's transportation capacities. It aggregates the microplans into a systemic plan, not in any simple additive way but by iterative interfacing and rerouting. Knowledge-driven planning ranges along a continuum of contexts from more to less feasible. Levels of planning influence where on the spectrum a given process falls. The more value-laden the context and objectives, the less rational the process of choosing options can be. The sophistication of information-systems design for planning cannot exceed the degree of structure of the planning environment—one cannot have decision-support systems, for example, without accepted cause-and-effect relations describing processes in the system for which one plans, and reliable translations of such relations into software. Transportation planning, for example, may assume an infrastructure of superhighways, availability and stable cost of private transport, potentially available federal funds for construction and maintenance, energy policies, and unchanging consumer preferences over the planning time frame. Given such assumptions, much of a "transportation plan" (for example, management of rush-hour traffic during a summer season of road repair) may be reduced to engineering choices. Additional knowledge about growth trends, neighborhood demographics, topography, and highway technologies can further automate decisions. But planning for urban neighborhood-renewal projects—or setting up and managing the research, development, and production systems of a multipurpose industrial project in technological innovation—are far less amenable to knowledge-intensive planning. Professional planners seeking to evaluate the potential for their specialty to be more knowledge-driven must make several kinds of judgments. They need to evaluate the structuredness of their planning contexts, the intensity and complexity of value choices implicit in selection of planning options, and the possibility of information-processing technology support favoring successful planning in that specialty.

Limits of Planning

Planning is generally occasioned when there is a recognized and justifiable concern that, without some intervention, the present state or situation will get worse, or that with some appropriate intervention it could get much better. Most commonly, neither the set of all possible states, nor the set of actions (interventions), nor the utilities (or disutilities) associated with each state and action, nor the probabilities of various states, are known (decision making under uncertainty); occasionally, these are believed to be known or knowable, and it becomes decision making under risk. At any rate, an effort can be made to obtain the desired knowledge. But there may be situations in which these things are unknowable.

Consider a Russian roulette player who holds a six-shooter to his head, loaded with one bullet and the chamber spun to randomize its location. The player bets *all* his assets, say $60,000 initially, that will be multiplied by 10 if he lives. He can plan to play three rounds, after which he will have $60 million if he lives, and to stop thereafter. He can calculate the risk, which is the loss of his life, with probability:

$$(1/6 + (5/6)(1/6) + (5/6)^2(1/6) \doteq 5/12$$

or an expected gain of $25 million. He can make the plan before starting but cannot know whether he will be able to carry it out. If he did not even know how many bullets the revolver holds, how many bullets are now in it, and what the multiplier of his assets is, he could not even assess his risk.

Yet he knew the rules of the game, the arena, and at least some of the stakes. That is what made it possible to plan. If completely unanticipated state transitions can occur with great suddenness, we clearly cannot plan. We cannot even prepare for such contingencies. It has been realized for some time that the greatest danger facing us is that of multiple interacting crises that occur simultaneously, or even trigger one another. [To prepare for this, a global-resource-trends simulation program was developed for the Joint Chiefs of Staff of the Defense Department (*Science*, 1983). The forecasting tool incorporates the possibility of multiple state-change discontinuities while assessing international conflict potential and its effects.]

To quote Wittgenstein, "worüber mann nicht sprechen kann, darüber muss man schweigen." The limits of planning are the limits of our imagination and our expressive or representational powers at any time. Ancient man could not imagine a spherical world and could not plan to circumnavigate the globe. We cannot give an example of an unanticipated state or event, for the moment we think of it and write it, it will cease to be unanticipated. Yet, in retrospect, there are numerous unanticipated states and events—for example, the transistor, integrated circuits, and the dramatic lowering of computer costs and increased capacities.

The ability to anticipate does not imply the ability to plan. We must, in addition, be able to shape events, to control the state transitions to some extent. Information is necessary but not sufficient. Even though many anticipated World War II, as some now anticipate another world war (possibly involving nuclear weapons), and have information to justify their beliefs and to enlighten proposals for prevention, no sufficiently powerful intervention instruments were or are available to planners. Similar comments may apply to a warmer climate due to carbon monoxide accumulation and a global greenhouse effect; the Environmental Protection Agency report on this matter includes a much stronger urgency for planning to cope with the event than the report issued shortly after by the National Academy of Sciences. We can, however, *prepare* for such changes with a view to adapting, even if we cannot plan.

An important consideration is the speed of anticipated changes relative to our capacity to assimilate information fast enough when the changes occur. Most accidents or disasters are due to the "suddenness" with which we are required to respond, and our state of preparedness is generally not up to the demand. We can be cognitively prepared to react if a car were to fall off the car-hauler on a superhighway in front of us, but our reaction time, presence of mind, and state of alertness may not be such as to enable us to avoid disaster; a trained, automatic reaction may be required, not one resulting from thought, and even the physiological parameters of the automatic response may be unequal to the situation. When they are, we can plan to be prepared by training ourselves in a small number of automatic emergency reactions. Ideally, we would like to plan so as to avoid such circumstances. But if we cannot, we can at least plan to be prepared.

Limits to Intervention

Beliefs about our ability to shape the future hinge on a distinction between planning and intervention. Planning a trip or the solution to a technical problem differ importantly from planning the treatment or medical management of a depressed person. In the latter case, such procedures as drug regimen, psychotherapy, and electroconvulsive therapy intervene into ongoing biochemical, psychological, and neurophysiological processes. They may interfere constructively or detrimentally. The changed state of the patient is not due solely to the planned treatment; changes may have occurred without treatment, and the intervention may have altered sensitively adjusted self-regulating mechanisms that were not completely understood.

Most of the urban and social planning done by professional planners is intervention. This applies particularly to the planning of technological interventions. It is important to keep in mind that we deal with an existing system that is usually complex. That system has numerous mechanisms that keep it functioning as it does. An attempt to plan for improving one aspect of the system may cause unintended dysfunction or disequilibrium in some other aspect of the system, or it may even cause unanticipated threats to the system as a whole. This applies equally to the built (man-made) as well as to the "natural" environment.

If system dynamics were understood there would be no problem (Zadeh, 1965; Zeleny, 1981), *provided* planners are not part of the system.

To plan technologies that are to be grafted onto complex systems, particularly sociotechnological systems with human participants, it is necessary to be able to say something about the system's behavior. The limits of what can be said, however, are governed by the remarkable principle of compatibility that is at the core of the theory of fuzzy sets (Zadeh, 1965; 1973). It states that, "as the complexity and human content of a system increase, the observer's ability to make precise and yet significant statements about the system's behavior decreases" (Zeleny, 1981). Thus, precision and relevance of our descriptions of human systems become increasingly incompatible in most cases of interest to planners. This is particularly the case when the observer is part of the system, and planners/observers often are part of the sociotechnological systems they intervene in.

An even deeper principle limiting what can be known about complex systems is an extension of the uncertainty principle beyond Elsasser's extension to biological systems (Elsasser, 1958). This states that to observe a complex system requires so many simultaneous measurements on the system that the state of the system is fundamentally changed; the act of observation alters the observed system so that it is impossible to know what state it was in. If we cannot ascertain a complex system's state, we cannot expect to know the effect of a proposed intervention. Observer and system are as inseparable as observation and intervention.

The discussion so far has dealt with planning of technologies that must function in concert with ongoing mechanisms of a complex societal system. But we should also discuss the effect of societal changes on technologies. This issue is important after technologies have become so pervasively and inextricably embedded in a societal system as to change our lifestyle; the technologies appear as if they had taken on a life of their own. An example is a military computer-based, communication-command control and intelligence system (C^3I), which is often so complex (10^6 lines of code) that it will almost certainly and always contain undetected (perhaps undetectable) bugs that are beyond the capacity of any one mind to completely understand and control in all circumstances. Here, societal trends—such as the need to maintain stability in managing conflicts by maintaining nuclear arsenals and associated C^3I systems—drive the technology. Another example is a societal trend toward *self*-service (Kochen and Zeleny, 1981) and a shorter workweek, with implications for technologies that support self-service, leisure activities, and values that shift from traditional productive activities, perhaps to knowledge-related ones.

To illustrate the danger of planning sociotechnological interventions of even the simplest kind, consider another possible system aimed at reducing traffic accidents. Given that an unacceptable number of traffic accidents are caused by impaired drivers (under the influence of alcohol, drugs, diminished reaction times due to advanced age, or emotional stress), it would be easy to equip motorists with a conventional device for recording the license plate of any driver observed to behave dangerously in traffic (nearly caused an accident, disobeyed traffic regulations, or endangered others). If enough independent reports about a car with a given plate accumulate in the control system, the driver of that vehicle is carefully examined. Critics will easily recognize in this an Orwellian "Big Brother" scheme of the kind practiced by the citizens of some totalitarian countries to control subversive, politically dissident, socially parasitic or otherwise "undesirable" elements. Abuse of the system could possibly be kept within acceptable control limits so that the expected social benefits outweigh the expected social costs. But deciding on such a system resembles decision making under uncertainty rather than under risk: the possible outcomes and their probabilities cannot always be specified well enough in advance to permit the calculation of expected social benefits and costs. There will be successful cheats under any system, of course. Possibly the system could be made self-planning and self-adjusting as in the case of the congestion-control example, but this requires new ideas that might alter the transportation system even more drastically and unpredictably.

A knowledge-intensive model of planning could, as in this transportation-oriented application, draw on many disciplines for its configuration. An understanding of the social behavior of drinking and alcoholism and the sociology of private automobile ownership and use would frame the human contribution to the rate of traffic accidents. A legal information-tracking system can shed light on concerns for privacy, as well as individual, municipal, and liquor-serving establishments' responsibilities and liabilities in drunk-driving accident data can highlight high-risk locales for heavier time-sensitive enforcement of speeding and safety laws. In Hawaii, for example, local police set up roadblocks and test sobriety on New Year's Eve. Many actions are possible short of transforming the system that the planning-decision context has assumed. A major challenge to planning information system design and performance is to help identify the frontiers at which cumulative interventions shift the total system into quite different patterns. Such performance is well beyond either our present social sciences or information-system art. If we do not know enough to reliably predict whether an intervention will have catastrophic, irreversible consequences, we should probably err on the side of caution.

Conclusion

"The Day After" was shown on television in November 1983. What is hopefully a widely understood fact was the primary lesson to be learned from that dramatic presentation of a nuclear holocaust. It is that our political leaders reached their positions by virtue of skills in persuading people to vote for them, to cooperate with them, to accept policies about who gets what; these skills do not qualify them to make *plans* about complex and important issues, such as nuclear weapons or C^3I systems, unchallenged. Of course it is the defense establishment, not elected politicians, who manage weapons planning and largely manage the system of providing information to informed debate over weapons planning. It may be this extra leverage, combined with politicians' need to delegate these issues to such experts (Yarmolinsky & Foster, 1983) that shapes the outcomes of weapons policies. (The locus of leverage is shifting stress from the megatonnage to the sensitivity and reliability of the C^3I system that controls these enormous packages of destructive power.) Leaders in totalitarian centrally planned societies achieved their rank by skills in acquisition of power and binding others to their will with any means toward that end, and this qualifies them even less for knowledge-intensive planning. The business and professional leaders also reached the top by winning competitive races of increasing challenge, and such skills have little relevance for knowledge-intensive planning, which they entrust only to themselves (Benveniste, 1977).

For a broad spectrum of planners, the growth of knowledge-intensive planning in an increasingly complex and powerful information-processing context will reward those with greater computer literacy. IBM, for example, has designed and disseminated a powerful PC for its engineers and planners; its information retrieval methods include the call-up of multi-layered diagrams and maps of high resolution with zooming and highlighting capability. If the planning profession is to participate in guiding or providing leadership to resolve the critical problems of rapid change in sociotechnological systems, it must master information-technology change too.

If knowledge on which to base plans exists, even if it is buried and scattered in the world's libraries or experts' brains, we, for whose "benefit" planning is to be done, will not settle for plans or planners that fail to utilize such knowledge. The message of this chapter is that we should not settle for less than what can be done to retrieve, evaluate, screen, synthesize, and utilize such knowledge. We should demand even more: When lack of knowledge needed for important plans is identified—and there must be a deliberate effort to check this—resources are to be allocated to acquire the needed knowledge through research.

The problem with this last exhortation is that decision-making powers confront not only demands for resources to better characterize possible problems, but also demands for resources to address problems that have already been identified. This second class of problems, with higher visibility, will have accrued advocates voicing demands for continuity of action. One can quickly degenerate into circular reasoning: the criteria for defining an "important plan" may largely be evolved from present understanding of the problems it is to address. A good example of the cognitive gaps this can lead to is the United States–Canada debate over acid rain pollution control needs and policy action timetables. The United States does not support action because of the costs it would incur and claims, consequently, that the need for action is unproven.

A second problem is that within the short and intermediate time horizons for planning activities, it is rare to have acquired the "needed knowledge" in forms that are accurate, comprehensive, noncontroversial, and suitable for the decisions to be made. Either the knowledge is derived indirectly from research findings, which distorts the knowledge's utility for planning purposes, or it is derived from efforts specifically commissioned for planning, in which case its acquisition and application are liable to being heavily value-laden.

An important idea to accomplish this has been slowly developing (Wells, 1938; Kochen, 1967). The time may be ripe within this decade to implement an on-line, continually updated knowledge based with a powerful man-machine interface. It will enable planners, as end-users, to be reasonably certain that they have used all the relevant existing knowledge in justifying their policies and plans, and that needs for new knowledge have also been identified.

These ideas were presented in the core seminar of the UTEP program. They were well received. It stimulated one capable student to write a paper on intelligent decision support systems and to focus her doctoral research in this direction. The first author chairs the Sociotechnological Systems Area, one of the three concentration areas that comprise the UTEP program, and this approach is reflected in his thinking about the area. Consideration is now being given to restructuring the core of the UTEP program, and the direction this takes may be influenced by the lines of inquiry expressed in this chapter.

References

Alexander, Christopher. 1965. "A City Is Not a Tree." *Architectural Forum,* Whitney Publications, Inc.

Benjamin, Daniel K. 1976. "Circumstances of Time and Place: Environmental Aspects of the California Coastal Plan," in, *The California Coastal Plan: A Critique.* San Francisco, CA: Institute for Contemporary Studies.

Benveniste, Guy. 1977. *The Politics of Expertise* (2nd edition). San Francisco, CA: Boyd & Fraser Publishing Co.

Dandekar, Hemalata, ed. 1982. *The Planner's Use of Information.* Stroudsburg, PA: Hutchinson Ross Publishing Co.

De Mey, Marc. 1982. *The Cognitive Paradigm.* Hingham, MA: Kluwer Academic Publishers.

Drake, William, Roy Miller, and Donald Schon. 1983. "The Study of Community-Level Nutrition Interventions: An Argument for Reflection-in-Action." *Human Systems Management,* Volume 4, No. 2, pp. 87–97.

Elsasser, William. 1958. *The Physical Foundation of Biology.* New York, NY: Pergamon.

Fisher, Roger and William Ury. 1981. *Getting to Yes: Negotiating Agreement Without Giving In.* Boston, MA: Houghton-Mifflin Co.

Friedman, John. 1973. *Retracking America—A Theory of Societal Planning*. Garden City, NY: Doubleday & Co., Inc.

Friend, J.K., J.M. Power, and C.J.L. Yewlett. 1974. *Public Planning: The Inter-Corporate Dimension*. London: Tavistock Publications.

Fuller, R. Buckminster. 1982. *Critical Path*. New York, NY: St. Martin's Press.

Goldsteen, Joel. 1981. "These Agencies Are Leading the Way," *Planning*, Vol. 47, No. 10, October 1981, pp. 12–15 (special issue on computers).

Hoaglin, David C., et al., eds. 1982. *Data for Decisions: Information Strategies for Policymakers*. Cambridge, MA: Abt Books.

Kochen, Manfred. 1967. *The Growth of Knowledge: Readings on Organization and Retrieval of Information*. New York, NY: Wiley.

———. 1983. "Barriers to Planning in Business: Toward Information Systems to Help Overcome Them." *Human Systems Management*, Vol. 3, No. 4.

———, and Barr, C. 1984. "Distributed Expert Systems for Planners." Presented at Workshop on Utilization-Focused Research and Planning, Eindhoven, The Netherlands, December 10–14.

Kochen, M. and K.W. Deutsch. 1980. *Decentralization: Sketches Toward a Rational Theory*. Cambridge, MA: OGH.

Kochen, M. and M. Zeleny. 1981. "Self-Service Aspects of Health Maintenance: Assessment of Current Trends." *Human Systems Management* 2:4, 259–267.

Lee, Douglas B., Jr. 1973. "Requiem for Large-Scale Models." *AIP Journal*, May.

Lumsden, Charles J. and E.O. Wilson. 1981. *Genes, Mind, Culture: The Coevolutionary Process*. Cambridge, MA: Harvard University Press.

Mautz, R., A. Merten, and D. Severance. 1983. *Senior Management Control of Computer Based Information Systems*. Morristown, NJ: Financial Executives Research Foundation.

Michael, Donald. 1973. *On Learning to Plan and Planning to Learn: The Social Psychology of Changing Toward Future-Responsive Societal Learning*. San Francisco, CA: Jossey-Bass, Inc.

Minsky, Marvin. 1961. "Steps Toward Artificial Intelligence." *Proc. IRE*, January, pp. 8–30.

———. 1961. "A Selected Descriptor-Indexed Bibliography to the Literature on Artificial Intelligence." *IRE Trans. of Human Factors in Electronics*, pp. 39–55.

National Research Council. 1983. *Procedures and Standards for a Multipurpose Cadastre*. Washington, D.C.: National Academy Press.

Ouchi, William. 1984. *The M-Form Society: How American Teamwork Can Recapture the Competitive Edge*. Reading, MA: Addison-Wesley.

Schank, Roger C. and Robert P. Abelson. 1977. *Scripts, Plans, Goals, and Understanding*. Hillsdale, NJ: L. Erlbaum Associates.

Schon, Donald A. 1973. *Beyond the Stable State*. New York, NY: W.W. Norton & Co.

———. 1983. *The Reflective Practitioner: How Professionals Think in Action*. New York, NY: Basic Books.

Science. 1983. "World Model for the Joint Chiefs." 11 November. Vol. 222: No. 4624, p. 595.

Wells, H.G. 1938. *World Brain.* Garden City, NY: Doubleday & Co., Inc.

Wilson, Edward. 1975. *Sociobiology: The New Synthesis.* Cambridge, MA: Harvard University Press.

Yarmolinsky, A. and G.D. Foster. 1983. *Paradoxes of Power: The Military Establishment in the Eighties.* Bloomington, IN: University of Indiana Press.

Zadeh, Lotfi A. 1965. "Fuzzy Sets." *Information and Control,* Vol. 8, pp. 338–353.

_____. 1973. "Outline of a New Approach to the Analysis of Complex Systems and Decision Processes." *IEEE Transactions on Systems, Man and Cybernetics,* Vol. SMC-3, No. 1, January, pp. 28–44.

Zeleny, Milan. 1981. *Autopoiesis: A Theory of Living Organization.* New York, NY: North Holland.

3

Rational Processes
for Environmental Planning

Jonathan W. Bulkley

Introduction

To address the topic of this chapter, namely, rational processes for environmental planning, it is important to examine a specific aspect of environmental planning. In this chapter, planning for water resources is chosen as the vehicle to illustrate the component of environmental planning. The rational elements and processes identified for water-resource planning will not be generally transferable to all other aspects of environmental planning. However, it is anticipated that the ideas communicated regarding rational elements may be modified, extended, or otherwise serve to suggest concepts which will be generally constructive as one considers other topics of environmental planning.

An Initial Concept

Water as a renewable and essential natural resource has certain characteristics that enhance the need for careful planning and evaluation to assure the most efficient use of the resource. It is often useful to consider the water resource in a specified region, which may be defined by the watershed or watersheds that drain the region. The water resource to be considered would include both surface and ground water. The water resources in the region can be described in terms of their spatial (S) availability, their temporal (T) availability, and the associated quality (Q) characteristics. The natural or present

48

representation of the water resources of a region could thus be represented in vector notation as follows:[1]

$$
\begin{matrix}
\text{Water resources} \\
\text{Region} \\
\text{(existing)}
\end{matrix}
\qquad
\begin{bmatrix} S \\ T \\ Q \end{bmatrix}
$$

As a consequence of a planning effort which considers present and future needs for the water resources in the region, a desired alternative of the existing conditions of the regional water resource is identified. This desired charge may be represented as follows:

$$
\begin{matrix}
\text{Water resources} \\
\text{Region} \\
\text{(desired)}
\end{matrix}
\qquad
\begin{bmatrix} S' \\ T' \\ Q' \end{bmatrix}
$$

where S' represents a different spatial availability of the water resource, for example, through a diversion to move the water from a present location to a more desirable future location. T' represents a different temporal availability of the water resources. For example, one might consider a dam to establish a reservoir to store water which is available at one time of year for use later in the year. Another temporal variation could be to place excess surface water into a ground-water aquifer for subsequent use at a different time. Q' may reflect different quality characteristics of the water within the region. The present Q may not provide water of appropriate chemical and/or biological characteristics such that the water may be used for its intended purpose even if the spatial characteristics are satisfactory and the temporal characteristics are appropriate. Consider, for example, water to be used for irrigation purposes. There may be a sufficient quantity of water available at the desired location (spatial condition satisfied). Furthermore, the timing of the availability of the water with regard to the growing cycle of the crop is appropriate (temporal condition satisfied). However, if the water has excessive salinity, it will not serve as an appropriate water for irrigation purposes. Plans will need to be developed to provide cost-effective means to achieve the desired quality characteristics (Q') of the water resources to serve the regional needs for irrigation water. Accordingly, the rational basis for water resource planning is established by a recognition that the present spatial, temporal, and/or quality characteristics of the water resources in a specified region are not capable of meeting the identified water needs within the region. Water-resource planning is the process to seek cost-effective and environmentally desirable means to meet the water needs within the region.

Additional Considerations

1. Properties of Water

Before examining the rational elements which have been developed for the planning of water resources, it is desirable to provide a framework of factors and other considerations which have impacted upon water-planning processes through the years. First of these additional considerations would be to consider six general properties of water.[2]

A. Water is a renewable resource with the hydrologic cycle circulating the water from the oceans and other surface water bodies into the atmosphere. Precipitation returns water from the atmosphere to land and water bodies. At any given moment nearly 98 percent of the water on the planet is located in the oceans of the world. Nearly 2 percent of the water is associated with land—for example, in lakes and rivers, subsurface (ground water)—and the balance of this water is in the ice caps and glaciers. It should be noted that over 75 percent of the water associated with land is contained in ice caps and glaciers. Only a small fraction of the world's water is in the atmosphere at any given time.

B. Water is ubiquitous, i.e., there are few places on earth totally without water. It may be located in the ground in subsurface reservoirs or it may be available in very limited amounts. For example, in Africa the Bushmen of the Kalahari have evolved as a people who can survive in a very water-limited environment.

C. Water is heterogeneous in that it can exist as a liquid, solid, or as a vapor. The chemical and biological characteristics of different water sources may vary widely. It should be clear that beneficial use of water often requires a match not only of water of sufficient quantity but also of appropriate quality.

D. An important characteristic of water is that it may be a common property. In contrast to mineral rights which can be clearly defined, water rights may be, ill-defined or non-existent. In the United States, for example, two separate legal systems operate for control of surface waters. In the humid East, the riparian system of water rights, which associates rights to water use with owning of property along a waterway, is dominant. In the semi-arid and arid West, the prior appropriation system of allocation of water rights is dominant. In this latter situation, the user derives a right to the water from a date of withdrawal of the water from a river or stream for a beneficial use. Ground water is a whole new subject for control and regulation.

E. Water is used in vast quantities. In the United States alone, the water withdrawn from either surface or ground-water supplies for domestic use (urban and rural areas) is 35 billion gallons/day. Water withdrawn for irrigation purposes is the largest single use in this country—165 billion gallons/day. Water used for energy production—especially as cooling water—is 150 billion gallons/day. Water for mining and manufacturing is withdrawn at a rate of 45 billion gallons/day.

F. Historically, water has been provided as an inexpensive resource in terms of the cost charged to the typical domestic user. For example, 1,000 gallons of premium lead-free gasoline at a local service station cost about $1,300 in Ann Arbor, Michigan in early 1985. In contrast, 1,000 gallons of premium lead-free water can be delivered to your home in Ann Arbor at a cost of $1.15; it is over 1,000 times cheaper than the comparable quantity of gasoline. This water is used for domestic purposes such as drinking, cooking, washing, waste disposal, and for lawns and gardens. If one were to consider water for irrigation purposes (which as we have seen is the single largest use of water in this country), one normally speaks of a charge for water per acre-foot. The farmers seek irrigation water at the lowest possible price per acre-foot. In some regions of the country, federally supplied irrigation water may cost the farmer $7.50/acre-foot. In contrast, if one were to purchase an acre-foot of Ann Arbor water ($1.15/1,000 gallons), the cost for one acre-foot would be $375. In other words, irrigation water may be obtained in certain areas of the country through federally supported programs at a cost of $.023 (2.3¢) per 1,000 gallons. This is a very inexpensive price for a very valuable resource.

In addition to these six properties and characteristics of water, one needs to be aware of several themes which have arisen over the years with regard to water resources development and utilization in the United States.[3] One must recognize that from the earliest days of our country and elsewhere throughout the world, rivers provided not only the water necessary to support populations, but also the same rivers were the transportation means to enable commerce and development to take place. Furthermore, as settlements took place along or adjacent to rivers, the various units of government became concerned not only about sufficient water in the river for water supply and navigation, but also on those occasions when there was too much water in the river and flooding took place. Finally, it has long been the practice in this country for the federal government to provide water for irrigation purposes as a means to settle and otherwise make useful for development vast areas of land in the West which otherwise would not be productive. Provision

of flood control, navigation, water supply, and irrigation water often resulted
from major dam construction. These multiple-purpose projects also provided
the potential for development of electrical energy through hydroelectric
power generation. All of these development activities have taken place in this
country especially throughout the 20th century, but the foundations for these
activities were laid well back in the 19th century. Water as a resource was
to be developed for its economic potential and the economic contribution it
could make to the well-being of the country as a whole.

Planning Themes

It is against this historical orientation that one needs to consider the
themes which now are operating as elements of water-resource planning in
the United States. Clearly, these themes are not necessarily transferable to
other countries/other locations. Nevertheless, the following seven themes
incorporate information which water planners need to consider during their
planning activities.

   A. The first theme that has emerged is that the level of future demands
       for water is not inevitable but derives in large part from policy
       decisions within the control of society. It is important to keep in
       mind the distinction between a *requirement* for water which may
       reflect the quantity of water required to maintain life itself, and the
       demand for water which may reflect the quantity of water which
       would be used at the price provided. To illustrate the idea that
       "trend is not destiny," water planners are encouraged to project a
       series of alternative futures associated with the water development
       issue under study. This consideration of alternative futures is criti-
       cal since water projects tend to be highly capital-intensive, have
       long physical and economic lives, and are highly irreversible. For
       example, one cannot find alternative uses for a dam and reservoir.
       Water planners seek to minimize the risk of failure to meet unanti-
       cipated demands for the water resource versus the risk of a prema-
       ture commitment of large economic and other resources to the solu-
       tion of problems which fail to materialize.
   B. A second theme relevant to rational water planning has emerged
       over the period of time since the early to mid-1960s. This theme is
       a shift in national priorities in this country from the development of
       water resources to the restoration and enhancement of water qual-
       ity. The emphasis on development of water-resource projects often
       meant that large projects were constructed with a significant federal
       subsidy. We have moved from the time in this country where

periodic fires on industrial rivers made front-page news. Environmental values have been incorporated into the planning and policy processes which require industrial and municipal wastes to be cleaned up prior to discharge to receiving waters. Planning has now been altered to incorporate these more environmental or noncommercial uses of water, i.e., water for recreation, esthetics, and the preservation of the balance of nature. It is recognized that an explicit balancing process is required to identify the conflicting interests at stake. The planning process must identify and make clear the consequences of alternative courses of action. Procedures must be developed to provide for public hearings and the consideration of divergent points of view. Appropriate decision-making bodies need to be developed to assess and evaluate benefits, costs, risks, and potential gains from alternative water-development projects. Basically, by the late 1960s, the mood of the public in the United States had changed; it rejected the traditional economic assessment of a proposed water project as the sole determinant of whether or not it should be implemented. Other values beyond economic development must be considered as well.

C. A third theme which has emerged is the recognition that water-resource planning must be tied more closely to land-use planning. In research done on units of government having jurisdiction over the Great Lakes' shorelines in both the United States and Canada, land use is the independent variable that offered the strongest explanation of in-shore water quality.[4] Certain land-use activities may have a significantly adverse impact on the water quality of both surface and ground waters in the area if the water-resource planning and the land-use planning are not carefully coordinated. The pollution of the ground-water aquifers on Long Island, New York as a result of both urban land use and rural land use is a classic example of this important interrelationship.[5]

D. A fourth theme which has been given emphasis since 1980 is that sound economic principles should be applied to decisions on whether or not to build water projects. The basic idea is that one should employ user-charges as a measure of the willingness to pay and thus a measure of the actual need for the project. Historically, in this country many water projects—especially navigation, flood control, hydropower development, irrigation projects in the West and, more recently, municipal waste-water treatment plants—have received federal funding assistance to encourage the projects to be implemented. The criticism is that rational economic analysis may be distorted in the face of these federal financial subsidies, and projects which should be rejected on economic grounds are allowed to be implemented. The change in the water industry in England

and Wales with the creation of the ten Regional Water Authorities in 1974, and the reliance on user-fees in place of grants from central governments are good examples of this theme actually being put into practice.[6,7]

E. A fifth theme which has been accepted and implemented in other areas of the world, and which is gaining acceptance in this country, is that water-resource policies and plans must be devised which will lead to the conservation of water. Plans and policies are needed which will motivate better (more efficient) use of existing water resources and reduction of existing water losses. The federal government incorporated this concept into the regulations associated with the provision of public funds to build, expand, and upgrade publicly owned waste-water treatment facilities. As one requirement to receive federal funds for these projects, the municipality needed to demonstrate that their sewage collection system had been studied to identify and correct any excessive infiltration and inflow to the system. Otherwise, public funds would be spent to treat infiltrating ground water through cracks and other failures in the collection system, or these funds would be spent to treat excessive inflows of storm water into a combined sewer system. Rational planning certainly requires efficient and effective use of available resources. In older cities, excessive leaks from aging water distribution systems generate an excessive demand for additional water resources. In some cases, this may mean additional trans-basin diversion to supply a system which is wasting a significant portion of the resource because of poor standards of maintenance and failure to replace old and outworn distribution equipment.

F. A sixth theme which has direct impact upon rational planning of water resources is the need to reexamine laws and legal institutions in the light of contemporary water problems. For example, the prior-appropriation doctrine which has developed in the West provides little incentive for transferring water rights to more valued uses. Rather, the incentive is to maintain present inefficient use—a "use it or lose it" concept. Until recently, little protection has been available for instream water uses—for example, fishing, recreation, and esthetics. Also, a major set of issues needs to be resolved with regard to Indian water rights. Until the Indian claims for water are resolved, it does not appear that rational planning can proceed. In the East, the riparian system of water rights does not necessarily provide a solid foundation for long-term resource planning and development. Finally, the failure to provide effective control of ground water pumping creates a potential for a "tragedy of the commons" condition.[8] The absence of effective institutional mechanisms results in a very strong incentive for each individual to pump ground water at an excessive rate and use it before another individual pumps the water and takes the resource.

G. Finally, the seventh theme which has emerged for water planning and policy is that the development, management, and protection of water resources should be controlled by that level of government nearest the problem and most capable of representing the vital interests involved. Historically, the federal government has had a major responsibility for water resource planning and project implementation. At present, pressures exist to devolve many of these federal responsibilities to the state level. However, the requirement remains for uniform federal standards to assure that certain minimum levels of performance are achieved. The need exists to be able to bring together the appropriate units of government within a "problem-shed" which may cross established political boundaries. This task is a difficult and challenging one which has only a few precedents in the field of water resources in this country. Issues of funding, enforcement, representation, conflict resolution, and project implementation all need to be resolved.

Rational Water Planning: The Principles and Standards

Historically, the federal government has invested significant funds in a variety of water projects including navigation, flood control, irrigation, hydropower development, municipal and industrial water supply, water pollution control, and water-based recreational activities. The federal Flood Control Act of 1936 specified that flood control projects should be implemented where benefits are greater than the costs of the projects. A variety of techniques have been employed since 1936 to encourage rational elements in federal water planning. In 1965, the federal Water Resource Planning Act established the Water Resources Council whose task, among others, included the preparation of Principles and Standards for federal water planning and water-project evaluation. These Principles and Standards were first announced in 1973 and then subsequently revised and designated as Rules (1980) by the Carter Administration. The major changes in the Principles and Standards implemented by the Carter Administration included the following:

1. The objective of National Economic Development was made co-equal with the objective of Environmental Quality.
2. The new procedures specified for evaluating benefits and costs were considered to use the best techniques available and were believed to ensure consistency and accuracy among agencies in the economic evaluation of federal water resource agencies.[9]

3. In addition, the revised Principles and Standards required conservation techniques to be fully integrated into the planning and review process.

4. Finally, the revision included the requirement that at least one nonstructural alternative be included in plan preparation. Basically, the nonstructural alternative was required to assure that demand modification policies were considered as well as more conventional project alternatives.

In order to provide a sense of the thrust of the Principles and Standards as revised by the Carter Administration—especially in the context of rational water planning-processes—consider the following information taken from the Rules:

Summary of the Planning Process[10] (emphasis added)

711.100 Introduction

The planning process consists of a series of steps that identify or respond to problems and opportunities and culminates in the selection of a recommended plan. The process involves an *orderly* and *systematic* approach to making determinations at *each step* so that the *interested public* and the decision makers in the planning organization can be *fully* aware of:

The basic assumptions employed;
The data and information analyzed;
The reasons and rationales used; and
The full range of implications of each alternative plan.

711.101 Major Steps

(a) The Planning process consists of the following major steps:
    (1) Specification of the water and related land resources problems and opportunities (relevant to the planning setting) associated with the National Economic Development and Environmental Quality objectives.
    (2) Inventory, forecast, and analysis of water and related land resource conditions within the planning area relevant to the identified problems and opportunities.
    (3) Formulation of alternative plans.
    (4) Evaluation of the effects of the alternative plans.
    (5) Comparison of alternative plans.
    (6) Selection of a recommended plan based upon the comparison of alternative plans.
(b) Plan formulation is a *dynamic* process with various steps that should be iterated one or more times. This iteration process, which may occur at any step, may sharpen the planning focus or change its emphasis as new data are obtained or as the specification of problems or opportunities changes or becomes more clearly defined.

In the author's view, the elements of the planning process specified above constitute one description of a rational planning process associated with water resources. It is important to note how the themes initially identified by the National Water Commission were reflected in these revised Principles and Standards. For example,

- The Environmental Quality Objective was made co-equal with National Economic Development (Theme 2).
- The specification of basic assumptions requires the planners to address the policy issues associated with future demands (Theme 1).
- The specification of water and *related land resource* problems and opportunities associated with the several objectives (Theme 3).
- The evaluation of the effects of the alternative plans. Note: These evaluations were to be done in terms of four separate accounts— National Economic Development (costs and benefits), Environmental Quality (positive/negative impacts), Regional Economic Development and Other Social Effects (Themes 2, 3, and 4).

Finally, note that these Principles and Standards required a multi-objective framework in order to accomplish the planning process.

The Reagan administration viewed the Principles and Standards as too rigid in the form of Rules implemented by the previous administration. Accordingly, in November 1982 the Reagan administration revoked the former Rules and issued a new version as Principles and Guidelines. Besides revoking the Rules' provisions, the new Guidelines require only a single National Economic Development Objective, and a secretarial exemption if a plan other than the NED is selected. Nevertheless, the procedures established in the Rules in September 1980 may yet serve as examples of the basic elements to be considered as one considers rational planning processes for the field of water resources.

Multi-Objective Analysis

The Principles and Standards as developed from 1973 until 1982 required multi-objective evaluation in the development of federal water plans. As a consequence, the techniques of multi-objective analysis which developed as a result of the stimulus of the U.S. Water Resource Council (Principles and Standards) and the associated Basin Planning Commissions are still available for use. In fact, multi-objective analysis (MOA) is a methodical and systemic approach or process where trade-offs are made among noncommensurate objectives which are often in conflict and/or competition.[11] The literature makes a distinction between multi-objective planning and multi-objective programming.[12] Planning is a process which contains all of the elements of a systemic approach to problem solution. For example, planning includes problem identification, formulation of goals and objectives, specification of measures of effectiveness, generation of alternative solutions, evaluation of alternatives, selection of an alternative, and, finally, implementation of a selected alternative. These are the elements which were specified in the Principles and Standards.

Multi-objective programming (MOP) is a highly structured formal mathematical procedure for identifying a range of attractive solutions to the planning problem at hand. In contrast to a single-objective programming model, MOP generally does not identify a single solution for the decision makers. Rather, it identifies a range of possible solutions that satisfy the constraints in the planning problem and leaves to the decision makers the choice of a solution point along a frontier of non-dominated solutions. The actual decision point chosen by the decision maker thus reflects the relative value which the decision maker attaches to the several objectives included within the problem. Any movement along the frontier of non-dominated solutions means that improvement in one objective—for example, reduced risk of an environmentally related illness as measured by the decrease in concentration of a known causative agent in a water supply, can be achieved only as a result of a trade-off with another objective. An example would be an increase in cost for pollutant removal prior to discharge into the receiving waters.

The major contribution of MOA to rational environmental and water planning is to display the consequences of choice to the decision makers. If the environmental planners have done a thorough and complete analysis, the generation of a set of non-inferior solutions of a multi-objective analysis provides information to the decision maker(s) upon the consequence of choice of trading one objective for another in choosing a solution for the specific problem under study.

An example which illustrates this concept of non-inferiority is taken from a recent Ph.D. dissertation at the University of Michigan. Dr. H. D. Wicke[13] explicitly considered the uncertainty associated with the prediction of a desired trophic state in Lake Ontario. This uncertainty arises from both the uncertainty associated with the computer model used to predict the total phosphorous concentration in Lake Ontario from a variety of loadings, and the uncertainty in the different experts' opinions as to what total phosphorous concentration is necessary in Lake Ontario to achieve the desired trophic

FIGURE 3.1

Risk Analysis and Water Quality
Management: Lake Ontario

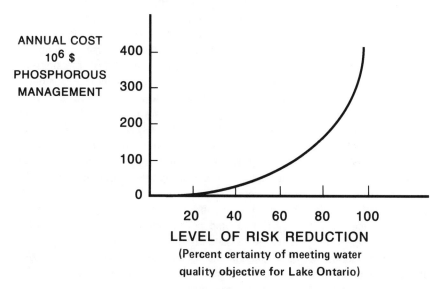

Source: Wicke, H. D., Ph.D. thesis, School of Natural Resources, University of Michigan, Ann Arbor, Michigan, 1983.

state. Furthermore, Dr. Wicke coupled this uncertainty of achieving a desired trophic state with the estimated cost of reducing phosphorous loadings to Lake Ontario. Her work illustrates the explicit trade-off required between increasing the certainty of achieving a desired environmental goal—a desired trophic state in this case—and the increased costs that are directly associated with decreasing the uncertainty associated with the desired goal (see Figure 3.1). This type of analysis requires the decision makers to explicitly consider the trade-off between risk reduction and the increased commitment of limited financial resources to achieve the acceptable level of risk.

Risk–Benefit Analysis in Environmental Planning

In December 1984 the world learned of a great tragedy in India where over two thousand citizens, young and old, lost their lives as a consequence of a failure in a chemical-processing facility. The environmental planner needs to utilize techniques of risk analysis and risk assessment to provide and display important information to decision makers. It is recognized that one may examine risk from a historical perspective—namely, identify incidents both natural and man-made which produce undesirable consequences. These adverse consequences may include fatalities, early illness, latent illness, reduced productivity, property damages, and/or environmental damage. The frequency of occurrence of the events producing these adverse consequences can be examined as well. The resulting cumulative distribution functions will display the frequency (events/unit time) of observing an incident leading to an undesirable consequence greater than or equal to a specified magnitude.

The problem becomes more complicated when the environmental planner is dealing with issues and situations for which there may not be a long historical record base on which one could build risk (probability) curves. In this latter case, the risk assessment procedure still follows two basic procedures. First, one undertakes a quantitative processing and evaluation of information through well-developed procedures and methodologies including the quantification of risk and the development of alternative policy options. Once the risk is quantified and policy options developed (to reduce the risk/increase the safeguards), a second step is needed. This second step is the introduction of value judgements by the decision makers concerning the identification of acceptable risks and their associated trade-offs. Here the task for the decision maker is to determine which selections are preferred and what policies are desirable.[14]

To accomplish this quantification of risk and to separate low frequency-high damage events from high frequency to low damage events for the decision maker, techniques have been proposed.[15] Basically the analyst or environmental planner generates outcome scenarios which describe a specific occurrence of a causative event. The purpose of these outcome scenarios is to describe as completely as possible all of the ways in which failure leading to damage may occur. With each of the outcome scenarios, one would need to estimate the frequency of occurrence of that event. Finally, with each outcome scenario, one may identify an anticipated damage as a result of the occurrence of the event. The resulting information may be plotted as damage versus frequency of occurrence in order to obtain an insight into the risk (frequency and damage) for the system under examination. In providing such information to the decision maker, the environmental planner has established a basis for the decision maker to respond and decide either that the present risk is acceptable or further safeguards are needed to reduce the risk. An explicit trade-off is then required where economic cost is increased as safeguards are introduced to reduce the identified risk to a more socially acceptable level.

Concluding Observations

This chapter has presented elements of rationality in planning for water resource development and use. Important characteristics of water resources have been noted; important themes which have developed in the planning and policies for water resource development in the United States have been identified. The elements of rationality that have been incorporated into water resource planning reflect the growth in knowledge, experience, analytical capability, and overall use of water as a critical life-sustaining resource not only in our country but throughout the world.

The techniques of multi-objective programming and planning are particularly well-suited to issues of environmental planning in general, and water resource planning in particular. A special challenge to the environmental planner who utilizes these techniques is *not* to project themselves into playing the role of decision makers. The analytical techniques of multi-objective programming and planning are complex. However, the results obtained from these studies have the potential to demonstrate to the decision maker the consequences of choice, and make clear the trade-offs between worthy but competing objectives. The chapter also identified the need for environmental planners to extend their ' training into the important area of risk-benefit analysis. Risk analysis offers a further element of rationality in both water resource planning and environmental planning.

Finally, the importance of diverse educational experiences contributing to the training of environmental planners has been noted. The challenges that face environmental planners and those individuals choosing to study in this critical professional area are immense. One expects that the rational elements of environment planning will expand and develop in the future to enable these challenges to be met and resolved in effective and efficient ways.

Notes

1. Buras, N. *Scientific Allocations of Water Resources,* America Elseview, New York, 1972.
2. U.S. Council on Environmental Quality and U.S. Department of State. *The Global 2000 Report to the President,* Vol. 1 and Vol. 2, U.S. Government Printing Office, Washington, D.C., 1980.

3. National Water Commission. *Water Policies for the Future,* U.S. Government Printing Office, Washington, D.C., 1973.
4. Bulkley, J.W., and Mathews, A.P. "Water Quality Relationships in the Great Lakes: Analysis of a Survey Questionnaire," Proceedings, 16th Conf. on Great Lakes (IAGLR) 1973.
5. Kimmel, G.E. "Nonpoint Contaminant of Groundwater on Long Island, New York," in *Groundwater Contamination,* National Academy of Science, Washington, D.C., 1984.
6. Bulkley, J.W. and Gross, T.A. "An Innovative Organizational Arrangement for Comprehensive Water Services: The Thames Water Authority as a Model for Complex Urban Areas of the Great Lakes," Research Project Technical Completion Report (OWRT USOI) 1975.
7. Bulkley, J.W. and Gross, T.A. "Innovation Management Concepts for 208 Planning," *Journal of the Technical Council,* ASCE, August, 1980.
8. Hardin, G. "The Tragedy of the Commons," *Science,* Vol. 162, 1243 (1968).
9. Viessman, W. and Welty, C. *Water Management Technology and Institutions,* Harper & Row, New York, 1985.
10. Rules and Regulations, *Federal Register,* Vol. 45, No. 190, September 29, 1980, p. 64399.
11. Haimes, Y. and D. Allee (editors). *Multi-objective Analysis in Water Resources,* American Society of Civil Engineers, New York, 1984.
12. Cohon, J., *Multi-Objective Programming and Planning.* New York, NY: Academic Press, 1978.
13. Wicke, H.D. *Risk Analysis and Water Quality Management.* Ph.D. Thesis: School of Natural Resources, University of Michigan, Ann Arbor, Michigan (1983).
14. Haimes, Y. "Risk Assessment for the Prevention of Groundwater Contamination," *Groundwater Contamination,* National Academy of Science, Washington, D.C., 1984.
15. Kaplan, S. and B.J. Garrick. "On the Quantitative Definition of Risk," *Risk Analysis,* Vol. 1, No. 1, 1981.

4

Technology Planning in Industry: The Classical Approach

Domenic Bitondo

Introduction

There is need today more than ever for industry to be more innovative and to couple this with better planning of technical resources.[1] This appears to be a dichotomy since innovation denotes change, disruption, and freedom while planning denotes control and well-defined courses of action. During the 1950s there seemed to be a blind faith in R&D, and plenty of resources were made available with no questions asked. During the late 1960s and the 1970s increasing inflation and a rapid rise in interest rates caused many businesses to measure their R&D expenditure in terms of its return of profitability. Therefore, we went into a period of many questions asked of R&D, but no resources supplied. R&D became remote from the mainstream of business planning. Today industry has reached the limit where neither the freedom of the 1950s nor control of the 1970s is providing the solution. It has become necessary for the successful businesses to learn to live with technological change and learn to manage risk with better planning, implementation and integration of their R&D programs. In the 1980s and '90s many questions will continue to be asked, but resources must be made available.

Corporate managements have helped successful corporations come to learn that the careful management and planning of science and technology are necessary ingredients of their business plans. On the other hand, it has been found that the methodology and structure for planning of technology and its integration into business planning have not been well developed in industry. It is the purpose of this chapter to provide a structure for the planning of technology so that it can be integrated into the business plans of a corporation. At the root of technology planning in a corporation is the requirement to provide the freedom scientists and engineers desire, yet to provide the direction that management insists upon so that management knows that the work being funded will produce eventual research results which benefit the corporation and its customers.

Planning to a scientist usually denotes constraints and lack of freedom, while to management it is a necessity. This dichotomy between scientists and management must be solved through the methodology used to plan technology. It is usually said by the scientist that research cannot be planned because of the unknown factors in invention and research. This is true if we are talking about research results—such results cannot be planned. On the other hand, research planning can provide direction to scientists and engineers so that their research work is consistent with the goals and objectives of the corporation and that the fruits of research are exploitable by the business units of the corporation. This is the crux of technical planning. It is not to force scientists to produce unknown results on a given schedule, but to provide direction to the research group so that its efforts are integrated into the corporation's goals, objectives and business plans. At the same time, with this direction, the scientists and engineers can pursue their work with the freedom which they so dearly desire by increasing their motivation in the accomplishment of the objectives.

Technical Planning

Technical planning is a logical thought process that is used to come to an agreement within a business on (a) its important technology areas, and (b) the technical strategies. This is done in order to formulate and/or to support (1) corporate objectives, (2) business goals, and (3) product and market strategies. From this an R&D program can be configured consisting of R&D projects staffed with people and the proper facilities. This results in an R&D program that is consistent with the business and its goals.

A number of ingredients are important to the technical planning process. First, it is necessary that the various functional groups such as planning, finance, marketing, product development, engineering, manufacturing, and R&D participate with top management in the thinking process to plan an R&D program. Management must ensure that these groups communicate on an equal basis. Second, the important technology areas of the business must be carefully defined using a common language so that they are commonly understood within the organization. Third, technical strategies have dimensions, and these dimensions have ranges. The technical strategies are a function of, and must be consistent with, corporate objectives, business goals, and market and product strategies. Fourth, there is a need for iteration between product and market strategy and technical strategy. Fifth, R&D, as well as being reactive to corporate objectives and business goals, must also be proactive in providing an input into those objectives and goals. And, sixth, the head of the R&D group must become an equal partner of the top management team rather than just a technical advisor.

Technological Innovation

Why discuss innovation? Technology brings about change; R&D is the agent of change and as such provides the stimulus for innovation. It upgrades products, solves problems in businesses and in society, brings about new products based upon new and old technologies, and starts new businesses/undermines old businesses by introducing new technology (changing the products within those businesses). R&D, as change, should provide a creative tension within the corporation. Successful businesses resist change—the "don't-rock-the-boat" syndrome—while technological change creeps up to cause those businesses to decline. R&D has the responsibility for the future and must consider the technological changes that are coming and how they affect the business options that are available to the corporation, as well as how technology might affect society as a whole. The introduction of new technology sometimes is not to the overall benefit of society. It is necessary, also, to consider those societal forces that create need as well as opportunity for technological innovation.

We, therefore, have a convergence of public- and private-sector planning which must draw on the interface between technology assessment and technology planning.

Technology assessment and government regulations brought about by societal needs also provide a stimuli for technological change. As we will note later, "a clearly defined need" (by the customer) is one of the greatest stimuli for innovation. Societal forces have been witnessed as strong needs during the past 12 years by the automobile companies where the "societal need" for fuel economy, emission control, and safety stimulated technological change in the automotive industry. In the book, *Technology and Social Institutions* (1974) by Professor Kan Chen, it was pointed out how Honda used the EPA regulations as an opportunity to innovate and invade the U.S. market with their new automobile engine.

Thus, in recent years there has been an increasing concern with technology assessment—the environmental impact of technology; and appropriate technology—relating the technology to the needs of a culture or society. All of these factors emphasize the need for corporations to ensure that technological advancements not only satisfy their corporate or business objectives, but are channeled so they contribute to the overall solution of the societal problem, yet are not detrimental to society as a whole.

The technological innovator must be sensitive to all these forces— corporate customers and societal—and the organization must provide the tools so that technological planning can factor the needs from the public and private sectors and still maintain a climate of creativity and innovation. Therefore, before a planning framework is described, it is necessary to consider those factors that produce successful innovation in a corporation so that technical planning can support and stimulate innovation rather than stifle it.

Technological innovation is not just the discovery of an idea, but it is the whole process from discovery to widespread adoption of it commercially. Technology planning must, therefore, support the whole innovative process. The need for continuing innovation is quite obvious. Many well-entrenched businesses have lost their markets—vacuum tubes to semiconductors, mechanical to electronic calculators—to name a few of the obvious ones. If innovation is important to a corporation, and technical planning must be done so that it stimulates successful innovation, what are the factors that are important to successful innovation? Studies by James Bryant Quinn[2] have indicated that the following patterns are important in successful innovation:

1. A strong incentive—by the company.
2. A clearly defined need.
3. Multiple competing approaches.
4. User guidance and participation during the development of the idea.
5. High technical expertise in the important technology areas.
6. Time horizons in organizations are longer than those most common in their fields.
7. Committed champions who carry forward the major developments.
8. Top-level, risk-taking support. Some top executive must be willing to take the risk.
9. Morale and discovery. High morale occurs when teams share a goal of creating a significant technical advance.

A planning process for technology must be such that it takes these nine factors and ensures that they are not violated.

Donald R. Schoen, in his paper written in the *Harvard Business Review* in 1969,[3] showed that top management involvement is a key ingredient in the management of technological innovation and, therefore, the involvement of top management must be a key requirement for successful planning of technology. Technology planning can no longer be relegated by top management to a planning group or to an isolated R&D group hidden away in some corner of the corporation. The head of R&D must be part of the management team. The heads of all the functional departments must be involved in developing the technological plan. Otherwise, innovation cannot occur in the organization. The planning methodology must make sense to the business manager as well as to the R&D scientist. A common language which both are comfortable with must be used in technology planning.

During the 1960s there was an increasing emphasis on return-on-investment types of quantitative analysis for determining the allocation of resources to technological developments. This short-range planning practice was detrimental to the future growth and competitiveness of corporations. This was especially true when competition came from foreign shores. The 1970s and 1980s have seen the growth of a more global matrix type of analysis or strategic management as described by Dr. Igor Ansoff.[4] Dr. Ansoff describes the principles important in integrating technology into strategic business planning/management.

There has been no single comprehensive framework to emerge, however, for strategic technical planning. Many researchers and authors have described the important principles necessary to be followed in developing such a planning framework for technology. Many of these results were based on the study of innovation. The technical planning framework described in the following sections incorporate these principles. Several corporations have incorporated this framework in whole or in part to suit the format of their strategic business management and have found it quite useful. However, as in any strategic planning concept, it requires several years of use before quantitative results can be obtained proving its ultimate benefit. In the meantime, several groups have found it a useful tool to stimulate their strategic analysis of the technological posture of their businesses.

Input Ingredients to a Technological Plan

Business, Market and Product Strategies

Where does one start in developing a technical plan? The starting points are corporate objectives, business goals, market, and product strategies. It is not the purpose of this particular chapter to present the methodology for the development of these strategies. There are many references describing methodologies used in industry to develop market and product strategies. One such example is *Strategic Market Planning* by Abell and Hammond.[5]

Product Definition

In order to properly plan a technological program in support of a market, the product areas must be properly defined. It has been found that in order to expand the horizons of technical innovation and still maintain management direction, the most effective basis for the definition of products is to use a definition based on "economies of service." This provides a functional distinction rather than one of product hardware or user characteristics. The Boston Consulting Group[6] has developed a method of product description for the definition of markets and market segments. This product description also proves useful to technology planning. This is best described with an example.

Minicomputers are well-defined product hardware from a technical standpoint, and there is no difficulty in identifying this class of hardware from among computer products ranging from personal hand-held calculators to super-computers. If the organization defines its product line as minicomputers, it could well receive competition from other hardware areas. For example, a minicomputer designed to be a low-cost, small-memory programmable computer can well receive competition from desk calculators, microprocessors, minicomputers, and stripped-down, medium-scale computers, depending on how the product is to be used by the customer—all quite different products, but competing to do the same job for users. Furthermore, the company that insists on defining its product as minicomputers may well lose its market if, for example, microprocessors and desk calculators can better satisfy its customer's requirements. Finally, such a narrow definition of its product line also puts a narrow definition on the technologies that are important to them. Therefore, it is much better to define the product line as "a low-cost, small-memory programmable computer." In this way the R&D group can expand its search for the best way of satisfying the customer's needs through its technological avenues. The R&D group is able to direct its program on how to satisfy that customer need, using any type of technology or hardware and not necessarily be constrained to a unique hardware configuration. Furthermore, if the marketing group uses these classifications for definition of its markets and the market segmentation, then there is consistency in planning between marketing and R&D.

The Technical Planning Process

Definition of Technologies Important to the Business: Strategic Technology Areas

The first step in developing a technical plan is to determine the technologies which are important to the business, thus providing a framework for the R&D projects. As in product definition, technologies also must have a common, uniform definition that stimulates innovation. In the past, technology definitions usually used the subdivisions represented by major departments in a university—such as mechanical, chemical, electrical, metallurgical, etc. These major divisions of technology have been further subdivided into a myriad of branches and sub-branches and formed into technology trees. A major area like chemistry is subdivided into organic and inorganic and on down to 30 or 40 branches. If organizations tried to define their important technology areas using these technology trees, a multitude of technology areas would result which would produce confusion, frustration, and difficulty for analysis by managements in an organization. A better definition is required for technologies important to the business. In order to differentiate from the past definition used for technologies, I have chosen to call the technology areas important to the business "Strategic Technology Areas," or "STAs."

A Strategic Technology Area is defined by a combination of the technical discipline or skill it represents and the product line it serves. In other words, the definition consists of four parts that include (a) the technical discipline or skill (for example, "heat transfer"), (b) how the skill or discipline is used (for example "to design"), (c) the product on which it is used (for example, "a device for cooling the temperature of a liquid"), and (d) how this device is used (for example, to cool the liquid in an engine in order to maintain a proper engine temperature for an automobile). Furthermore, the same technical discipline or skill—"heat transfer"—could be used to design the protective shield on a re-entry manned spacecraft in order to prevent burn-up of the spacecraft during re-entry. Although the scientific discipline is the same, the type of R&D for these two cases would be different.

It is important to restrict the number of STAs to some manageable number. This usually turns out to be the case, because the four-part definition forces a combination of various disciplines and functions that naturally come together under one STA. Some of the clues that are important in determining STAs are:

1. An STA is usually a core technical skill that has been foremost in the proliferation of products in the business unit over many, many years. It is a skill that has been used in almost every product that the business unit has developed. For example, a particular business unit was adept in mechanical engineering skills, having particular competence in the field of precision design, manufacture, and assembly of very high-quality, precise, miniature parts. This mechanical engineering STA could be seen in the primary product of the unit, which was altimeters, but it was also present in the oxygen-supply systems, which required accurate pressure regulators made of small, precise, mechanical parts.
2. That is usually why (from a technological competency standpoint) the customers come to that organization for its products. It is usually what the organization understands best technically, and is adept in the use of the STA in the design of its products or services for its customers.

The process of determining the STA of the business must include participation by research, product development, marketing, general management, manufacturing, and other functions of the organization that are in a position to supply the necessary information to develop the STAs. It also requires sufficient time. It cannot be done simply by listing the areas: It requires a lengthy thought process to develop the list. Lowell W. Steele[7] stresses "the importance of a classificatory language and the difficulty in developing it." He goes on to say "it must represent a hierarchical system that begins at the level of work performed by the individual scientist and engineer" (the technical skill part of the STA), "and from this totally technical point of view, it must move to the higher levels of aggregation that have utility in planning" (the product part of the STA), "but that continues to appear sensible to the practitioners." In essence, he is describing the use of the four-part definition of the STA given herein as a planning tool for R&D.

The development of the STA classificatory language is difficult and frustrating. This language must be developed internally with the direct involvement of the managers who must make it work. The process of the development of the list of STAs, although slow and frustrating, is an indispensable part of technical planning methodology, and it is rewarding and satisfying once the classification has been achieved—it cannot be done in a few days or even a few weeks. Some corporations have taken the STA definition and redefined it through two to three yearly planning cycles. This does not mean that it is not useful in its first years of use. Just the opposite is true. The very fact that effort and time are taken to develop this classificatory language causes the organization to obtain a better understanding of its important technology areas as well as developing its technical strategies.[8]

Development of the STA Strategy

Before proceeding to the development of the technical strategy, the next step is to determine the STA strategy. By this it is meant how each STA is (a) utilized, (b) acquired, and (c) compared with competition. The STA strategy for utilization requires determination of whether the STA will be (1) applied, (2) replenished, or (3) exploited. These three terms are defined as follows: "Apply" means that the STA will be used by the organization to continue to develop and improve existing products using the existing skill level of the STA that resides in the firm. "Replenish" means that the organization must increase its skill level within that particular STA either by catching up or pushing the state of the art. "Exploiting" means that the skill levels of the STA will be used to develop new products or new businesses in new markets, and the STA will be used in an innovative and different way from that in which it is already being utilized. Comparing these three terms to terminology usually used by most organizations, "apply" can mean product development, "replenish" is research, and "exploitation" is advanced development.

The second item of STA strategy is acquisition. This merely requires a statement on how the skill level of an STA will be acquired: It may already be available within the organization, or it will be developed by the hiring of experts and/or through the acquisition of another organization.

Finally, a competitive analysis can be made by STA using the same STA classification for the competitors. In this way, a more valid comparison between the skill level of the organization and its competitors can be made by STA rather than by trying to determine the competitive position of a competitor in general terms.

Development of the Technical Strategy of the Business

Having determined the areas in which to work, the next step is to determine the Technical Strategy to pursue. For example, is it necessary to be an aggressive leader or a follower, etc.? The Technical Strategy appropriate to each business strategy can be determined by considering the three dimensions of Technical Strategy. The dimensions of Technical Strategy are: (a) R&D strategy, (b) R&D posture, and (c) R&D objectives. These three dimensions have ranges along which they vary as a function of the market and product strategies of the particular product line.

R&D Strategy.   The R&D strategy dimension varies as a function of the attractiveness of the business and the position of the organization in that business. For example, if an organization has products in a rapidly growing market and enjoys a large market share in that market, usually it is of advantage to the corporation to maintain its position by means of an offensive R&D strategy where continuous long-range R&D should be supported. On the other hand, if the organization has a large market share in a business that is growing at only a very small or negative rate, then its R&D Strategy should take a defensive position where R&D would be accomplished only if needed. This might occur, for example, if competition is likely to make any inroads into its market share. The organization may want to conduct R&D in order to better its position by either reducing cost or increasing the performance of its product. The range of the R&D Strategy dimension is then determined by the range of the market attractiveness and the business position of the organization.

R&D Posture.   This dimension is a function of the product-line need and the market-share strategy of the organization. The R&D Posture of the STA skills will vary from a high level of inventiveness to "avoider" of technology. For example, if an organization wants to enter a new market with a new product, it must use skills in the appropriate STA that are inventive or at least innovative in order to successfully enter the new market and compete with the existing products already in the market. On the other hand, an organization merely wishing to maintain market share with existing product lines would maintain an R&D Posture of "technology avoider" and not spend any R&D funds on those STA skills applicable to those products.

R&D Objectives.   This dimension applies to products as well as the manufacturing processes, and the range will vary from the innovative development of a new product or process, through performance improvement of the product or process, to cost reduction of the product or process, to no effort at all. This particular dimension is tied to the product life cycle. For example, as a product matures and reaches the top of its growth curve, the usual R&D objective is to improve performance and/or reduce the cost of the product. On the other hand, during the early stages of product development, product innovation is required. During the rapid growth stage process, innovation is required.

The technological strategies appropriate for each business strategy can vary along these dimensions and are illustrated in Figures 4.1–4.4:

1. Varying the R&D strategy from offensive to defensive depending on the market attractiveness and business position (Figure 4.1)
2. Varying the R&D posture from invention to minor application of existing technology as a function of product-line need and market-share strategy (Figure 4.2)
3. Determining product-line strategy, from eliminating products to developing new products (based on new specifications) for new markets as a function of market-share strategy and product-line needs (Figure 4.3)

FIGURE 4.1

Research and Development Strategy

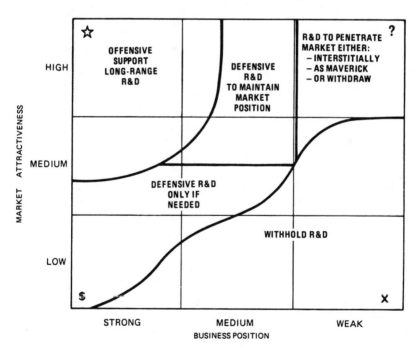

Source: Adapted from Derek F. Abell and John S. Hammond, *Strategic Market Planning* (Englewood Cliffs, NJ: Prentice–Hall, Inc., 1979).

FIGURE 4.2

R&D Posture for Each Product Line

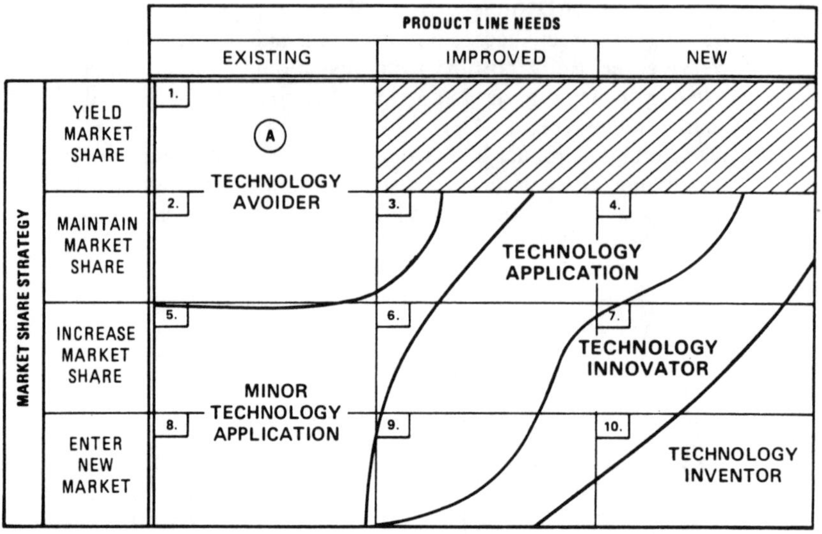

Source: Adapted from S. Johnson and C. Jones, "How to Organize for New Products," *Harvard Business Review* 35 (May–June 1957), pp. 49–62.

4. Determining the objectives of R&D as a function of the product life cycle requiring R&D for product innovation and/or process innovation, to performance improvement and cost reduction (Figure 4.4).

How does a mature, slowly growing or stagnant business develop new ideas or direct attention to new technologies when the Technical Strategy calls for withholding R&D and avoiding technology? The question arises: Where do our new ideas come from?—a lightning bolt from the sky? New ideas, besides being born through a spark of creativity, also require perspiration. Where is this perspiration or work generated? From the Strategic Technology Areas! How is this possible? Although the Technical Strategy may have dictated the withholding of any work in applying the skills of an STA to a particular product, STA Strategy reminds us that a decision must be made whether or not the STA skill needs to be replenished and exploited as well as applied. Although market and product strategy may dictate the strategy of withholding R&D effort in a given STA on behalf of a given product or business area, the fact that the skill in that STA was considered to be a

FIGURE 4.3

Product Line Strategy

		PRODUCT LINE NEEDS		
		EXISTING	IMPROVED	NEW
MARKET SHARE STRATEGY	YIELD MARKET SHARE	1. REDUCE PRODUCTS	/////////	/////////
	MAINTAIN MARKET SHARE	2. CONSOLIDATE PRODUCTS	3. MINOR PRODUCT IMPROVEMENT (IF REQUIRED)	4. NEW PRODUCT EXISTING SPECIFICATIONS
	INCREASE MARKET SHARE	5. REDUCE COST OF PRODUCTS	6. PRODUCT IMPROVEMENT	7. NEW PRODUCT IMPROVED SPECIFICATION
	ENTER NEW MARKET	8. APPLY PRODUCTS TO NEW USES	9. PRODUCT REDESIGN AND IMPROVEMENT	10. DIVERSIFICATION
	FUNCTIONAL RESPONSIBILITY	↑ MARKETING: MARKET STRATEGY	↑ ENGINEERING: PRODUCT DEVELOPMENT	↑ RESEARCH: BASIC AND APPLIED R & D

Source: Adapted from Johnson and Jones "How to Organize for New Products," pp. 49–62.

core skill area for the organization requires that management see that there is continuing work in replenishment and exploitation of these major core STAs. This is the core technical-skill area upon which the business was built. Since these STAs were central to the development of the organization's products (this is what the organization is good at technically) and became a competency resulting in past innovations, it remains that the organization will continue to be innovative through continuing R&D in its core STAs.

If the STAs have been properly defined by using the product definition given earlier, and if the technical skill competency that has been core to the business, R&D programs, or replenishment and exploitation remains, planning within these STAs will generate new ideas and provide insight into new and changing technologies (new STAs) and will undermine the old technologies with the STA.

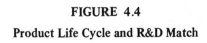

FIGURE 4.4

Product Life Cycle and R&D Match

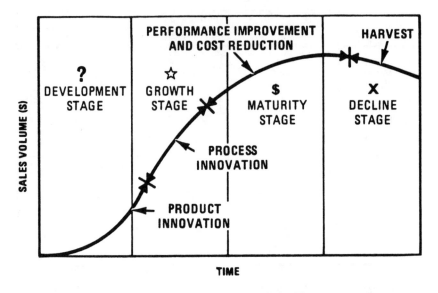

Source: Adapted from Abell and Hammond, *Strategic Market Planning.*

The whole process of determining the STAs and defining them—deciding on the STA strategies and developing the dimensions and ranges of the Technical Strategy—is a stimulating and dynamic one. It forces discussion of new business strategies when new and different technical inputs and strategies are seen to be important. The data in the charts that are illustrated in this chapter are merely a snapshot in time. For example, at the yearly long-range planning time, if the proper strategy were selected, the charts would show a better business picture in the following years. If they do not improve, the strategy isn't paying off and should be changed. Using these kinds of displays provides a common language within the management team that helps develop the proper Technical Strategy to support the business. By developing the STAs, and the STA Strategy and Technical Strategy, management understands why some STAs are funded more than others, and how the funding is linked through the technical strategy to the business strategy and to the STAs that are important to the organization's customers and markets. Management also understands that if it lets its research scientists free to work within these STAs, the ideas that flow will be useful to the business and can be marketed.

Management can, therefore, request project proposals from the R&D group in each of these STAs which they know will be consistent with the Technical Strategy as outlined by the planning document. The STAs tie technology to customer need. The R&D scientists have the freedom to roam within these STAs and do not feel constrained. They have plenty of room within which to determine what they should work on. As the requested R&D project proposals are approved for funding, the project's cost estimates can be recorded under each STA and the total R&D program can be summed by STA as well as by product line. The elements of the Technical Planning process are summarized in Table 4.1.

Corporate Technical Priorities

With the kind of information developed within a multi-divisional corporation, corporate management can guide a central corporate research laboratory. A survey of all business units can be conducted where each is asked to define and describe their most important STAs and also to list those STAs which are new to it, but which will be important to their future. All these divisional STAs can be reviewed, and because many are similar, the total can be reduced to a manageable list. A survey of a large corporation consisting of 45 separate divisions in different businesses produced a list of 242 STAs. By combining similar STAs this list was reduced to 85. Continued aggregation and analysis of the 85 STAs produced 22 corporate STAs which were defined as being important to the corporation's future. It turned out that eight of these STAs were long-range research areas, while the others were areas of technical expertise important to the corporation. The first eight were provided as direction by management to the central corporate laboratory where R&D proposals were accepted for funding within the laboratory. The remaining 14 areas were designated as "centers of expertise" and assigned to divisions who were competent in those areas to monitor and support.

Formulating the Research Program

In formulating the research program, one of the first questions that a manager brings up is whether the work should be basic, applied or developmental. However, the most meaningful descriptors to the decision maker are those that characterize the output of R&D in terms of the strategy to be followed rather than the type of R&D to be carried out. In essence, this is the STA structure, the STA Strategy and Technical Strategy described herein as

TABLE 4.1

Structure for Technology Planning

Technologies
- STA Definition
  and Selection
- STA Maturity
- STA Strategy

    Utilization

       Apply
       Replenish
       Exploit

    Acquisition
    Competitive
    Analysis

Technical Strategy
- R&D Strategy

    Offensive

       Continuous
       Interstitial
       Maverick

    Defensive

       Continuous
       Only if needed

    Withhold
- R&D Posture

    Inventory
    Innovator
    Major Applier
    Minor Applier
    Avoider
- R&D Objectives

    Product

       Development
       Performance Improvement
       Cost Reduction

    Process

       Development
       Performance Improvement
       Cost Reduction

    Withdraw

---

the necessary classification system required by the businessman. The proper mix of basic, applied, or developmental work would be determined by the R&D group based on the STA, STA Strategy, and Technical Strategy direction consistent with the business, market and product strategy. If the Technical Strategy in support of the organization's business strategy requires that basic research be accomplished, then that work must be accomplished in order to successfully meet the requirements of the basic strategy. The classification system developed herein allows the executive to make the proper business decisions based on whether the R&D expense will be consistent with the strategy and the ultimate return in sales and profit, and removes the need to discuss the details of each R&D project. Whether or not the business should support basic research is a moot question.

In implementing the technical program it is also necessary to understand the technological culture of the organization. For example, if an organization is not a risk-taking, innovative culture, then developing a technical plan with high technological risks and a need for innovation will not be successful. It is important to know the technological culture and innovativeness of the business so that a proper R&D program can be planned and administered. The important characteristic parameters in determining the innovativeness of a business[9] are: (a) its research intensiveness versus development intensiveness, (b) the downstream coupling from research to customer, (c) the shape and duration of the product life cycle curve, (d) the R&D investment–expense ratio, and (e) the proximity to the state of the art.

Using these five characteristic parameters, at one end of the spectrum is the technological risk-taking, innovative organization. It works with indefinite design specs, broadcasts objectives and market data throughout its organization, has nondirective work assignments, has continuing project evaluation and selection, and stresses the perception of significant results, values, and innovation over efficiency. In this innovative organization the downstream coupling between R&D manufacturing and the customer is very tight: The product life cycle is usually very short and is in perpetual chaos, has a high ratio of R&D investment to expense which means that it requires serious and continuous evaluation of technology procurement by management, it accelerates product and process change, is in a very dynamic product market, and finally, pushes the technological state of the art.

The less innovative, low risk organization culture usually works with well-defined specifications, has fairly high and direct supervision, organizes its tasks in sequential arrangement, is vulnerable to disruption and change, and values efficiency over innovation where schedule and cost are more important than changing the course and costs to pursue a new idea. Since the product life cycle is usually long, the downstream communication between marketing and R&D is very slow and formal, since information has sufficient time to travel through the various bureaucratic functions. Investment ratios are usually low and, therefore, efficiency of projects rather than effectiveness is more important. This also results in the development of internal technology over a long period of time and/or the purchase of capital equipment with new technology built in. It organizes as a functional organization as opposed to a project organization, and is characterized by formal planning and control which moves slowly and ponderously. They are quite far from the state of the art, and technological risk is low.

It is important to recognize where the organization is in the spectrum within these two cultural extremes because different administrative management and control methods are necessary for such diverse organizations. What is important is to recognize when the shift occurs from one side of the spectrum to the other, because management must change its methods of administrative control. This usually occurs when a new technology is starting to surpass an old technology. Clues to a coming shift in a business are obtained from the shift in STA Strategy in Utilization toward replenish from apply, in R&D Strategy toward offensive long-range R&D from defensive, in R&D Posture toward inventor/innovator from minor technology applier, and in R&D Objectives toward product innovation from cost reduction or performance improvement. Competitors, on recognizing the shift, enter the market and find it easy to compete because the old competitors are unwilling to shift to the new administrative management and control methods.

Finally, in the implementation of the R&D plan, there are certain important factors[10] that are necessary in order to have a successful R&D group. These are: (a) a properly defined role understood and supported by top management as well as all the business units, (b) appropriate organizational structure linked with the business units it serves, (c) joint planning with the business unit using the methodology described herein, (d) stable, centralized funding based on corporate priorities rather than parochial interests of the business unit, and (e) proper working environment that allows freedom but maintains a sense of urgency required to support the corporation in its goals.

Technology Planning to Stimulate Innovation

How are factors important to successful innovation[11] supported by this planning methodology? The four-part STA definition ties scientific skills and disciplines to need through the product definition, thereby placing a "clearly defined need" in the forefront of the determination of the business unit's

STAs. Marketing participation in the determination of STAs, STA Strategy and the connection of Technical Strategy to market, and product strategy guarantee "user guidance."

Organizing the R&D group and its program by STA ensures "committed champions" for each STA tied through its definition to the products. With top management seeing that replenishment occurs when dictated by business goals, "high expertise" is built up in each STA. Top managements using this planning methodology are able to give direction to their R&D group without having to delve into the minute details of an R&D project and are "comfortable with the risk" in that they have a well-understood methodology for planning, review and control. Furthermore, since they have sufficient understanding of the technical plan and its strategy, they have more "realistic time horizons" as to the length of time that will be required to meet the goals.

By the participation of all the functional groups in the technology planning process, using a common, well-understood language with a methodology integrated into the business planning structure, the groups build up a "strong incentive" to support the technology plans and the culture turns to a "discovery mode" innovative climate.

Finally, the technology planning methodology's primary function is to allow the management team to ask relevant questions. It is not to produce a book that decorates the chairman's shelf. Because of this question-forcing methodology, the management team remains alert about "competing technological approaches" and changing STAs. They are less likely to be superseded by a new competitor using a new technology to win over an old market.

Notes

1. Brian Twiss, *Managing Technological Innovation,* 2nd ed., Longman Group, Ltd., England, 1978.
2. James Bryant Quinn, "Technological Innovation, Entrepreneurship, and Strategy." *Sloan Management Review,* Spring 1979.
3. Donald R. Schoen, "Managing Technological Innovation," *Harvard Business Review,* May/June 1969.
4. Igor Ansoff, *Implementing Strategic Management,* Englewood Cliffs, NJ: Prentice-Hall, Inc., June 1984.
5. Derek F. Abell and John S. Hammond, *Strategic Market Planning* (Englewood Cliffs, NJ: Prentice-Hall, Inc., 1979).
6. Boston Consulting Group Concept of Competitive Analysis and Corporate Strategy—HBS Case 9-175-175, Rev. 6/76.
7. Lowell W. Steele, *Innovation in Big Business.* New York, NY: Elsevier Publishing Co., Inc., 1975.

8. Dr. Graham R. Mitchell, Director of Planning, GTE Laboratories, private communication.
9. Ansoff H. Igor and Stewart, J.M. "Strategies for a Technology-Based Business," *Harvard Business Review*, Nov./Dec. 1967.
10. D. Bitondo, "The Bendix Approach to Corporate R&D," *Advanced Management Journal of the Society of American Management Associations,* Fall 1977.
11. Quinn, *op. cit.* "Technological Innovation, Entrepreneurship, and Strategy."

5

Clarifying Complex Public Policy Issues: A Social Decision Analysis Contribution

Kan Chen and J.C. Mathes*

Policymakers at all levels—national, regional, state, and local—often are not able to make decisions acceptable to a wide spectrum of relevant interest groups. On the surface, this is a result of diverse and conflicting values as well as perceptions of the issue at hand among the various interest groups.[1] The more complex the issue, the more diverse and irreconcilable the various positions seem to be. An issue such as import quotas on automobiles therefore becomes oversimplified so that the diversity can be made more tractable. With certain issues, such as nuclear power, oversimplification takes the form of ideological poles around which the various groups coalesce.[2] The diversity of specific values becomes obscured in the ideological context that reduces the complexity of the public issue to almost mutually exclusive dichotomies. Oversimplification of any sort results in a public decision that is suboptimal in a decision analysis sense or unduly satisficing in a decision-making sense.

In the face of complex issues, a variety of constituencies, and insufficient information about the issues, values, and interests involved, public decision-making bodies often must rely on hearings in an effort to clarify the issue, collect the relevant facts, identify the various values and interests involved, explore the goals and trade-offs at stake, and identify the range of policy alternatives available.[3] In such situations, the amount and diversity of information available can become formidable, as the case study discussed below illustrates. Among the policy makers and the various constituencies and interest groups in these exploratory and information-gathering situations prior to actual policy formulation, the problem essentially becomes a com-

---

*This chapter incorporates material prepared by Dr. Kenan Jarboe, who participated in the research project.

munication problem: the need for an effective process for determining, sorting, interpreting, and disseminating the relevant information.

To address this communication problem, various conflict resolution methods and rational information tools may be especially useful. In an effort to address some of the factors of public decision making that have not yet been completely addressed by the existing tools, we have developed a value-oriented social decision analysis (VOSDA) procedure to enhance the mutual understanding required for effective resolution of certain types of public policy issues.[4] We have applied this procedure in extended pilot projects and conclude that, despite mixed results, the procedure could be developed further and make a distinct contribution to informed public decision making.

Our VOSDA procedure essentially is designed to use multiple-criteria decision-making techniques to increase communication among multiple interest groups and multiple decision makers in a public decision-making process.[5] Whereas social decision analysis procedures heretofore have been designed to rationalize the actual act of decision making by some public decision maker or decision-making body, we have used these procedures to enhance the communication processes that precede the actual decision-making stage. Social decision analysis methodologies could make considerable contributions to the process of public decision making by:

- Enhancing the quality of information publicly available to all parties;
- Educating all parties to the multiplicity of values and uncertainty perceptions appropriate to the issue at hand; and
- Sensitizing all parties to the trade-offs that must be made by each of them in any resolution of the issue.

We assume that communication to increase the rationality of the public decision-making process while at the same time allowing multiple decision makers and interest groups to interact within the accepted political process will reduce conflict and facilitate a decision that is widely accepted as well as more optimal than otherwise would be the case. The actual use of VOSDA to enhance communication will be illustrated by what we did in a pilot project. Our VOSDA procedure can also be a prerequisite to a search for Pareto-superior alternatives on a quantitative basis. The potential use of VOSDA to aid Pareto-optimum social decisions will be illustrated by a semi-hypothetical example.

Nuclear Energy Policy Analysis: A Pilot Project

One of our pilot projects was to help analyze alternative state energy policies by a special joint committee of the Michigan State Legislature.[6] The co-chairs of this special joint committee authorized us to act in the role of staff advisor to the committee and to conduct a social decision analysis for them. The committee heard 75 witnesses at 13 hearings over a seven-month period and received over 100 additional documents. On the basis of the hearings and the numerous additional documents, our value-oriented social decision analysis of Michigan's electrical energy future provided a detailed outline of the alternative energy policies as well as the numerous trade-offs that must be made among various interest groups and associated social values.

The electrical energy situation is complex indeed, and presents at least five alternative policy positions or alternative futures. A decision tree outlining the policy paths to alternative energy futures yields a spectrum of eight hypothetical electrical energy programs with various mixtures of coal, nuclear, and renewable energy sources according to various assumptions about future energy demand. Any evaluation of alternative programs requires the identification of various consequences of each program and then exploration of trade-offs among a number of attributes, which are given various weights (or value trade-offs) by various individuals, interest groups, and institutions according to the policy position or alternative future they advocate. The VOSDA procedure helps to systematize the communication of such group evaluation.

The Value-Oriented Social Decision Analysis Procedure

The VOSDA procedure consists of three stages:

1.   Clarifying the problem
2.   Identifying alternative actions and possible consequences
3.   Determining and describing the preferred policies of individual parties and interest groups

The role of the decision analyst throughout this procedure is to describe and communicate, rather than interpret and evaluate, the positions and viewpoints of the various interest groups.

1. Clarifying the Problem

Stage One of the VOSDA process serves three functions. The primary function of Stage One is to develop a classification of the various positions held toward the issue at hand and to clarify, codify, and communicate each participant's or group's views of the problem. The two secondary functions of this stage are to teach the project team the substantive and procedural content of the project and to establish a working relationship based on understanding and trust between the project team and the participants. In other words, stage one functions as a clarifying tool for the participants, a learning tool for the project team, and a trust building tool for both.

We first analyzed and classified the views made public before the committee. Out of the materials and testimony we were able to identify five policy viewpoints.

1.   A Utility Cost Energy Supply Policy
2.   A Unified Michigan Energy Supply and Conservation Policy
3.   A Regulated Energy Supply Policy
4.   A Coordinated Energy Demand Policy
5.   An Alternative Energy Resources Policy

This classification was developed in terms of four factors that emerged as central to the formulation of electrical energy policy: regulatory context, energy mix, future energy demand, and supply-demand policy (Table 5.1).

Then we created a composite Situation Analysis Map—an unstructured cognitive map—to describe all of the policy variables and causal linkages mentioned or alluded to in the documents or testimony (Figure 5.1)[7] A Situation Analysis Map is a graphic representation of the causal linkages between policy variables. It traces out the cause-and-effect logic in various interpretations of a problematic situation, and can be used to clarify the rationale behind individual viewpoints. After the five policy viewpoints had been identified, the individual map for each of these viewpoints was developed with the composite map as the base. Thus, the situation-analysis map served as a device by which to communicate the similarities and differences in interpretations of the energy problem among all of the interested parties and policymakers.

The five viewpoints and the situation-analysis maps were circulated among all the participants after each individual had had an opportunity to review our representation of his or her position and interpretation of the situation. Before dissemination, one description was revised extensively while the others were revised or edited less extensively. When the revisions were completed to his or her satisfaction, we obtained each participant's permission to make public the descriptions, quotes, and situation-analysis map representing their positions.

FIGURE 5.1

Situation Analysis Map for Describing Michigan Electrical Energy Future Alternatives

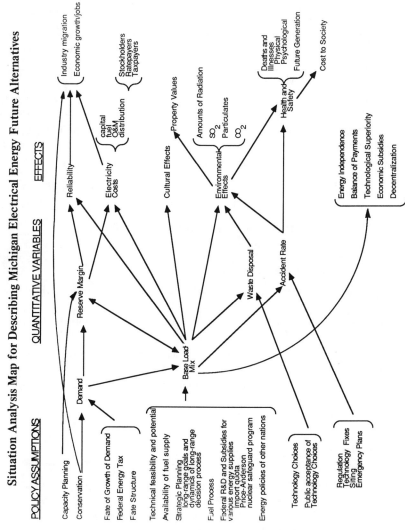

TABLE 5.1
Five Michigan Electrical Energy Policy Alternatives

1. A Utility Cost Energy Supply Policy

Policy is formulated primarily in economic terms, on the basis of minimum cost to the customer, and aims to supply reliable service in an environmentally acceptable manner.

Regulatory Context: Utilities have the responsibility for energy planning and policy, within federal, state and local regulations.

Energy Mix: The energy mix relies on coal and nuclear power for base load generating facilities to meet projected future energy needs and replace existing plants as necessary.

Future Energy Demand: Continued growth in energy demand is assumed, although at a lower rate than before 1973.

Supply-Demand Policy: The policy focuses on the energy supply variable, while encouraging conservation efforts.

2. A Unified Michigan Energy Supply and Conservation Policy

Policy is formulated at the State level on the basis of social as well as economic factors because of the complexity of the energy problem, and aims to insure reliable sources of future energy supply and encourage energy conservation.

Regulatory Context: The State coordinates energy planning and policy, in close cooperation with the utilities.

Energy Mix: The energy mix relies on nuclear and coal as primary sources but assumes conservation and alternative energy resources as well.

Future Energy Demand: A steady growth in energy demand is assumed, dampened as conservation measures take effect.

Supply-Demand Policy: The policy focuses on the energy supply variable, but also encourages energy conservation to lessen demand.

3. A Regulated Energy Supply Policy

Policy is formulated to counterbalance past utility growth and nuclear energy.

Regulatory Context: The State assumes responsibility for energy planning and policy by regulatory direction of utility planning.

Energy Mix: The energy mix continues present energy sources and introduces conservation and alternative energy sources.

Future Energy Demand: A significant decrease in rate of growth of demand is assumed, relative to historical rates.

Supply-Demand Policy: The policy focuses on the energy supply variable, assuming demand is a dependent variable.

TABLE 5.1 (continued)

4. A Coordinated Energy Demand Policy

Policy is formulated in terms of a comprehensive social systems approach to limiting energy supply.

Regulatory Context: The State coordinates energy planning and policy on a state-wide basis.

Energy Mix: The energy mix stresses conservation, especially end-use conservation, to supplement the current energy supply mix and assumes no further investment in nuclear power.

Future Energy Demand: A significant decrease in rate of growth of demand – or even decline – is assumed as well as planned.

Supply-Demand Policy: The policy focuses on the energy demand variable – policy to limit and reduce demand.

5. An Alternative Energy Resources Policy

Policy is formulated in terms of a comprehensive social systems approach to energy supply and demand, based upon matching end-use demand with appropriate energy resources.

Regulatory Context: The State assumes responsibility for state-wide energy planning and policy.

Energy Mix: The energy mix stresses energy efficiency and alternative energy resources and a gradual phasing out of non-renewable energy technologies.

Future Energy Demand: A reduction in energy demand through increased efficiency is assumed.

Supply-Demand Policy: The policy focuses on both supply and demand as interdependent variables in a social system.

2. *Identifying Alternative Actions and Possible Consequences*

Stage Two of the VOSDA process bridges the gap between the descriptive analysis of the policy issue (Stage One) and the quantitative decision analysis of probabilities and utilities (Stage Three). Stage Two is the translation of the verbal descriptions and situation-analysis maps into specific decision options and consequences. The output of Stage Two is a description of the problem in a decision-analysis format. This decision-analysis framework is used to identify specific areas of agreement and disagreement over the implications or impacts of alternative energy policies (Stage Three).

In our work with the Special Joint Committee, we broke Stage Two down into three steps. First, we outlined, in a preliminary fashion, the decision options and attributes of the consequences as we saw the situation, based upon the output from Stage One. Second, we conducted a second set of interviews with the participants. The purpose of the interviews was to obtain their views as to relevant decision options and consequence attributes. During the interviews, we were guided by three questions:

- What attributes of the consequence do you feel are important in considering the social decisions on Michigan's electrical energy future?
- Which attributes are measurable by specific numbers and what are those quantities?
- For those attributes which cannot be pinned down to a quantifiable variable, how should they be measured?

For example, we asked: What is the best way to measure liability? What measures are best for costs? Is the question of obtaining permits a yes/no question?

Third, we synthesized the inputs of the participants and our delineations of the attributes and options. We first developed a decision tree (Figure 5.2) and outlined eight alternative electrical energy programs that were implicit in the five viewpoints or positions (Figure 5.3). We then established a complete list of relevant consequence attributes and developed probability measures for each of the attributes. All of this information was then collated into a worksheet packet for the participants to use in the actual social-decision analysis (Stage Three).

3. Determining and Describing the Preferred Policies of Interest Groups

Stage Three of the VOSDA process involves the actual social decision analysis and the synthesis and communication of the decision-analysis results. The first step of Stage Three was a third interview with the participants to have them fill out the worksheets on probability measures for different levels of the attributes in each scenario in Figure 2. After a brief meeting to explain the procedure, we left the worksheet packets with the participants. Thus, the participants had ample time to consider their answers carefully.

The process of filling out the worksheets for Michigan's electrical energy alternatives consisted of five tasks. The first task was to select the policymaking process option at the beginning of the decision tree which best described the current situation. The second task was to select those attributes considered to be important in deciding among the eight electrical energy programs. The third task was, for each attribute selected, to estimate the

FIGURE 5.2

Policy Paths to Alternative Energy Futures: A Decision Tree

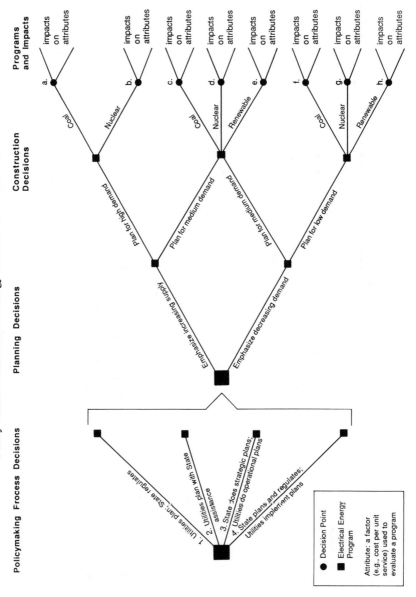

FIGURE 5.3

Eight Alternative Michigan Electrical Energy Programs

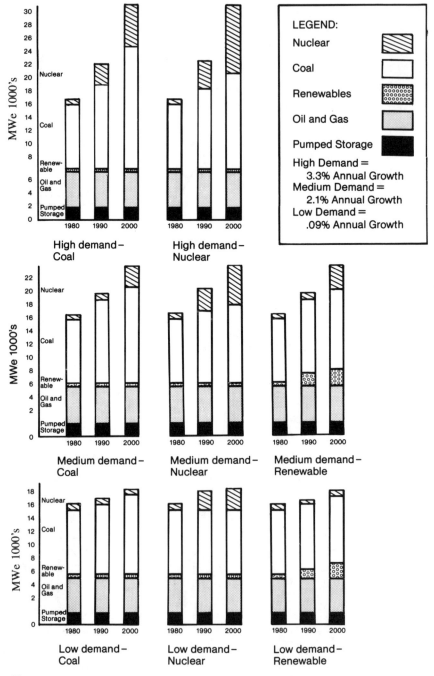

LEGEND:

Nuclear

Coal

Renewables

Oil and Gas

Pumped Storage

High Demand =
    3.3% Annual Growth
Medium Demand =
    2.1% Annual Growth
Low Demand =
    .09% Annual Growth

High demand –
Coal

High demand –
Nuclear

Medium demand –
Coal

Medium demand –
Nuclear

Medium demand –
Renewable

Low demand –
Coal

Low demand –
Nuclear

Low demand –
Renewable

probability of each event occurring for each of the eight electrical energy programs and to estimate the utility ranking for that event, on a scale between 0 and 100, relative to the other events for that attribute. The fourth task was to distribute 100 points among those attributes selected earlier to reflect the relative importance to the interest group of the attributes (to change from one extreme to the other) in the choice of electrical energy programs. The last task was to determine which policymaking process is most likely to apply in the future and to estimate how such a shift in the policymaking process would affect the probabilities estimated earlier.

The second step of Stage Three was a standard decision analysis for each of the participants. We calculated the expected utility for each of the decision options for each of the participants. To calculate the expected utility, we used the additive multi-attribute utility model:[8]

$$U = \sum_i \sum_j w_i p_{ij} u_{ij} \quad \text{where}$$

U is the program's expected utility

w_i is the weight assigned attribute i

p_{ij} is the probability of event j in attribute i

u_{ij} is the utility of event j in attribute i (1)

After the standard decision analysis had been completed, we went back to each participant to explain the results, along with our interpretation of those results. The participants were strongly urged to carefully study the results and bring to our attention any results they felt uncomfortable with. Since the purpose of our project was to use decision-analysis techniques as a communication tool, not as a direct decision tool, it was important that each participant's decision analysis results be satisfactory to him. Likewise, it was important that the participants felt the probabilities, utilities, and weights reflected their own beliefs, values, opinions, and viewpoints with sufficient accuracy. In those cases where the participants felt the results did not adequately describe their views, we allowed them to revise their earlier answers until they were satisfied with the results of their individual decision analysis.

When the revisions were completed, we asked each participant for permission to circulate his/her decision analysis results, clearly labelled as their viewpoints. These results were then circulated among the participants.

The final step of Stage Three of the VOSDA procedure was our analysis of the decision analysis results to identify similarities and differences. We made analyses in a number of areas. First, we examined how the participants differed in their composite rankings of the eight alternative electrical energy programs (the expected utilities for each option). We also examined how the participants differed according to fuel type and demand level. We then examined the various trade-offs each participant made among the attributes when their composite rankings were calculated. Next we analyzed in detail how the participants differed on each individual attribute. Finally, we described how the participants differed as to which attributes they chose as important and how much weight they assigned to the incremental changes of each attribute. Our descriptive analysis then was circulated in report form among all the participants as well as the policymakers.

Evaluation of the VOSDA Procedures

As our project evaluation concluded, in the present application the VOSDA process was not a consensus building technique in the sense that it did not lead to a negotiation, bargaining, or trade-off stage of the policymaking process whereby modification of the interest groups' positions should occur in order for an acceptable political decision to emerge.[9] At the same time, the process enabled the interest groups or stakeholders as well as the policymakers to identify and clarify the issues and positions on a complex issue. Furthermore, it established an intergroup communication procedure within a rational context that enabled participants to address the substantive issues in an initially cooperative rather than adversarial mode. As such, it seems to hold promise as a prelude to subsequent informed negotiation procedures or actual social decision-making exercises.

In terms of participants' attitudes toward alternative energy programs, the primary result of the project was to reveal the inconsistencies between generalized or composite policy positions and the particular judgments upon which those policy positions are based. The composite rankings of the alternative energy programs clearly indicated that the participants (e.g., interest group representatives) could be divided into two groups. One group tended to prefer medium- and high-demand coal and nuclear electrical energy programs. The other group tended to prefer the low-demand coal and low-demand renewable energy programs. At the generalized level, therefore, a polarity of positions appeared that corresponded rather predictably with an ideological interpretation.[10]

The particular judgments of the participants varied considerably, however. As far as we can determine, the two distinct groups suggested by the composite rankings bear no relationship to the individual choices and weights of the attributes separately (Table 5.2). For example, only four attributes are weighted heavily by two or more participants. The dissimilarities in weighting priorities indicated that the participants have a wide range of values when it comes to evaluating alternative electrical energy programs.

The dissimilarities are apparent when the choices and weights are examined. The number of attributes chosen varies similarly among the participants in each group. In addition, only five attributes are chosen by four or more participants, and these seem to be distributed equally between the two groups. Furthermore, only one attribute is heavily weighted by four (a majority) of the participants, two from each group. The weights assigned to the attributes seem to vary as randomly between the two groups as do the attributes chosen. Finally, although all of the attributes we identified were chosen by the participants themselves or introduced in testimony before the committee, eight were not chosen by any participant when it actually came time to choose and weight attributes.

The pilot project suggests that a VOSDA procedure can be helpful in demystifying the rhetoric of various interest groups in regard to any specific issue, especially when that rhetoric assumes ideological overtones. In American society, especially in a political context, all interest groups subscribe to the same basic American values. They differ in the relative weights they put on the various values, as manifested by the weights assigned to the incremental changes in the attributes of the possible consequences resulting from competing policies or programs. Through the explication and sharing of the differences in these relative weights and subjective probabilities, VOSDA can help identify and generate Pareto-superior (or win-win) policy/program options, as illustrated by the following example.

Potential Application of VOSDA to Pareto Optimization: A Numerical Example

To illustrate the quantitative aspect of VOSDA and its potential application to Pareto optimization, we present a numerical example based on a semi-hypothetical dispute between the business and environmentalist communities on a jobs-versus-health issue.[11] Both communities want jobs and health, two basic American values. However, they differ on the relative weights put on the number of jobs to be created and on the environmental quality to be

TABLE 5.2

How Seven Participants Weight Attributes

Attributes	Participants' Decision Attribute Weights (% of 100)*				
	Policy 1	Policy 2	Policy 3	Policy 4	Policy 5
cost per unit service	20	8	20	10	7.4
industrial climate a) due to supply	20	13	12.5(a)	12(b)	
b) due to price			12.5(b)	5	
ability to meet demand		20			
acceptability to public at large	x	20	15		
impact on environment	11		10	10	22.2
overcapacity			10		
reliability			10		
dependency on fuel imports					
acceptability to communities	14	7			
flexibility	13	12		5	29.6
capital costs					3.8
willingness to finance		10			
availability of capital		10		10	7.4
ability to obtain permits					
amount of government intervention in business				5	
nuclear proliferation				5	14.8
risk from nuclear wastes			10	10	14.8
operating costs					
availability of fuel	22				
risk of nuclear accident				8	
availability of labor and resources				10	
amount of government intervention in individual lives				5	
CO_2 increase				10	
interstate electricity marketing					
energy-related employment					
centralization					
acid rain					
energy-related occupational injuries and fatalities					
radiation exposure					
air quality					
thermal pollution					

*For policy positions of participants refer to policies on Table 5.1

x Considers this attribute primary

preserved. They may also differ on the uncertainty (probabilities) in the consequences of alternative programs for a production plant construction.

To be specific, we can consider a decision tree with two alternative programs, A and B (Figure 5.4). Program A, proposed by the business community, has a higher potential for job creation than Program B has, but also has a higher potential and likelihood of environmental damage which would result in adverse impacts on public health. In the event of environmental damage, a later remedy is possible. However, the remedial action would result in a higher cost of production, making the plant less competitive and eventually reducing the number of jobs created. The two programs thus have different impacts or consequences.

FIGURE 5.4

**Decision Tree for Business and Environmentalist
Communities in Dispute Over a Job-Versus-Health Issue**

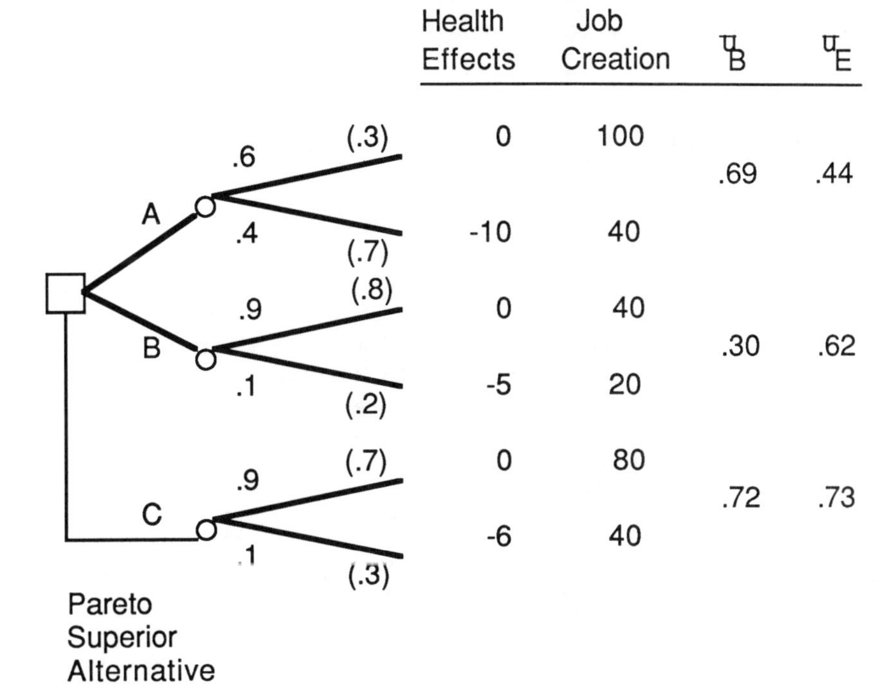

	Health Effects	Job Creation	U_B	U_E
A .6 (.3)	0	100		
			.69	.44
A .4 (.7)	-10	40		
B .9 (.8)	0	40		
			.30	.62
B .1 (.2)	-5	20		
C .9 (.7)	0	80		
			.72	.73
C .1 (.3)	-6	40		

Pareto
Superior
Alternative

The two communities will have different probability assessments of the various impacts, as are illustrated by the numbers adjacent to the branches emanating from the event (circular) nodes. The numbers without parentheses are the probabilities assessed by the business community, and those within the parentheses are those by the environmentalist community. These differences are particularly prominent for the uncertainty in the impacts of Program A, the plan advocated by the business community. The value differences between the two communities are evidenced by the differences in the relative weights within their utility functions:

$$u_B = .9u_{BJ} + .1u_{BH} \tag{2}$$

$$u_E = .4u_{EJ} + .6u_{EH} \tag{3}$$

where

u_B is the utility function of the business community

u_E is the utility function of the environmentalist community

u_{BH} is the business community's utility function for health

u_{EH} is the environmentalist community's utility function for health

u_{BJ} is the business community's utility function for jobs

u_{EJ} is the environmentalist community's utility function for jobs

The business community assigns a greater weight to job creation and the environmentalist community to impacts on public health.

In actuality, u_{BH} and u_{EH} would be nonlinear and different, and so would u_{BJ} and u_{EJ}. However, for the sake of simplicity, we assume these four single-attribute utility functions to be linear. On a normalized basis, $u_{BH} = u_{EH}$ and $u_{BJ} = u_{EJ}$ (Figure 5.5). The two attribute utility functions, u_B and u_E (multiattribute utility functions in the general case), are additive. These two utility functions also are normalized (i.e., relative weights add up to 1: their ranges are between 0 and 1 within the ranges of job creation and health impacts under consideration).

The expected utility of each program for each community is computed in terms of its probability assessments. For example, the expected utility for the environmentalist community of Program B is:

$$\bar{u}_E(B) = .8(.4 \times .25 + .6 \times 1) + .2(.4 \times 0 + .6 \times .5) = .62$$

FIGURE 5.5

Normalized Single-Attribute Utility Functions
for Health Effects and Job Creation

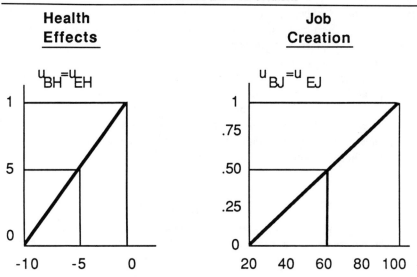

The expected utility computations are:

	Program A	Program B
Business Community	.69	.30
Environmentalist Community	.44	.62

Since each community prefers the program with a higher expected utility for that community, the business community prefers Program A and the environmentalist community prefers Program B. With VOSDA, the quantitative analyses would be available to both communities. Thus, they could understand why and how much they differ from each other. (Note that "interpersonal utility comparison," a concept unacceptable to most decision theorists, has not been invoked in our example. Each community uses only its own utility function to choose between Programs A and B.) The potential of such an approach to optimizing public policy decisions is not restricted to enhancing communication between just two interest groups, as our pilot project on nuclear energy illustrates.

Because the VOSDA procedure involves open communication between two or multi-interest groups in the public area, it could provide the foundation for trade-offs or compromises between the groups that might result in a Pareto-optimal policy (at least qualitatively speaking). A social decision analyst or a third-party mediator would help both (all) sides to explore Pareto-superior alternative programs, which may be preferred by both sides to the existing programs. In our example, Program C would be a Pareto-superior alternative to Program A and Program B (Figure 5.4). Although the consequences of Program C do not dominate those of Programs A and B at first sight, careful calculations of the expected utility of C indicate that it is superior to A and B from the standpoints of both communities. The joint evaluation of all three programs may be plotted on the $\bar{u}_B\bar{u}_E$ plane (Figure 5.6). The fact that point C lies to the northeast direction from points A and B

FIGURE 5.6

Joint Evaluation of Alternative Plans on the $u_B u_E$ Plane

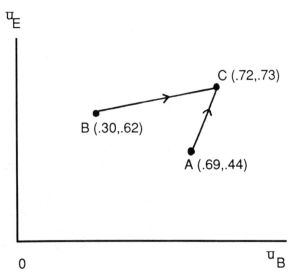

Business: C>A>B
Environmentalist: C>B>A

C is Pareto superior to A and B

indicates that Program C is Pareto-superior to Programs A and B. In other words, the dispute between the business and environmentalist communities in choosing between Programs A and B may be transcended by their cooperation in searching for a "win-win" situation represented by Program C. A VOSDA process could facilitate this cooperation by overcoming the unimaginative polarization that might lock opposing interest groups into an "A or B," win-lose decision-making situation.

We realize that, in spite of recent progress in Paretian analysis,[12] the search for Pareto-superior and Pareto-optimal solutions that are feasible within practical constraints is not a straightforward procedure. The fact that we did not incorporate Paretian analysis with our VOSDA procedure in the pilot project on Michigan's alternative energy policies was partly due to the profound problem of an N-person game, where N was many more than two, and partly due to the difficulty in generating new energy policies that might be Pareto-superior. However, the sharing between interest groups of probability assessments and value trade-offs reflected in utility functions, as described in the VOSDA procedure, is a *prerequisite* to the search for Pareto superior alternatives on a quantitative basis.

Conclusions

The application of social-decision analysis or multiple-criteria decision making in public contexts is in a preliminary stage; traditional politics, negotiation, bargaining, and debate still dominate the decision-making process. However, "in a multiobjective view of the world, achieving less with respect to one objective means that more can be attained with respect to other objectives. It is the balance achieved with respect to all objectives, rather than the linear pursuit of the quantitative maximum of a single objective, which leads to an enhanced sense of prosperity, well-being, and quality of life."[13] The VOSDA procedure holds promise for contributing to the development of a social decision-making process that can generate decision alternatives consistent with a multiobjective awareness of the world.

If the VOSDA procedure were extended to an interactive fourth stage, such as an interpersonal workshop mode, perhaps movement would occur, the possibility of compromise and trade-offs increase, and Pareto-superior alternative scenarios develop. The extended VOSDA format could be a four-step procedure: (1) clarifying concepts and arriving at agreement on definitions of consequence attributes, (2) "anchoring" alternative choices and weights of attributes among participants, (3) sensitivity analyses, and (4) alternative policy or program generation and evaluation. This would be an alternative to a computer simulation procedure, such as the adaptive environmental assessment approach,[14] which depends on a model building procedure to handle the complexity of the variables and quantified relationships. The VOSDA procedure would be an open-ended rather than bounded alternative, as each participant could formulate his or her own conceptual model of reality in choosing and weighting attributes. The sharing of these value and reality judgments among the representatives of the interest groups would be used to generate Pareto-superior options.

At present, however, the VOSDA procedure remains primarily a communication tool that provides a means of clarifying problems and positions on complex public issues. It facilitates mutual understanding on public issues among various interest groups, institutions, and policy makers. It creates a detailed understanding of a complex issue by the parties that might not otherwise be possible. By doing so, it can enhance the possibility of mutually acceptable trade-offs in the subsequent public decision-making act.

Notes

1. Public policy literature formulates the problem in various ways. Lloyd C. Irland says, "We have inherited from a simpler past and from the Multiple-Use Act a belief that the public lands can be managed to 'harmonize' conflicting uses. This is no longer true, if it ever was. . . ." "That assumed harmony among user groups does not exist." "Citizen Participation—A Tool for Conflict Management on the Public Lands," *Public Administration Review,* May/June 1975, pp. 263–64. Joseph L. Coates says, "There is no public but only publics with regard to any particular issue. . . . There is no general constituency for the future." "Public Participation in Technology Assessment," mimeo, pp. 2–3.
2. "The nuclear debate is something more than conflicting attitudes and beliefs about nuclear power *per se,* and . . . its essence actually is rooted in significant ideological cleavages and differences in world views of the partisans involved." Steven L. Del Sesto, "Conflicting Ideologies of Nuclear Power," *Public Policy,* Winter 1980, p. 40. See also, Dorothy Nelkin and Michael Pollak, "Ideology as Strategy: The Discourse of the Anti-Nuclear Movement in France and Germany," *Science, Technology, and Human Values,* Winter 1980, pp. 3–13.
3. We assume an interest group or group-theory model of the political process, although we have not modelled the specific situation embodied in our case study or examined it according to specific theorists. See J. David Greenstone, "Group Theories," *Micropolitical Theory,* ed. Fred I. Greenstein and Nelson W. Polsby, Addison-Wesley, Reading, Mass., 1975, pp. 243–317, and Robert H. Salisbury, "Interest Groups," *Nongovernmental Politics,* ed. Fred I. Greenstein and Nelson W. Polsby, Addison-Wesley, Reading, Mass., 1975, pp. 171–228.

4. Kan Chen, J.C. Mathes, Kenan Jarboe, and Janet Wolfe, "Value Oriented Social Decision Analysis: Enhancing Mutual Understanding to Resolve Public Policy Issues," *IEEE Transactions on Systems, Man, and Cybernetics,* September 1979, pp. 567–80; Kan Chen, J.C. Mathes, and Kenan P. Jarboe, "Clarifying Energy Debates: Preliminary Results of a Social Decision Analysis," *Proceedings of the International Conference on Cybernetics and Society,* October 8–10, 1980 (New York: IEEE), pp. 213–18; Kan Chen, J.C. Mathes, Kenan P. Jarboe, and Sydney Solberg, "Alternative Energy Futures: Interest Group Tradeoffs," *Proceedings of the International Conference on Cybernetics and Society,* October 26–28, 1981 (IEEE: New York), pp. 548–52. These articles and associated reports are products of the University of Michigan Value-Oriented Social Decision Analysis Project (NSF Grant No. SS77-16294). We are indebted to Kenan P. Jarboe, Janet Wolfe, and Sydney Solberg for their contributions. Additional art for this chapter was prepared by Mary Schoenfeldt and Cy Barnes.

5. We have, of course, compared our approach to the application of decision analysis in the public sector by Ward Edwards, Kenneth Hammond, Scott Barclay, and Cameron Peterson, among others. VOSDA, despite similarities, differs in fundamental ways: it addresses the problem of multiple decision makers (as well as of multiple game players or stakeholders), it allows for disagreements over problem definition and reality judgments (and does not assume value-free facts), it allows for disagreement over value trade-offs, and it does not force or even assume that consensus is possible.

6. The project is documented in our report, *Michigan's Electrical Energy Future.* We are grateful to the co-chairs of the Special Joint Committee of the State of Michigan Legislature, Senator Doug Ross and Representative Mark Clodfelter, for allowing us to assume a staff role in order to conduct this pilot project. We are indebted to Dr. William Scanlon, Staff Director for the Committee, for his advice and significant contributions.

7. R. Axelrod, ed., *Structure of Decision,* Princeton University Press, Princeton, NJ, 1976.

8. Ralph L. Keeney and Howard Raiffa, *Decisions With Multiple Objectives,* John Wiley & Sons, New York, 1976.

9. The evaluation here is our own, although we incorporate some of the suggestions from the external reviewers for our VOSDA project, Lawrence Susskind and Andrew Sage. We appreciate and are indebted to their detailed review and constructive criticism, which we hope to be able to incorporate in future development of the VOSDA process.

10. See note 2.

11. This numerical example was inspired by the EPA experiment to get the public involved in environmental risk management in Tacoma, Washington, as described in "Environmental Risk: Power to the People," by Barnett N. Kalikow, *Technology Review,* Vol. 87, No. 7, October 1984, pp. 55–61.

12. Howard Raiffa, *The Art and Science of Negotiation,* Harvard University Press, 1982.

13. Milan Zeleny, *Multiple Criteria Decision Making,* McGraw-Hill: New York, 1982, p. 490.

14. C.S. Holling, ed., *Adaptive Environmental Assessment and Management,* John Wiley & Sons, Chicester and New York, 1978 (IIASA Applied Systems Analysis Series, Volume 3). See also, Richard L. Johnson, "A Multiple Objective Decision Process for Environmentally Related Energy Development Decisions," *Proceedings of the International Congress on Applied Systems Research and Cybernetics,* Acapulco, Mexico, December 1980.

Part III

Planning Roles

6

Steering the Path Between Ambiguity and Overload: Planning as Strategic Social Process

Stuart L. Hart

As we approach the late 1980s, our social, environmental, and economic problems seem only to have become more perplexing. Shifting population dynamics, changing social values, growing international economic competition, sagging industrial productivity, increasing resource dependencies, accelerating technological innovation, and continuing concern for the "quality of life" have and will continue to spur major structural changes in the framework of our society.

Increasingly, the issues and problems faced by organizations seem to defy resolution by the decision tools and planning techniques that have been developed over the past 40 years, primarily in the areas of operations research, quantitative modeling, and formal planning (e.g., McKenna, 1980; Steiner, 1979). These techniques were designed primarily to aid or solve problems that occur repeatedly in the operation and management of organizations. Social and economic turbulence, however, has conspired to make the utility of such techniques questionable in many of today's decision situations.

More and more, we read about the importance of enhanced "strategic" analysis and decision making on the part of U.S. firms and government agencies. Indeed, many of today's most perplexing problems (e.g., toxic waste, acid rain, starvation, industrial decline) are attributed to poor strategic planning or shortsighted policy analysis. In increasing numbers, observers and analysts of public administration and business management have become critical of the rigid and unadaptable techniques of formal planning that emerged and blossomed during the 1960s and 1970s (e.g., Ansoff, 1979; Quinn, 1980; Dunn, 1981; Tichy, 1983). In fact, it is becoming a widely accepted tenet that formal systems of planning and analysis have proven to

107

be major disappointments (e.g., Mason and Mitroff, 1981). The very foundation of the field of planning is being shaken.

In the past ten years numerous analysts and commentators have
expounded multiple and often conflicting roles for the "planner." These have
ranged from technical analyst to political coalition builder, from staunch
advocate to impartial intermediary, and from creative designer to humble
implementer (see Hudson, 1979; Schon, 1981). In an effort to help grapple
with this complexity, important strides have been made toward the development of a contingency theory of planning roles. For example, Bryson and
Delbecq (1979) showed that some planners do appear to behave con-
tingently—to change their strategies or tactics as the situation dictates—and
that political concerns generally take precedence over technical concerns for
all but the most simple situations. Despite these advances, however, "planning" still means different things to different people.

Perhaps in reaction to this seeming state of confusion, Mintzberg (1981)
has raised the question, "What is planning, anyway?" After highlighting
several competing images of planning, none of which seemed adequate from
a conceptual or operational point of view, he concluded that planners find
their roles more on either side of the decision-making process than at its
center. On the front end, planners supply ad hoc, predecision analyses, and
on the back (output) end, planners program the decisions reached by others
into implementable tactics. In essence, planning and decision making, according to this image, are separable activities accomplished by separate people.

Recognizing that Mintzberg's (1981) analysis was meant to fuel debate
more than it was to resolve the issue, this chapter argues for a more integrative, multidimensional role for the planner in society. While it may never be
possible to define operationally what *planning* is, it will always be possible to
identify who the *planners* are in any given situation. It is their collective
behavior that determines how planning is perceived by other organizational
actors and by society at large.

Given the great complexities that face us, it is argued that to have any
positive impact, planners can no longer afford to be unidimensional. Whether
in the private or public sectors, planners must be more than good analysts
and technicians. Their activities must include more than mere policy implementation or intermediation. An integrative model, informed and guided by
analysis but inextricably dependent upon social interaction and political process, is advocated. Under this model, planning becomes synonymous with
effective management of complexity and uncertainty.

The discussion begins by describing the characteristics of today's complex problems that force the field of planning to redefine its role. It closes
with some thoughts about how to operationalize this integrative image.

The Changing Context for Planning

The classic statement of the traditional "rational" approach to planning and problem solving in organizations can be found in Meyerson and Banfield (1955, p. 314):

> 1) A decision maker considers all alternatives open to him; 2) He identifies and evaluates all of the consequences which would follow from the adoption of each alternative; 3) He selects that alternative, the probable consequences of which would be preferable in terms of his most valued ends.

March and Simon (1958) and, later, Ray (1970) outlined the assumptions made by this rational approach to problem solving:

1. The problem is given and defined;
2. The options or alternative solutions are given;
3. There is complete and accurate knowledge of the outcomes for each of the options (under conditions of certainty); knowledge of the probability distribution of outcomes (under conditions of risk); or a set of exhaustive decision rules (under conditions of uncertainty);
4. There is a utility function or preference ordering for all decision makers that is exhaustive, consistent and commensurable in a single ordering system.

According to this approach, the planner's job is seen as solving analytically an assortment of problems that appear to be readily definable and understandable. The planner, in effect, is hired to eliminate those conditions that are consensually judged to be undesirable. As Rittel and Webber (1973, p. 156) have observed, the record has been quite spectacular. Contemporary urban society stands as clear evidence of professional prowess: "The streets have been paved, and roads now connect all places; houses shelter almost everyone; the dread diseases are virtually gone; clean water is piped into nearly every building; sanitary sewers carry wastes from them; schools and hospitals serve virtually every district, and so on."

Recently, Geurts, Hart, and Caplan (1986) developed a framework for organizing the different problem types faced by organizations; it contained two main dimensions—decision phase and state of knowledge. The first dimension (phases of the decision process) was subdivided into three general categories: (1) problem recognition and formulation, (2) option generation and evaluation, and (3) option selection and implementation.

The second dimension (state of knowledge) referred to the perceived extent and quality of information available regarding a particular problem. It was conceived of as having four levels:

1. *Certainty:* all relevant variables regarding a problem and the relationships among them are considered to be known;
2. *Risk:* all relevant variables regarding a problem are considered to be known but their relationships can only be estimated (probabilities);
3. *Uncertainty:* all relevant variables regarding a problem are considered to be known, but some cannot be measured and the relationships among others are unknown; and
4. *Ambiguity:* all relevant variables regarding a problem have yet to be identified.

Combining these two dimensions produced a typology of 12 cells, each representing a particular type of decision or planning problem (Table 6.1). Using the typology as an organizing framework, it was shown that most existing planning tools and techniques are applicable only for problems in the *upper,* and particularly the upper *right* portion of the typology.[1] These are the relatively well-defined problems mentioned above, involving choice among a finite set of detailed options.

But now that most of the well-defined problems have been dealt with, and organizations are faced with increasingly turbulent and interconnected environments, the traditional, rational–analytic approach has been the target of growing criticism. Indeed, today's complex planning problems generally do not meet any of the assumptions outlined above—very seldom are such problems given, alternatives or outcomes clearly defined, or do people have complete preformed images of preference or utility. More often, today's problems are *complicated* (innumerable interacting variables), *interconnected* (a decision in one area is affected by choices made in others), and *conflictual* (the values or assumptions of those involved in or affected by the decision are in conflict). In short, most emerging planning problems occupy the *lower* part of the typology, particularly the lower-left portion (Domain of Complex Problems).[2] These planning problems require both different skills and new approaches to be successfully dealt with.

The literature has recognized these types of problem situations with a variety of different descriptors. March and Simon (1958) characterized them as "unprogrammed" or "innovative" decisions. Rittel and Webber (1973) labelled them "wicked" problems (in contrast to the more "tame" programmable types). Radford (1977) straightforwardly chose to name them "complex decision problems," while Mason and Mitroff (1981) dubbed them situations of "organized complexity." Ackoff (1974) simply called them "messes"—complex mixtures of highly interdependent problems that by definition cannot be formulated, let alone solved, independently of one another.

TABLE 6.1

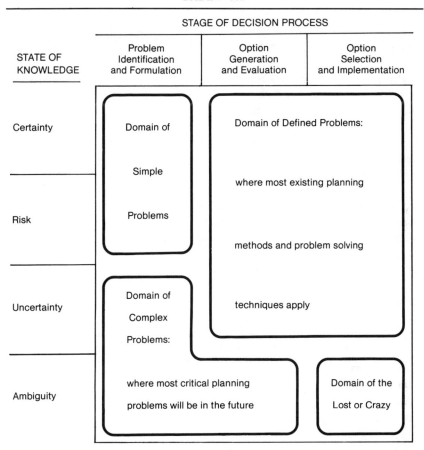

Such problems contain not only a large number of quantifiable variables but also the qualitative considerations (values, aspirations, hopes and fears) of those involved in and affected by the decision process. Indeed, Cartwright (1973) distinguished "simple" problems (upper portion of the typology) from what he called "metaproblems" (lower portion) using two fundamental dimensions. First, he asked whether the number of variables in the problem could be specified completely in its definition; if so, the problem was determinate and not open-ended. Second, he asked whether the variables themselves could be meaningfully quantified; if so, the problem was reducible to a common calculus. Complex (meta) problems are thus problems that are both open-ended and not completely quantifiable.

Thus, complex planning problems are subjective constructions of what Boulding (1956) called "images" of the real world; each stakeholder in the decision process has his own perception of the situation derived from his previous experience and the information available to him (Berger and Luckman, 1966; Mitroff, 1983). As a result, the way in which such problems are formulated is the key to their resolution since, while no one perception of the problem is more correct than another, some perceptions can be more useful than others for planning purposes. There are two principal reasons for this: (1) the way in which a problem is perceived determines the range of possible solutions to that problem, and (2) the way in which a problem is perceived determines the kind of strategy that is appropriate for its solution (Cartwright, 1973).

Another way of stating the above is that today's complex planning problems are not problems at all, but *problematic situations*; converting such situations into problems requires that the complexity and uncertainty of the situation be reduced by focusing on particular elements and relations. The application of rational–analytic problem-solving techniques to such situations may therefore be misleading because it suggests that the value aspects inherent in such decisions can somehow be taken out of the process. As Pressman and Wildavsky (1979, p. 190) observed:

> When problems are puzzles for which unique solutions exist, technicians take over. But when problems are defined through the process of attempting to draft acceptable solutions, then analysts become creators as well as implementers of policy. . . . Implementation includes not only finding answers, but also framing questions.

Thus, planning problems are never solved but only *resolved*. Ross (1979) captured this notion with his "law of the indestructibility of problems"—old problems do not disappear, they simply turn into new problems. Because of the interconnectedness of complex issues and problems, any "solution" will generate second- and third-order repercussions over an extended period of time. The objective should therefore be to make the problems you create (as a result of intervention) less severe than the problems you solve. In this light, modern planning is an activity oriented toward creating problems that can be solved. It must define problems that decision makers are able to handle with the variables under their control and in the time available.

In summary, today's planning problems increasingly diverge from the assumptions associated with the traditional rational–analytic approach: seldom do the situations, options, or outcomes come clearly defined in strategic settings. Instead, such problems are complex and interconnected, involving multiple perspectives and assumptions. Whereas "simple" problems are determinant and quantifiable, complex problems are open-ended and highly judgmental. To a large degree, such problems are subjectively constructed by those involved in the decision process. In this sense, they are not problems at all, but problematic situations, requiring simplification and conversion into solvable problems. Such problems require a different approach if they are to be dealt with effectively.

Steering the Path Between Ambiguity and Overload

Simon's (1945) concepts of "bounded rationality" and "satisficing" form the foundation of a literature that stresses the inability of individuals or organizations to achieve intellectual mastery of complex problems. The capacity of the human mind for formulating or solving such problems is very small compared with their size and complexity. The result is that rather than searching for the "optimal" solution, the decision maker accepts the first formulation that is satisfactory. This approach to problem solving through simplification is similar to Lindblom's (1959) concept of "incrementalism": since the number of courses of action available may be large and comprehensiveness is not possible, the decision maker analyzes only those alternatives that differ incrementally from the existing situation. Lindblom (1979) aptly summarized the central message of this literature:

> No person, committee, or research team, even with all the resources of modern electronic computation, can complete the analysis of a complex problem. Too many interacting values are at stake, too many possible alternatives, and too many consequences to be traced through an uncertain future. (p. 518)

While the strategies of incrementalism and satisficing work well for complex problems when the nature of the problem and the means available for dealing with it do not change significantly, they have been criticized in situations where radical changes appear to be necessary (Radford, 1977) or where turbulence has rendered past actions inapplicable in the future (Schon, 1971). Pure satisficing and incremental decision making may also be overly pessimistic about the role of analysis in complex planning problems. Michael (1973), for example, pointed out that Simon's notion of satisficing need not be absolutely limiting in its application. The level of satisficing can be determined by society or an organization; therefore, if we want more "informed" decisions, we must set the standards of satisficing higher. Quinn (1980) has extended this idea with his concept of "logical incrementalism." Etzioni's (1967) concept of "mixed scanning" is also appropriate in this regard as it constitutes a synthesis of both large (synoptic) and small (incremental) decisions into a single framework. This approach consists of a mix of broad surveys (scanning) of the overall problem area and in-depth investigations of only those areas that are judged to merit such attention. Such an approach is consistent with the "heuristic" characteristics of human information processing outlined by Simon and Newell (1971, p. 149):

> The problem solver's search for a solution is an odyssey through the problem space. . . . To a major extent, the power of heuristics resides in their capability for examining small, promising regions of the entire space and simply ignoring the rest. We need not be concerned with how large the haystack is, if we can identify a small part of it in which we are quite sure to find a needle.

Lindblom himself has more recently (1979) refined and extended his initial dichotomy between incremental and synoptic decision making. While still denouncing the impossible and unproductive ideal of synoptic analysis, Lindblom recognized an approach (strategic analysis) lying between simple incrementalism and comprehensive analysis. Thus, while it is not possible to be synoptic in dealing with complex planning problems one can at least be well informed and thoughtful in the choice of methods for problem simplification.

In addition to not being able to collect and analyze all relevant information about the problem, much potentially useful and important information is simply not available at the time the decision must be made. Since planning problems are inherently long-term in their orientation, they require anticipating the outcomes of cause and effect chains stretching five to ten years into the future, where causes are individual management decisions, environmental influences, and organizational actions, and the effects are highly uncertain or totally unknown (Hosmer, 1982). In a sense, then, the organization faced with a complex problem is caught in a "Catch-22": on the one hand, it cannot hope ever to gain a complete understanding of the situation no matter how much energy is expended in the effort. On the other hand, long before acquiring what data are needed, it will be overcome with more information than can be digested. Thus, as Lindblom (1980) regretfully made clear: "Everyone who wants to think through a policy problem must steer a course between too little and too much information. There exists no path between the two that is not highly fallible" (p. 21).

In addition to the above paradox, much of the information immediately available to those faced with complex planning problems may consist only of symptoms and hunches rather than detailed description. It was this dilemma that probably led Thompson (1967) to the conclusion that coping with uncertainty was the central task facing the administration of large organizations. Other writers suggest that the challenge may be even greater. Ansoff (1965), for example, characterized such situations as decision making under "partial ignorance":

> In technical terms, used by mathematical decision theorists, specification of strategy is forced under conditions of partial ignorance, when alternatives cannot be arranged and examined in advance, whereas under conditions of risk (alternatives are all known and so are their probabilities) or uncertainty (alternatives are known but not the probabilities), the consequences of different alternatives can be analyzed in advance and decision made contingent on their occurrence. (p. 121)

Similarly, Mintzberg (1976) described such situations as decision making under "ambiguity":

> . . . a strategic decision process is characterized by novelty, complexity and open-endedness. . . . Only by groping through a recursive, discontinuous process involving many difficult steps and a host of dynamic factors over a considerable period of time is a choice made. This is not the decision making under uncertainty of the textbook, where alternatives are given even if their consequences are not, but decision making under ambiguity, where almost nothing is given or easily determined. (pp. 250–51)

Ansoff (1979) noted that the timeliness of an organization's response depends upon two variables: the rapidity with which the problem affects the organization and the amount of time needed to plan and effect the response. Since the 1950s, however, these two variables have been on a collision course: the rate of environmental turbulence has accelerated while the organization's response has been made slower by growing size, complexity, and regulation (Hosmer, 1982). Thus, if the organization waits until information is adequate to use traditional forecasting or modeling techniques, it will be increasingly surprised by crises; but if it accepts the vague information, the content will not be specific enough to drive the traditional planning and decision-aiding techniques.

A possible solution to the above problem is to make better use of strategic or "weak" signals (Ansoff, 1975). Instead of letting the formal planning process determine the information needs, an organization should determine what planning and action are feasible as strategic information becomes available. This would mean that at "lower" states of knowledge, personal intuition, managerial judgment, expert opinion, and social preferences (elicited through surveys or direct participation) would have to be used, whereas at later stages, the more information-demanding forecasting or modeling techniques become usable.

To sum up, today's planning problems are increasingly characterized by high levels of complexity such that it is not possible to gain full understanding before needing to act. It is possible, however, to be well-informed and thoughtful in the choice of methods for problem simplification. Indeed, without "scanning" capabilities, organizations will be overcome with more information than can be digested. Furthermore, much of the information available consists only of hunches or symptoms rather than detailed data, rendering most traditional decision aids unusable. Thus, effective planning entails going beyond the coping with uncertainty to that of dealing with ambiguity and partial ignorance.

Planning as Strategic Social Process

While numerous planning approaches have gained prominence in the literature, there has been little consideration of the match between approach and the nature of the problem faced. With the exception of a few analysts such as Thompson (1967), Cartwright (1973), Vroom and Jago (1974), Bryson and Delbecq (1979), Nutt (1976, 1981), and Geurts, Hart, and Caplan (1986), all of whom have suggested models to match planning strategies to the context of the decision situation, much of the literature has been preoccupied with the direct translation of physical science and engineering approaches to planning problems—including those involving rapidly changing, open societal systems. Indeed, as noted earlier, many analytical techniques built upon concepts of comprehensiveness and rationality have become important tools in planning and decision making by default.

Despite the widespread use of such techniques, however, there is mounting evidence that for all but a circumscribed set of relatively well-defined organizational problems, such approaches can be in serious error. On the one hand, there has been a growing willingness on the part of decision makers to perceive problems in a broader context—as being more than just "simple" problems; on the other hand, planning techniques and decision strategies over the past few decades have improved far more rapidly in the opposite direction. As a result, planners and managers often find themselves in the position of wanting to broaden their simple definitions of problems, yet they are offered only better and better techniques to solve the original simply defined problem (Cartwright, 1973). Indeed, to many managers and planners, the availability of formal problem-solving procedures serves only to highlight those parts of the job with which these procedures do not deal: problem identification, the assignment of problem priority, and the allocation of scarce resources to problems (Pound, 1969).

More recently, Mitroff and Emshoff (1979) emphasized that while strategy and policy making are processes of treating ill-structured problems, the tools of planning that have been used most frequently have been those which were developed generally for well-structured issues and problems. Lyles and Mitroff (1980) presented empirical evidence supporting this argument. Mintzberg et al. (1976) conducted an investigation of how organizations go about making "unstructured," strategic decisions. They concluded:

> Researchers of administrative processes have paid little attention to such decisions, preferring instead to concentrate on routine operating decisions, those more accessible to precise description and quantitative analysis. . . . But it is at the top levels of organizations where better decision making methods are most needed; excessive attention by management scientists to operating decisions may well cause organizations to pursue inappropriate courses of action more efficiently. (p. 246)

Since uncertainty spurred by turbulence is now the dominant characteristic of most organizational environments, it is not surprising that some emphasis in recent literature has shifted away from *algorithmic* approaches (i.e., quantitative programming and modeling techniques) and toward *integrative* problem-solving approaches (iterative approaches emphasizing the interaction of technical analysis and human judgments). Integrative problem-solving approaches recognize the impossibility of rational-comprehensive analysis and/or the maximization of some overall measure of benefit when dealing with complex problems. Thus, integrative approaches are not as utopian as rationalism but not as conservative or pessimistic about the role of analysis as the classic incrementalists (e.g., Lindblom, 1959).

The integrative approach envisions the planner as neither the pure technical analyst nor the neutral implementer of decisions made by others. Rather, the complexity of emerging problems necessarily places the planner at the crossroads between analysis and politics, as the facilitator of a *strategic social process*. Planning in this mode requires a gentle blend of targeted, strategic analysis and structured interaction among stakeholders with different perspectives and varying kinds of knowledge and information. Analysis is used to inform the interaction by key actors rather than substitute for it. Analysis provides information but does not attempt to synthesize or aggregate. Synthesis of values and actions is left to the interaction process among the parties of interest.

An important element in integrative approaches to complex problems is the *procedure* used to arrive at the results. Radford (1977) suggested that

there are four broad specifications that such procedures should meet in order
to be readily acceptable to those with responsibility for resolution of complex
decision problems:

   1) the decision procedure should incorporate the most appropriate characteris-
      tics of existing approaches developed in practical experience and in the
      analytical, behavioral and political sciences;
   2) it should be readily understandable by those who may be involved in (or
      have responsibility for) complex decision problems;
   3) it should be sufficiently broad and flexible that it can be used appropriately
      in a wide range of problem situations, in diverse areas of management and
      administration, and in government, business, and community affairs;
   4) the decision procedure should be one that can be introduced unobtrusively
      into an organization, causing a minimum of disruption of existing pro-
      cedures. (pp. 14–15)

Extending this discussion, Rittel and Webber (1973, p. 162) stated that
the resolution of "wicked" problems should be based on a "model of planning as an argumentative process in the course of which an image of the
problem and of the solution emerges gradually among the participants, as a
product of incessant judgment, subjected to critical argument." Friedmann
(1973) has suggested that the facilitator of such a process is not a person
having superior knowledge in some field, but rather a superior ability to
explore complex situations and integrate diverse points of view. Michael
(1973), in making a similar argument, also emphasized the importance and
difficulty of overcoming the psychological resistances to embracing uncertainty and learning from mistakes.

Evaluating the outcomes from such a planning process is no easy task.
Hart (1985) proposed a set of quality criteria for such collective processes
that includes both process and content items. Dunn (1981) has suggested
some criteria for determining the effectiveness of solutions to complex planning problems. Rather than obtaining correct technical solutions to self-
evident problems, the process and outcome must be *creative* in one or more
of the following ways:

   1. The process of analysis must be sufficiently *unconventional* that it
      involves modification of previously accepted ideas,
   2. The process of analysis must take place with high *intensity* or over
      long periods of time,
   3. The solution must be sufficiently *novel* that most people could not
      have arrived at it independently, and
   4. The solution must be regarded as *valuable* by analysts, policy
      makers, and stakeholders.

At the organizational level, Ackoff (1974) characterized such a process as "idealized redesign." The idealized redesign process unleashes creativity because it relaxes internally imposed constraints. Designers of such a process do not pretend to have the final answers; rather, they seek to design the process capable of finding answers—they create an "inquiring system," in the words of Churchman (1971). Such a process depends upon the widespread participation of those who are potentially affected by (as well as expert in) the subject of the decision (Ackoff, 1978).

Through such a process, organizations gain the capacity to become proactive (Ackoff, 1974). Rather than resisting change associated with environmental turbulence, the proactive organization attempts both to anticipate and to influence the changing environment. Thus, it not only seeks to align itself with the changing world (through the gathering of pertinent "intelligence") but also attempts (through exploration and creativity) to design a better one. Rather than viewing turbulence as a threat, the proactive organization views it as an opportunity. Furthermore, through self-evaluation and feedback, the proactive organization retains the ability to adapt and adjust as it proceeds. In so doing, it becomes a learning system capable of both gradual refinement of existing courses of action as well as more radical responses to major discontinuities and external change.

Discussion and Conclusions

Organizations can expect to be faced with increasing levels of uncertainty over the next decade. Turbulent social and economic conditions will continue to have a profound influence upon the ability of public and private organizations to remain viable, competitive, and socially responsive. As the issues and problems facing organizations become increasingly complex and ill-defined, the traditional tools and techniques of planning will become more and more inappropriate while the need for integrative approaches that aid in the formulation and clarification of complex problems will increase.

Planning must break from its traditional shackles that envision it as either a purely analytic set of decision-support activities or as the process of implementing decisions made by others. The need for integrative approaches to problems mandates that the planning profession adapt its role to one of facilitating a social process. This puts the planner at the center of the decision process, in the role of facilitator and integrator.

Technical analysis constitutes only one form of input to this process. There are diverse types and levels of inputs to the planning process, ranging from strongly held individual values and preferences to scientific and technical knowledge. To manage such diversity of input, the planner must create an "intermediary process" to: (1) mediate and integrate the different types of information and knowledge elements; and (2) create the necessary opportunities for interaction and learning among key actors (experts, policy makers, stakeholders). Planning can thus be envisioned as the strategic social process by which the supply of information for decision making is brought into alignment with the demand for consideration or analysis.

But, while analysts and commentators on such matters have been long on description of the nature of such problems and the broad characteristics of the integrative approach, there has been little in the way of practical prescription or method development. Few writers have wrestled with the down-to-earth realities of operationalizing the integrative approach. Most of the work that has been done in this regard has been in the development and use of specific decision aids (e.g., delphi, nominal group technique, decision analysis, gaming-simulation). Only a handful of authors have made efforts at developing and testing more integrative approaches to problem solving. Examples include Delbecq and Van de Ven's "Program Planning Model" (1971), Friedmann's "Transactive Planning" (1973), Warfield's "Task-Oriented Transient Organization" (1976), Ansoff's "Issue Analysis" (1975), Radford's "Integrated Strategy" (1977), Mason and Mitroff's "Strategic Assumption Surfacing and Testing" (1981), and Enk and Hart's (1985) "Eight Step Approach."

These efforts notwithstanding, there is a need for much more work in this regard. Indeed, it is sadly ironic that, in this age of the "information explosion," our sophistication in addressing complex planning problems is only marginally better than it was 40 years ago. Recognition in the academic literature of the existence and nature of such problems is only half the battle; we must now turn our attention to the challenge of integrating such capabilities into the structure and function of real organizations. This requires the fostering of planners with strong backgrounds in group and organizational processes as well as policy-analytic skills. Planners must not only be able to span the gap between the world of analysis and the political realities of organizational life; they must also be willing and able to understand and integrate the perspectives of diverse stakeholders into the problem-solving process. In short, the effective planner in the coming years must be not only *interdisciplinary* (capable of integrating different branches of scientific and technical knowledge) but also *interparadigmatic* (capable of integrating different knowledge systems).

Notes

1. Problem formulation under conditions of certainty is self-evident, hence the "Domain of Simple Problems."
2. Option selection and implementation under conditions of ambiguity is clearly an undesirable situation (although not without precedent), hence the "Domain of the Lost or Crazy".

References

Ackoff, R. *The Art of Problem Solving.* New York: John Wiley and Sons, 1978.

_____. *Redesigning the Future.* New York: John Wiley and Sons, 1974.

Ansoff, I. *Strategic Management.* London: MacMillan, 1979.

_____. "Managing Strategic Surprise by Response to Weak Signals," *California Management Review,* 18 (1975): 21–23.

_____. *Corporate Strategy.* New York: McGraw Hill, 1965.

Berger, P. and Luckman, T. *The Social Construction of Reality.* Garden City, N.Y.: Doubleday, 1966.

Boulding, K. *The Image.* Ann Arbor: University of Michigan Press, 1956.

Bryson, J. and Delbecq, A. "A Contingency Approach to Strategy and Tactics in Project Planning." *Journal of the American Planning Association,* 45 (1979): 167–79.

Cartwright, T. "Problems, Solutions and Strategies: A Contribution to the Theory and Practice of Planning." *Journal of the American Institute of Planners,* 39 (1973): 179–87.

Churchman, C.W. *The Design of Inquiring Systems.* New York: Basic Books, 1971.

Delbecq, A. and Van de Ven, A. "Group Process Model for Problem Identification and Program Planning." *Journal of Applied Behavior Science,* 7 (1971): 466–92.

Dunn, W. *Public Policy Analysis.* Englewood Cliffs, N.J.: Prentice-Hall, 1981.

Enk, G. and Hart, S. "An Eight-Step Approach to Strategic Problem Solving." *Human Systems Management,* in press.

Etzioni, A. "Mixed Scanning: A 'Third' Approach to Decision Making." *Public Administration Review,* 27 (1967): 385–92.

Friedmann, J. *Retracking America: A Theory of Transactive Planning.* New York: Anchor-Doubleday, 1973.

Geurts, J.; Hart, S.; and Caplan, N. "Decision Techniques and Social Research: A Contingency Framework for Problem Solving." *Human Systems Management,* in press.

Hart, S. "Toward Quality Criteria for Collective Judgments." *Organizational Behavior and Human Decision Processes,* 36 (1985): 209–28.

Hosmer, L. *Strategic Management: Text and Cases.* Englewood Cliffs, N.J.: Prentice Hall, 1982.

Hudson, B. "Comparison of Current Planning Theories: Counterparts and Contradictions." *Journal of the American Planning Association,* 45 (1979): 387–98.

Lindblom, C. *The Policy Making Process.* Englewood Cliffs, N.J.: Prentice Hall, 1980.

_____. "Still Muddling, Not Yet Through." *Public Administration Review,* 39 (1979): 517–26.

_____. "The Science of 'Muddling Through'." *Public Administration Review,* 19 (1959): 79–88.

Lyles, M. and Mitroff, I. "Organizational Problem Formulation: An Empirical Study." *Administration Science Quarterly,* 25 (1980): 102–19.

March, J. and Simon, H. *Organizations.* New York: John Wiley and Sons, 1958.

Mason, R. and Mitroff, I. *Challenging Strategic Planning Assumptions.* New York: John Wiley, 1981.

McKenna, C. *Quantitative Methods for Public Decision Making.* New York: McGraw-Hill, 1980.

Meyerson, M. and Banfield, E. *Politics, Planning and the Public Interest.* Glencoe, Ill.: The Free Press, 1955.

Michael, D. *On Learning to Plan and Planning to Learn.* San Francisco: Jossey-Bass, 1973.

Mintzberg, H. "What is Planning Anyway?" *Strategic Management Journal,* 2 (1981): 319–24.

Mintzberg, H.; Raisinghani, D.; and Theoret, A. "The Structure of 'Unstructured' Decision Processes." *Administrative Science Quarterly,* 21 (1976): 246–75.

Mitroff, I. *Stakeholders of the Organizational Mind.* San Francisco: Jossey-Bass, 1983.

Mitroff, I. and Emshoff, J. "On Strategic Assumption Making: A Dialectical Approach to Policy and Planning." *Academy of Management Review,* 4 (1979): 1–12.

Nutt, P. "Some Guidelines for the Selection of a Decision Making Strategy." *Technological Forecasting and Social Change,* 19 (1981): 133–145.

_____. "Models of Decision Making in Organizations and Some Contextual Variables Which Stipulate Optimal Use." *Academy of Management Review,* 1 (1976): 84–98.

Pound, W. "The Process of Problem Finding." *Industrial Management Review,* 11 (1969): 1–19.

Pressman, J. and Wildavsky, A. *Implementation,* 2nd ed. Berkeley: University of California Press, 1975.

Quinn, J. *Strategies for Change: Logical Incrementalism.* Homewood, IL: Richard Irwin, Inc., 1980.

Radford, K. *Complex Decision Problems: An Integrated Strategy for Their Resolution.* Reston: Reston Publishing Co., 1977.

Ray, P. "On Theories of Rational Optimizing." Ann Arbor: University of Michigan, 1970.

Rittel, H. and Webber, M. "Dilemmas in a General Theory of Planning." *Policy Sciences,* 4 (1973): 155–69.

Ross, G. "The Elusive Nature of Organizational Effectiveness." Ann Arbor: Institute for Social Research, 1979.

Schon, D. "Some of What a Planner Knows." *Journal of the American Planning Association,* 48 (1982): 351–64.

———. *Beyond the Stable State.* New York: W. W. Norton, 1971.

Simon, H. *Administrative Behavior.* New York: The Free Press, 1945.

Simon, H. and Newell, A. "Human Problem Solving: The State of the Theory in 1970." *American Psychologist,* 26 (1971): 146–59.

Steiner, G. *Strategic Planning.* New York: Free Press, 1979.

Thompson, J. *Organizations in Action.* New York: McGraw Hill, 1967.

Tichy, N. *Managing Strategic Change.* New York, NY: Wiley, 1983.

Vroom, V. and Jago, A. "Decision Making as a Social Process: Normative and Descriptive Models of Leader Behavior." *Decision Sciences,* 5 (1974): 43–769.

Warfield, J. *Societal Systems: Planning, Policy and Complexity.* New York: John Wiley, 1976.

7

Planning, Public Budgeting, and Politics: Maximizing the Impact of Advice Giving

Milan J. Dluhy

Many planners increasingly find themselves participating in public budgeting. The opportunity to shape public policy through the budget certainly is a challenge, but it can also be terribly frustrating. This chapter focuses on public budgeting at the national level and tries to illustrate how planners and, by implication, planning education can become more sensitive to the realities of influencing perhaps the most complex and least understood decision-making process in our society. After a brief comment about ideal decision-making situations, there will be sections devoted to the nature and context of the budgeting environment, how planners can realistically approach exerting influence in that environment, and finally the implications of this reorientation to public budgeting for planning education.

Ideal Decision-Making Situations

Planners strive to have their findings, recommendations, and advice accepted by decision makers. Ideally, planners are the most comfortable and satisfied in situations where:

- the decision makers seek answers to questions rather than numbers to legitimize their political positions;
- sufficient quantitative research and data are available to make decisions;
- there is a timetable and formalized process available for making decisions;
- there are other planners besides themselves with technical knowledge available to advise decision makers; and

- analytical tools are used by planners and these tools are accepted as legitimate by decision makers.

This optimal set of circumstances provides the planner with the greatest opportunity to have an impact on the ultimate choice made by decision makers.[1] However, the connection between research and public policy has been looked at closely in recent years, and the basic and somewhat disturbing conclusion of most of the studies on the use of research by decision makers is that this knowledge rarely (if ever) has a direct, immediate, independent, and instrumental effect on concrete decision making.[2] So the planner is left searching for the few situations or conditions where his/her advice will be used, or more typically withdrawing from serious debates about public policy. This essay argues that despite the frustrations of decision making that are present in almost all aspects of public budgeting at the national level, the planner can still be an important advice giver in that process if he/she will be realistic about that process and the role that can be played in it.

Context of Budgeting at the National Level

Numerous accounts of the budgetary process at the national level conclude quite persuasively that the formulation and enactment of the budget are inherently political.[3] The budget involves mainly the struggle over who gets the benefits and who pays the costs. While there may be formal goals, timetables, and schedules which guide the preparation of the budget, the process is a story of conflict, struggle, political trading, and ultimately the building of a political coalition which will support the final priorities established in the budget. The very revealing and much-quoted account of the budget process given a few years ago by David Stockman, the former director of the Office of Management and Budget, in *Atlantic* is worth quoting to illustrate the political nature of that process:

> The idea-based policies that he had espoused at the outset were, in the final event, greatly compromised by the constituency based politics that he abhorred. What had changed, fundamentally, was the list of winning clients, not the nature of the game. Stockman has said the new conservatism would pursue equity, even as it attempted to shrink the government. It would honor just claims and reject spurious ones, instead of simply serving powerful clients over weak clients. He was compelled to agree, at the legislative climax, that the original moral premises had not been served, that the new principles of Reaganism were compromised by the necessity of winning. "I now understand," he said, "that you probably can't put together a majority coalition unless you are

willing to deal with those marginal interests that will give you the votes needed to win. That's where it is fought—on the margins—and unless you deal with those marginal votes, you can't win."

In order to enact Reagan's version of tax reduction, certain wages had to be paid, and, as Stockman reasoned, the process of brokering was utterly free of principle or policy objectives. . . . Once the Reagan tacticians began making concessions beyond their policy-based agenda, it developed that their trades and compromises and giveaways were utterly indistinguishable from the decades of interest-group accommodations that had preceded them, which they so righteously denounced.[4]

This rather candid portrayal of the budget process at the national level implies that research, evaluations, and other forms of scientific knowledge have little if any impact on the preparation of the budget, and that by logical implication planners who translate and use this type of information have little credibility and influence in that process. In order to explore this proposition in more detail, it is helpful to understand the sequence that is used to prepare and adopt the budget. Table 7.1 provides a summary of the time sequence used in budgeting, the key actors involved at each stage in that sequence, and the principal activities taking place at each stage. There are a number of important observations to be made about this sequence. *First,* the number and variety of actors involved in the sequence make it complex but also accessible. The opportunity to exert influence can come at any point in that sequence so if planners fail at one stage, they can turn to another. For example, failure to influence an agency's budget or the President's budget may lead planners to turn to Congress to have their views listened to. Even within the Congressional stages of budgeting, planners may be more persuasive within the House as opposed to the Senate.[5] There are numerous points of access and multiple opportunities to present information. While it is true, as Allen Schick argues, that the bulk of the budget is determined by prior years' legislative decisions, in a budget the size of the federal government's, the disputes over margins can be translated into billions of dollars.[6] At this level there is a large enough stake for many actors to fight for and ultimately secure substantial benefits. And if actors think about the cumulative stakes over a period of time like five years, the rewards are indeed worth the fight.

A *second* observation about the budget sequence is that there are conflicting assumptions about the future. The budget must include at a minimum assumptions and estimates about spending, revenues, deficits or surpluses, and monetary policy (the rate at which money will be created) over a period of time. For example, revenue intake is contingent upon the economy. A healthy economy produces more revenue for the government at

TABLE 7.1

Budget Cycle and Timetable at National Level

Time Period (approximate)	Key Actors	Major Activities	Other Comments
August through October	"Bureaucrats", President, O.M.B., Secretary of Treasury	Agencies estimate and project needs of their individual programs for next two years.	Most activity takes place within agencies. President, O.M.B., and Secretary of Treasury set parameters only based on certain assumptions.
November through January	President and staff, O.M.B., Council of Economic Advisors, Secretary of Treasury, "computers"	Preparation of executive budget given agency estimates, the delivery of State of Union and Economic Message to Congress.	President and key advisors make critical assumptions about overall spending, revenues, and deficits or surpluses. The President's budget is produced.
February through May 15	House and Senate leadership, House and Senate Budget Committees, Congressional Budget Office	Budget committees pass in the form of resolutions ceilings on spending for major functional activities of government. These ceilings become the first concurrent resolution.	First attempt to reconcile executive budget and congressional budget and their different assumptions.
May 15 through October	House and Senate Appropriations Committees, other authorizing committees, House and Senate leadership, interest groups, O.M.B., media, President and staff	Passage of congressional spending bills. Thirteen appropriation bills are passed or a "continuing resolution" is passed until all 13 bills are passed by Congress and signed by President into law. On September 15 Congress completes action on second concurrent resolution.	Real bargaining and negotiation take place, especially near the end of this phase (October–November). The second concurrent resolution must coincide with appropriation bills.

Source: Adapted from Stanley E. Collender, *The Guide to the Federal Budget, Fiscal 1984 Edition* (Washington, D.C.: The Urban Institute Press, 1983).

current tax levels. The size of the deficit or surplus in turn is contingent
(among other things) upon the commitments to spending, revenue intake, and
monetary policy. In short, budgeting requires technical information and
analysis in order to make reasonable estimates. These estimates are based on
assumptions about things such as the unemployment rate, growth of the economy, and changes in interest rates. Tables 7.2 and 7.3 indicate the types of
assumptions and estimates that are made in budgeting. In order to illustrate
the conflicts and differences in these assumptions and estimates, these tables
show how the Reagan administration and the Congressional Budget Office,
two of the principal actors in the process, often differ. Each relies on
technicians or planners to provide them with information, and each interprets
and uses this information to develop concrete proposals that are included in
the budget negotiations. It is also important to remember that the budget
sequence is one where massive amounts of data are available to base estimates on, numerous technicians (staff) are present to analyze this data, and
various analytical tools have been developed and used to facilitate the reaching of decisions. In short, budgeting is not a mystical exercise based on
uneducated and impulsive guesses, but a process where information overload
and an abundance of technical personnel who can use analytical tools are

TABLE 7.2

Budget Projections, 1981

Congressional Budget	Billions of Dollars					
	FY81	*FY82*	*FY83*	*FY84*	*FY85*	*FY86*
Revenues						
Administration	600.3	650.3	709.1	770.7	849.9	940.2
Congressional Budget Office	611.9	709.1	810.2	919.6	1,033.2	1,158.2
Outlays						
Administration	655.2	695.3	732.0	770.2	844.0	912.0
Congressional Budget Office	659.8	738.7	792.5	843.3	894.9	949.9
Deficit or Surplus						
Administration	−54.9	−45.0	−22.8	.5	5.8	28.2
Congressional Budget Office	−47.9	−29.6	17.7	76.3	138.3	208.9

Sources: Office of Management and Budget, *Fiscal Year 1982 Budget Revisions*, March
1981, p. 11; Congressional Budget Office, *Baseline Budget Projections: Fiscal Years 1982–
1986* (Washington, D.C.: GPO, 1981), p. 10.

available to aid decision makers. The end result is that technicians armed with analytic tools and mountains of data do not make decisions for decision makers but merely provide a better way of organizing the search for answers.[7] The decision maker still must weigh these more analytic inputs against information on other dimensions that will come from political parties, clientele, interest groups, and others before they can arrive at a decision. Conflict is therefore inherent in budgeting. Data and research are important, but are just one input into the decision-making process which determines the final budget.

A *third* observation about the budget sequence is the length of time frame itself. Table 7.1 illustrates that the process begins in August (approximately) of one fiscal year and does not end until all the appropriation bills have been passed by Congress and signed into law by the President. On paper, this is supposed to occur the following October or 14 months later when the new fiscal year begins. In practice, Congress and the President fre-

TABLE 7.3

Economic Assumptions of Reagan Budget, Calendar Years 1982–88

Economic Indicator	Projected					
	1983	*1984*	*1985*	*1986*	*1987*	*1988*
Year-to-Year Change						
GNP in current dollars						
Administration	6.7%	9.3%	9.1%	8.8%	8.7%	8.6%
CBO	6.8%	9.6%	9.0%	8.1%	7.6%	7.4%
Consumer price index						
Administration	4.9%	4.6%	4.6%	4.6%	4.5%	4.4%
CBO	4.5%	5.0%	4.7%	4.1%	3.9%	3.7%
Annual Average						
Unemployment rate						
Administration	10.7%	9.9%	8.9%	8.1%	7.3%	6.5%
CBO	10.6%	9.8%	9.0%	8.4%	8.0%	7.5%
Treasury bill rate						
Administration	8.0%	7.9%	7.4%	6.8%	6.5%	6.1%
CBO	6.8%	7.4%	7.2%	6.6%	6.1%	5.9%

Sources: Budget of the United States Government, Fiscal Year 1984, pp. 2–9 and Congressional Budget Office, *The Outlook for Economic Recovery* (Washington, D.C.: GPO, 1983), p. 7.

quently are unable to agree by October, in which case Congress passes a continuing resolution which funds agencies and programs at the previous year's level. They continue to negotiate and may not actually obligate money for the new fiscal year until three or four months after the October deadline. In total, from agency estimates to final passage, the budget may take from 14 to 18 months to adopt. This lengthy process further magnifies the fact that changes can be and are made throughout a rather lengthy period of time. This reinforces the image of budgeting as complex, open to substantial negotiation, and accessible to many actors and influences. Additionally, assumptions and estimates can change dramatically in 18 months. The very parameters used to project future budgets are connected closely to the fluctuations in the world's economy, and these estimates of parameters have usually been subject to substantial error. Therefore, a lengthy budget sequence not only promotes conflict and negotiation, but it often makes assumptions and estimates which can become outdated and inaccurate quite easily.

A *fourth* observation about the budget sequence is that while various reforms have been adopted over the years, budgeting still remains an inherently political process.[8] At different times, reformers have introduced systems and analytic techniques which were designed to improve decision making.[9] While the 1960s introduced the PPB (planning–programming–budgeting) system to the federal government, the 1970s experimented with MBO (management by objectives), Performance Budgeting, Program Evaluation, and ZBB (zero base budgeting). Each of these formats yielded different information, and each had its own value set. While elements of each are still evident in the budget sequence, none of the reforms has been able to eliminate the underlying basis of budgeting—that it is inherently a political process. Rather it is more accurate to say that decision makers are now armed with more analytical methods and tools than ever before, and that these tools can provide useful information as an input to decision making, but they can not be made independent from other inputs. While there still appears to be a need to convince the public that budgeting is comprehensive, goal-oriented, efficient, equitable, and above all non-political, the reality is that incrementalism, constituency-based politics, political trading, and coalition building still best describe budgeting.

In sum, planners need to recognize that in order to have their advice accepted by decision makers in the budget sequence, they need to have a realistic perspective about how that process operates, so they can maximize their input. Above all, budgeting is political and, therefore, planners must view budgeting as a political process, not narrowly as an analytic exercise where formats, data, and analysis are the main ingredients of decision making. Given this political perspective, however, planners should not be discouraged from participating. The budget sequence is lengthy, it has multiple points of access, decision makers want and need quantitative information to make estimates and clarify their assumptions, and decision makers will use information generated according to analytic formats if it answers some of their questions or supports one of their political positions.

A Realistic Approach to Influencing Public Budgeting

It has been argued to this point that a realistic perspective on the budget is one that accepts the budget first and foremost as a political document produced by a political process. It is not the result of a set of formalized analytic exercises. Accordingly, data is rarely presented in a comprehensive and non-judgmental fashion. Data is almost never used instrumentally by decision makers; it is more common to use it symbolically.[10] In other words, data does not frequently influence the formulation of a political position (instrumental use) by a decision maker, but rather it is more likely to be used to legitimize a political position that is already held by a decision maker (symbolic use). These comments relate primarily to the use of data in making direct, immediate, and concrete decisions. This suggests that planners can often be caught in situations where decision makers seek their advice only because the decision makers know ahead of time that the planner will produce information that already supports their own political position. The view that the planner has a direct and immediate impact on what the decision maker chooses to do is not realistic. However, the planner, by presenting data, research, and other forms of knowledge, can indirectly impact on decision making. The opportunity to influence decision makers by presenting data and research, even in a highly politicized process like budgeting, comes when the planner takes a more realistic view of his/her role in the decision-making process. If the role of the planner is viewed in a more indirect way, i.e., that the planner should help to structure the search for answers to questions but not seek to actually make decisions for decision makers, the opportunity for influence can still be realized. For example, *data and research over an extended period of time can be used to help decision makers reconceptualize problems, their structural causes, and their most feasible solutions.* Results of social experiments like the Experimental Housing Allowance Program (EHAP) which began in 1973 and was finally evaluated in 1982 at a cost to the government of $200 million,[11] in the long run has influenced federal decision makers to move from production-oriented housing policy to consumer-oriented housing policy where housing allowances given to consumers are preferred to subsidies given to the housing industry or landlords. This shift in thinking took many years and did not occur in the short run. Only now are we at the point of reprioritizing housing policy through the budget based on years and years of research and experimentation in this field.[12]

Besides aiding in reconceptualization of problems and their solutions, planners can use data and research *to help decision makers rule out the worst options*. Again, the planner may not be able to recommend the best decision and have his/her advice accepted but may be able, through the use of data and research, at least to eliminate the most costly and least feasible options. The budget process in an era of retrenchment is most certainly interested in advice which shows decision makers which options will definitely not work, especially because they may be very cost-inefficient. Ruling out the worst options for the decision maker is a valuable service and one which gives the planner influence over the decision-making agenda. Closely associated with the task of ruling out the worst options is *the careful costing out for decision makers of all options being considered.* Planners can help to develop criteria for assessing options, actually collect data to assess these options, and present all of this information in a format that can be utilized by a decision maker. Here the decision maker applies the weights to the different criteria but the planner furnishes the hard-core information assessing each option. Again, the influence appears more indirect but it is still present.

Finally, the planner can also perform the task of *helping decision makers to see the trade-offs between options*. In this context, planners may have to mix both quantitative and qualitative information in order to show the costs or consequences of making a particular decision. The art of demonstrating what the trade-offs of different decisions are is perhaps the most challenging and rewarding task that can be performed by the planner since it comes the closest to actually making the decision.

Table 7.4 provides a summary of three different types of planning roles that can be played in a decision-making process like budgeting, which is so dominated by politics. Dramatists use data and research, but they use it in very one-sided ways and only to reinforce those decision makers who already agree with them. Rarely will a dramatist convert a decision maker whose mind is already made up to the contrary. The technician is a help. He/she helps to structure the agenda for the decision maker especially by laying out and evaluating the various options. However, the neutral tone of presentation results in advice being given in a way that decision makers will use it only for overall conceptual purposes, not for direct and immediate decision making. Pragmatists know how to use data and research very well. In fact, their key skill is that they are able to clearly show the trade-offs between options, especially as seen in a political context. The political consequences of action or inaction are critical knowledge for the decision maker. The ability to provide this knowledge tempered by the realities of the decision-making environment makes this role one which maximizes advice giving. The main shortcoming of pragmatists is that they can become too closely associated with political partisans and lose their professional identities and reputation for objectivity. In practice, planners can be influential using any of the three

TABLE 7.4

Three Types of Planning Roles

Dramatist	*Technician*	*Pragmatist*
"Appeals to values, emotions, ideology"	*"Appeals to objective need, sense of rationality"*	*"Appeals to feasibility or what will go"*
Uses clear, simple language, no jargon	Assumptions, biases, and criteria laid out	Brief but complete case
Dramatic use of data whenever possible	Neutral tone of presentation used	Data presented in simplified form
Tell stories to dramatize worst situations	Substantial documentation of problem and issues is presented	Only feasible options offered
Inflammatory language, consciousness-raising tactics	Focus on structural roots or causes of problem	Trade-offs between options are made clear
Discredits opposition	Explores a wide range of solutions and options	External support for solutions is evaluated
Action oriented so that specific next steps are clear	Evaluates options thoroughly	Both quantitative and qualitative data are presented
Only one solution is presented	Assesses options but no preferred one is emphasized	Data used to legitimize position
Feasibility of solution is down played	Aims at long-term conceptual reorientation of audience	Clear and implementable solutions are recommended
Value rationale is central to argument		

roles. As long as they are willing to influence decision makers in a more indirect way, they can have a real impact on public budgeting.

Implications for Planning Education

In my judgment, the task of training planners to be good researchers, analysts, and technicians is a straightforward proposition. Courses emphasizing research design, data analysis, and analytic techniques are quite common at the graduate level, and few Ph.D students escape heavy doses of each. However, this essay has argued that planners who hope to be influential in public budgeting must not only reorient themselves toward the political realities of budgeting, but they must be more cognizant of what roles they can play in the budget process. A careful examination of these three roles and the discussion of the context of budgeting presented here suggest that quantitative and analytical skills are not enough if a planner seeks to have a responsible amount of influence in budgeting. In addition, the planner will need considerable knowledge about the sociopolitical context in which he/she will be working, as well as a whole set of skills which will allow the connection between research and policy to be made more effectively. In this respect, training in document preparation, making oral presentations, decision theory, and political advocacy would be very valuable. In the end, planners will be more successful advice givers if they learn to make the connections between knowledge and policy in the context of the realities of political decision making.

Notes

1. For a more complete discussion of this issue, *see* Milan J. Dluhy, "Muddling Through or Thinking About the Problem Seriously . . .", reprinted in John E. Tropman, Milan J. Dluhy, and Roger Lind, *New Strategic Perspectives on Social Policy* (New York: Pergamon Press, 1981).
2. For a summary of this literature, *see* Carol Weiss, ed., *Using Social Research in Public Policy Making* (Lexington, MA: D.C. Heath, 1977).
3. For example, *see* Allen Schick, *Congress and Money* (Washington, D.C.: The Urban Institute, 1980); Howard E. Shuman, *Politics and the Budget* (Englewood Cliffs, NJ: Prentice–Hall, 1981), and Aaron Wildavsky, *The Politics of the Budgetary Process,* 4th ed. (Boston: Little, Brown and Co., 1984).
4. William Greider, "The Education of David Stockman," *Atlantic,* Vol. 248, No. 6, Dec. 1981, pp. 51-52.
5. John W. Ellwood and James A. Thurber, "The Politics of the Congressional Budget Process Re-examined," reprinted in Lawrence C. Dodd and Bruce

I. Oppenheimer, *Congress Reconsidered,* 2nd ed. (Washington, D.C.: Congressional Quarterly Press, 1981).
6. Schick, *Congress and Money,* p. 579.
7. For a discussion of this point, *see* Freemont J. Lyden and Ernest G. Miller, *Public Budgeting,* 4th ed. (Englewood Cliffs, NJ: Prentice–Hall, 1982), Introduction.
8. Shuman, *Politics and the Budget,* especially Ch. 8 and 10.
9. Lyden and Miller, *Public Budgeting,* Introduction.
10. Weiss, ed., *Using Social Research in Public Policy Making,* Introduction.
11. Joseph Friedman and Daniel Weinberg, *The Great Housing Experiment* (Beverly Hills, CA: Sage Publications, 1983).
12. *Ibid.,* Ch. 1.

8

Building Citizen Support for Planning at the Community Level

Barry Checkoway

Planning practice is changing. Previous years of economic growth contributed to an increase in federal, state, and local planning agencies, in addition to regional and special purpose bodies with territorial or functional responsibilities. In times of growth, planning was viewed by many as a type of urban engineering and applied social science characterized by objective fact-finding and the so-called rational model. Leading texts emphasized technical research methods and "hard data" analysis, while government guidelines described scientific application of facts (Krueckeberg and Silvers, 1974; Spiegel and Hyman, 1978). Planners were akin to technical experts who analyzed data for other people who considered alternatives and made decisions. Implementation was largely a matter of choice among technical alternatives. The plan, as a statement of reasoned deliberation and general public interest, was considered capable of generating support throughout the community. If some planners criticized contradictions between the rational model and actual practice, or used planning as a vehicle for power redistribution and social change, they were by no means typical in the field (Beyle and Lathrop, 1970; Burchell and Sternlieb, 1978; Davidoff, 1965).

Today planning operates in a changing context. Economic recession has replaced growth and reduced development. This has exacerbated conditions in central cities and metropolitan areas, some of which are slowing, even declining in population, employment, and other measures of urban activity. Private groups blame government for economic problems and planning agencies for a range of ills. They mobilize substantial resources, mount cam-

Forthcoming from Barry Checkoway, ed., *Strategic Perspectives on Planning Practice,* Lexington, MA: Lexington Books, D.C. Heath and Company, copyright 1986. Reprinted by permission of the publisher.

paigns to shape public attitudes, and elect representatives who reduce government and agencies. Planners no longer expect to generate widespread support, but instead may struggle for survival in the face of power (Checkoway, 1983; Clavel, et al., 1980; Forester, 1982).

It thus is no surprise that planning agencies may not implement their plans. Analysts have documented the shortcomings of implementation in diverse arenas for years (Alterman, 1983; Bardach, 1977; Lynn, 1980; Mazmanian and Nienaber, 1979; Thompson, 1981). The surprise for many planners is that the problem is not implementation alone but also their very future in the community. Austerity policies and adversarial power challenge planners to recognize sociopolitical change and develop capacity for the years ahead.

This chapter analyzes methods of building citizen support for planning at the community level. It draws on research and practice in several fields and includes cases of planners and agencies that apply innovative or exemplary methods. It does not suggest that these planners are typical in the field, or that these methods alone are sufficient to alter the context of practice. It does suggest that planning operates in a changing context, and that planners who want to influence implementation—and perhaps agency survival—must go beyond rational models to build support for planning at the community level.

Methods of Building Citizen Support

Building citizen support involves methods to plan programs, services, and resources with implementation in mind. It assumes that planning operates in a context of politics, and that planners wishing to influence decisions must apply methods appropriate to this context. Practitioners apply methods in public or private settings; at national, state, and local levels; and in housing, land use, natural resources, social and human services, and other fields. There is no single notion that characterizes all forms of practice.

There is nothing new about agency attempts to build support, but previous efforts often have contradicted stated aims or produced uneven results. For example, agencies for years have composed governing bodies, boards and committees to represent citizen interests and build support for plans, but these bodies have not always involved individuals accountable to diverse constituencies in the community (Checkoway, Marmor and Morone, 1980). Other agencies have adopted subarea planning aimed to decentralize decisions and programs to territorial subunits and local participants, but subarea planning has often served administrative ends and deconcentrated functions without real decentralization to local residents (Checkoway, 1984; Kasperson and Breitbart, 1974). Yet other agencies have employed programs and methods to improve communications, involve individuals, and activate participation in planning, but most agencies have not adopted singular driving objectives for participation and instead have favored safe methods like public hearings that satisfy minimal federal requirements and provide public relations without transferring power to or increasing support of citizens (Arnstein, 1969; Checkoway, 1981d). Exceptional agencies have represented interests and activated citizens with fervor, but most have not built significant support.

What methods could help build citizen support for planning at the community level? The following are not the only methods, but are among the most important.

Formulate Strategy

Strategy is the science and art of mobilizing resources toward goals. It includes steps to set goals and priorities, identify issues and constituencies, develop structure and organization, take actions, and evaluate results. It involves choice and sequence, staging and timing, and several styles and roles. Strategy shows commitment to think ahead, anticipate alternatives, and achieve results (Booth, 1977; Bryson and Delbecq, 1979; Steiner, 1979).

Corporate leaders formulate strategy to help assure success, but planning officials tend not to think or act strategically (Baum, 1983; Peters and Waterman, 1982). However, Bleiker (1978) instructs planners how to design programs and apply techniques that develop support for plans that are controversial, unpopular, and difficult to implement. Staples (1984) describes strategic analysis to help build winning organizations. Bryson, Freeman, and Roering (1984) describe cases of strategic planning in public agencies, including a health service which identifies issues, analyzes alternatives and implements plans; and a county government which prepares policy objectives, identifies internal and external environmental factors, forms task forces around issues, and selects alternatives for implementation.

Identity Issues

Issues express specific social concerns and affect people in deeply felt ways. They appeal to particular constituencies with concrete proposals, provide tactical handles and multiple phases, and help build support for organizations. Which is the most salient issue? Who are the constituencies? What tactics and actions will work? Where will it lead? Booth (1977) instructs planners to "cut" issues in ways which relate to constituencies, although many planners produce comprehensive plans with vague goals for some general public. Such plans may serve functions but diffuse constituencies and exacerbate implementation. Such goals may be good but too vague to stir imaginations and move constituents to action.

How can planners cut issues which build citizen support? Lancourt (1979) challenges planners to consider salience and self-interest in identifying issues for implementation. She assumes that people will act in the name of public responsibility and civic duty when it is in their self-interest to do so. Roche (1981) describes planners who took goals from agency plans, listed groups with identifiable stake and political strength, defined issues in terms of target groups, and used media to make issues come alive to these groups. For example, they built support of labor leaders by seeking their input and showing how proposed plans would maintain wages and minimize disruption to employees. They did not justify esoteric formulas or sell rationality, but appealed to self-interest and, as a result, leaders voted overwhelmingly to support the plan.

This does not suggest that issues alone will generate support. On the contrary, Krumholz (1975, 1982) describes planners who framed comprehensive plans in terms of specific issues and constituencies, but had uneven results because they lacked resources to activate participation or overcome opposition in the community. Issues are important but insufficient to build support without other methods.

Develop Constituencies

Building an organization involves caring about those who are affected. Whose issue is it? What do they see as their stake? Are they organizable? Constituencies are those who are affected by issues and may show support. Planners who represent some diffuse public interest rather than target supportive constituencies may do so at risk to themselves.

Constituencies are not random relationships but result from efforts to identify and develop them (Barkdoll, 1983; Beneviste, 1977; Lipschultz, 1960; Staples, 1984). In one innovative agency, for example, planners identify major constituency groups, invite them to select representatives to the governing body, and assist representatives in building support in the community. In another they create an independent organization with business, labor, professional, civic and consumer group members who build support beyond the governing body (Checkoway, 1981c). In yet another they analyze agency goals in terms of individual and group opposition, and then develop relationships and provide services to selected ones in expectation of loyalty and support in return (Roche, 1981).

Educate the Public

Citizens cannot be expected to support planning without understanding their problems and stake in the process and agency addressing them. The challenge is not public relations but popular education and community development. It is an older conception of planning in which planners help people to learn about themselves and their problems, and facilitate a process to involve people in the decisions which affect their lives (Freire, 1968; Goulet, 1971).

Planners recognize the importance of public education, but tend to emphasize public information programs including "safe" methods like annual reports, newsletters, and public hearings to inform the general public rather than target specific constituencies (Checkoway, 1982; Texas Municipal League, 1975; Winholz, 1968). Others lack educational objectives or rely upon obscure media like legal notices in newspapers, although studies show that these are among the least effective ways to communicate with the public (Rosener, 1975; Sinclair, 1977). Yet others use technical language which exacerbates difficulties in understanding and gives the impression that only professionals can present an adequate response (Friedmann, 1973; O'Rourke and Forouzesh, 1981; Smith and Borghorst, n.d.). Low income and minority citizens may have particular problems in understanding, ignore calls for participation, or withdraw their support (Checkoway, 1979).

There is a history of popular education in early agencies, which includes exhibits and displays in department stores and shopping centers, and popularizations of technical documents for mass distribution (Glenn et al., 1947; Scott, 1969). Several practitioners provide strategy and skills of popular education (Joslyn-Scherer, 1980; Gordon, 1978). One innovative agency provides extensive public notices of hearings, public service announcements, radio and television appearances, direct mass mailings, leaflet distribution, public presentations, and personal outreach by staff and board members, in addition to publishing a monthly multicultural, multilanguage newspaper. The newspaper has become the leading vehicle for planning information in the area. Another agency sponsors a speakers' bureau that facilitates board and staff member presentations to local groups, helps agency representatives exchange ideas and receive feedback, and facilitates board member education and leadership training. Another agency conducts training programs, publishes educational guides to develop leaders and activate citizens, and reaches the public through weekly columns in newspapers, public service announcements, and regular appearances on television and radio (Checkoway, 1981c). These agencies view education as central to their mission.

Find and Make Leaders

Citizen leaders show commitment to goals, develop a following, and stand up for planning in the community. They also attend board meetings and chair committees, but these are vehicles for leadership rather than leadership itself. Many planners retreat from the process by which leaders are selected or developed. Instead they consider leadership in the narrow context of meetings, or believe that some given process satisfactorily provides leaders to represent the population and account to constituencies, or "appropriate" leadership by promoting people who hold positions in established institutions. However, leadership appropriation also may promote people who are uncommitted to plans or who lack time to act like leaders.

There is no a priori justification for overrepresentation of business and other private interests in planning agencies. Their traditional overrepresentation is purely political and difficult to defend by leadership or implementation criteria. It would be ironic if agencies appropriated leaders with relatively little commitment to planning, although this happens in some communities.

How can planners find and make leaders? Bradley (1981) describes an innovative agency that seeks to identify potential leaders, recognize their talent, and develop their skills. He assumes that any citizen can function well when given proper support, that planners have responsibility to foster development, and that if citizens are not acting like leaders, planners may not be doing their job properly. Kimmey (1981) describes centers authorized to assist and consult with participants through orientation, reference, and other programs. These include training to overcome disparities in knowledge, present technical information and participation techniques, and develop leadership capacity and political skills. Yet others provide curricula to teach board members about the political economy of planning ideologies of the principal actors, distribution of benefits and problems of special clients and subpopulation groups, alternative delivery systems, and elements of planned social change. Lessons focus on skills with citizens and enlist their participation, set goals and formulate strategies, develop self-confidence and the ability to think independently (Checkoway, 1981c; Strauss et al., 1976). There is no science of leadership development in planning, but if planners themselves do not take this responsibility, then who will?

Establish Relations with Influentials

These key actors are able to exercise power and influence decisions that affect the agency. They are not random relationships but result from a plan for establishing or maintaining them. Who are the influentials? What are their political resources? What is their place in various institutions? What are the possible paths of influence?

How can planners identify, maintain, and develop relations with influentials? Tait, Bokemeir and Bohlen (n.d.) describe positional, reputational, decision-making and other methods to identify those who may gain from agency activity and marshal their support. They also identify possible opponents, analyze their interests, and anticipate ways to constructively channel their involvement. Roche (1981) analyzes ways to cultivate relationships through issue-based appeals to self-interest, or special efforts to involve influentials in decisions, or priority responses to requests for information and assistance in return for support. He describes planners who discuss issues with influentials to explain their stake; respond quickly to requests from public officials, labor unions, chambers of commerce, media, and community groups with large constituencies; and participate in political elections for officials who return favors by defending planning. There is no lack of published advice on personal or political approaches to win friends and influence others (Carnegie, 1936; Riordan, 1963; Twain, 1916).

Build Coalitions

Coalitions are working relationships to collaborate together and influence outcomes. They serve to mobilize individuals or groups around a common program and generate power to fulfill the program which is developed. They also help individuals share resources, help one another, and build mutual support. They may be short-term, shifting, or relatively permanent. Some are little more than occasional meetings, while others operate with staff of their own. They are important for individuals seeking to build support beyond reach of what each could accomplish alone (Dluhy, 1981; Pearce, 1983; Kahn, 1980; Schakowsky, n.d.).

Coalition-building methods vary from one case to another. For example, an agency covering a large rural area applies "coalitional planning" to build support among community leaders and public officials who can affect planning. Agency staff analyze power structures to identify influentials and then include them on the governing board, subarea councils, and committees. Another agency creates subarea councils with committees, subcommittees, and task forces to develop plans, review projects, and advocate change at the local level. Each council has staff who coordinate relations with constituent organizations. Another agency assists and funds groups forming community councils within subareas. These councils help identify local problems, lobby legislators, and support implementation (Checkoway, 1981c; Roche, 1981). Yet another agency targeted underserved groups and traditional non-participants, conducted community outreach and media campaigns, held training sessions on problems and prospects, and formed a coalition which continues to impact agency and community today (Glenn, Lipschultz, and Sherry, 1981).

Activate People in Planning

The benefits of citizen participation are well known. For agencies, participation can fulfill legislative mandates, improve communications, and build support. It also can open up the political process, involve low income and minority citizens, and develop community organization. For citizens, participation can offer opportunities to gain representation, exercise legal and political rights, and influence policy decisions. Done with knowledge and skill, participation can enhance participatory democracy and improve planning for social change.

Recent years have witnessed an increase in citizen participation programs and methods employed by agencies, although the overall record has been uneven. Many agencies have expanded the scope of participation, and exceptional ones have sought participation with fervor. But few agencies have adopted singular objectives for participation, favored methods that transfer power to citizens, or used participation to mobilize constituency support. Most planners view themselves as committed to participation, but work in the face of obstacles that remain.

Knowledge of participation also has increased over time. Agency catalogues count more than forty current or emergent methods; analyze selected methods according to function; and rationalize the design, implementation, and evaluation of practice (Advisory Commission on Intergovernmental Relations, 1979; Community Services Administration, 1978; U.S. Department of Transportation, 1976). Analysts have studied participation objectives and methods in use, identified major participants and obstacles, and evaluated impacts and factors influencing the field (Burke, 1979; Gil and Lucchesi, 1979; Glass, 1979; Rosenbaum, 1983; Rosener, 1979). Practitioners have provided perspectives and lessons from practical experience. For example, Creighton (1981) describes steps from empirically based practice to identify participation objectives and publics, formulate alternatives, assess internal and external resources, and match methods to purpose at each stage of planning. This is not to suggest that methods alone can activate citizens and build support. On the contrary, studies suggest that formal methods show little or no association with the quality or impact of participation, while other factors—including board and staff commitment and leadership—do correlate with quality participation (Checkoway and O'Rourke, 1983). But they provide lessons nonetheless.

What Are the Obstacles?

There are serious obstacles to building support for planning at the community level, although this is not my primary purpose and there already is extensive writing on the subject. However, it is important to recognize obstacles while also embracing the desirability and possibility of change.

It is difficult to build support for planning when agencies lack legitimacy in the community. Private economic interests often act like they should control local planning decisions, and resist efforts to get them to share their power with others. Citizens may accept the notion of private control over planning systems and show little support for public intervention. Only a fraction of the general public perceives planning as an activity in which they could participate or knows of the existence or functions of planning agencies (Foley, 1955; Lipsky and Lounds, 1976; Riska and Taylor, 1978). Citizens often receive information through networks dominated by private interests and hesitate to "intrude" in areas involving private power. The lack of public knowledge and support tends to lower the expectations for planning and reduce the incentives for public initiatives. This is not to suggest that public attitudes toward planning agencies necessarily arise from some independent group consciousness or are a given to be taken for granted. On the contrary, it would be as mistaken to take public attitudes as given as it would be to ignore private efforts to shape them or to reject the possibility that new initiatives could respond and alter the situation. Intervention could make a difference, as private interests have shown for years.

It also is difficult to build support when planners lack knowledge, skills, or attitudes conducive to practice. Studies find only a minority of planners who regard their work as properly or inevitably political, a majority of straightforward technicians who believe they are or should be concerned with objective fact-finding and rational analysis of information, and a substantial group who are ambivalent about acting political and who tend to emphasize technical skills as a result of this ambivalence (Baum, 1983). Other studies find planners who stress values of efficiency, economy, and control which often are the antithesis of citizen participation (Altshuler, 1972; Friedmann, 1973). They perceive ordinary citizens to lack knowledge and professional expertise; expect their participation to cause delays in action, expand the number of conflicts, or increase the costs of operations; and regard their inquiries as a waste of time and distraction from "work" (U.S. House Subcommittee on Health and the Environment, 1978). There are exceptional planners who activate citizens and build support with fervor, but they are not typical.

This image has implications for planning research and education. First, most planners do not perceive themselves as political, a situation which could be defined as a problem for research and education to address. Second, a minority of planners are political and their work could provide lessons for others. Third, a substantial group of planners are ambivalent and possible constituents or allies for changing practice. There is no a priori reason why planners could not develop capacity and skills to build support for their work in the community. Research and education could find excellent opportunities here.

Some analysts argue that research and education do not prepare people for effective practice. Hemmens, Bergman, and Moroney (1978) survey planning graduates who report that their jobs require analytic, communication, and process skills different from training received in the schools. Schön, Cremer, Osterman, and Perry (1976) survey other planning graduates who report that key skills in writing, negotiating, influencing, and consulting with clients are not usually available in planning curricula. De Neufville (1983) contends that planning schools agree on no common literature, raise questions which produce stale debate, and provide poor instruction to make planning work. She argues that planning theory is inconsistent with experience, irrelevant to application, and frustrates scholars and practitioners.

But it would be as mistaken to blame scholars and educators for not bridging the gap between knowledge and action as it would be to excuse practitioners from their responsibility to apply knowledge that is already available. Some planners have sought to build support and implement plans in the face of power, but others, perhaps most, have opted to sit tight and wait for earlier times to return rather than to play a more active role. Dyckman (1983) argues that although planners once may have been concerned with broad social policy, political action, and community leadership, they subsequently became entrenched in government bureaucracies applying instrumental rationality and mechanical skills to projects shaped by authoritarian regimes and powerful private interests. Marcuse (1983) decries the retreat of some planners from progressive ideals to instrumental or technocratic practice, from long-range planning to short-range expediency, from the broader public to narrow private interests, and from ordinary citizens to established powerholders. Schön (1983) observes that despite technical innovations in planning—for example, PPBS, cost-benefit analysis, computer simulations—most planners have not adopted behavior conducive to agency survival.

In the final analysis, planning agencies face the power of private economic interests, who mobilize resources and influence planning. For example, Pines (1982) describes heads of companies developing media campaigns and advertising drives against government agency initiatives; conducting economic education and antiregulatory programs in the workplace and classroom; formulating strategy and building coalitions to pack public hearings and lobby legislators. Citizen participation has increased in scope and quality around planning, but private economic interests are often the most active, organized, and influential participants. They challenge planners to respond and alter the situation, but even exceptional efforts still would operate in an imbalanced political arena.

Conclusion

Planning operates in a changing context. Austerity policies and adversarial power challenge planners to recognize sociopolitical change and to develop capacity for the years ahead. Planners who want to influence implementation must go beyond rational models to apply sociopolitical methods to build support for planning at the community level. These include methods to formulate strategy, identify issues, develop constituencies, educate the public, and activate citizens in planning. There are obstacles to practice, but exceptional agencies show possibilities and provide lessons for others.

Building citizen support can help influence implementation. This does not suggest that the answer to implementation is in these methods alone, for planning operates in an arena which requires more powerful methods than those described here. Nor does it deny that this approach might engender controversy and arouse reaction by groups that may emerge more powerful than before. Nor does it neglect that planning agencies offer only one vehicle to activate citizens and create change in the community. There are other means, one or a combination of which may be better ways to bring change. In the final analysis, building citizen support for planning at the community level might not make much difference. But then again it might.

References

Advisory Commission on Intergovernmental Relations. 1979. *Citizen Participation in the American Federal System.* Washington: Advisory Commission on Intergovernmental Relations.

Alterman, Rachelle. 1983. Implementation analysis: The contours of an emerging debate. *Journal of Planning Education and Research,* 3 (Summer) 63–66.

Arnstein, Sherry L. 1969. A ladder of citizen participation. *Journal of the American Institute of Planners,* 35 (July): 216–224.

Bardach, Eugene. 1977. *The Implementation Game: What Happens after a Bill Becomes Law.* Cambridge: MIT Press.

Barkdall, Gerald L. 1983. Involving constituents in agency priority-setting: A case study. *Evaluation and Program Planning,* 6: 31–37.

Baum, Howell S. 1983a. *Planners and Public Expectations.* Cambridge: Schenkman.

_____. 1983b. Politics and ambivalence in planners' practice. *Journal of Planning Education and Research,* 3 (Summer): 13–22.

Benveniste, Guy. 1977. *The Politics of Expertise.* San Francisco: Boyd and Fraser.

Beyle, Thad L. and George T. Lathrop, eds. 1970. *Planning and Politics: Uneasy Partnership.* New York: Odyssey Press.

Bleiker, Hans. 1978. *Citizen Participation Handbook.* Laramie: Institute for Participatory Planning.

Booth, Heather. 1977. *Direct Action Organizing.* Chicago: Midwest Academy.

Bradley, John. 1981. An educational approach to health planning. In Barry Checkoway, ed., *Citizens and Health Care: Participation and Planning for Social Change.* New York: Pergamon Press.

Bryson, John M. and Andre L. Delbecq. 1979. A contingent approach to strategy and tactics in planning. *Journal of the American Institute of Planners,* 45 (April): 167–179.

Bryson, John M., R. Edward Freeman, and William D. Roering. 1985. *Strategic Planning in the Public Sector: Approaches and Future Directions.* Minneapolis: Strategic Management Research Center, University of Minnesota.

Burchell, Robert W. and George Sternlieb, eds. 1978. *Planning Theory in the 1980's: A Search for Future Directions.* New Brunswick: Center for Urban Policy Research.

Burke, Edmund M. 1979. *A Participatory Approach to Urban Planning.* New York: Human Sciences Press.

Carnegie, Dale. 1936. *How to Win Friends and Influence People.* New York: Simon and Schuster.

Checkoway, Barry. 1984. Two types of planning in neighborhoods. *Journal of Planning Education and Research,* 3 (Winter): 102–109.

_____ ed. 1983. New perspectives on planning practice. *Journal of Planning Education and Research,* 3 (Summer): Special issue.

_____. 1982. Public participation in health planning agencies: Promise and practice. *Journal of Health Politics, Policy and Law* 7, (Fall): 122–133.

_____. 1981a. Citizen action in health ' planning. In *Citizens and Health Care: Participation and Planning for Social Change*, ed., Barry Checkoway. New York: Pergamon Press.

_____. 1981b. Consumerism in health planning agencies. In *Health Planning in the United States: Selected Policy Issues*. Washington: National Academy of Sciences Press.

_____. 1981c. Innovative citizen participation in health planning agencies. In Barry Checkoway, ed., *Citizens and Health Care: Participation and Planning for Social Change*. New York: Pergamon Press.

_____. 1981d. The politics of public hearings. *The Journal of Applied Behavioral Science* 17 (October–November–December): 566–582.

_____. 1979. Citizens on local health planning boards: What are the obstacles? *Journal of the Community Development Society,* 10 (Fall): 101–116.

Checkoway, Barry and Thomas O'Rourke. 1983. Correlates of consumer participation in health planning agencies. *Policy Studies Journal,* 3 (February): 296–310.

Checkoway, Barry, Thomas O'Rourke, and David M. Macrina. 1981. Representation of providers in health planning boards. *International Journal of Health Services,* 11 (4): 573–581.

Clavel, Pierre, John Forester, and William W. Goldsmith, eds. 1980. *Urban and Regional Planning in an Age of Austerity.* New York: Pergamon Press.

Community Services Administration. 1978. *Citizen Participation.* Washington: Community Services Administration.

Creighton, James L. 1981. *The Public Involvement Manual.* Cambridge: Abt Associates.

Davidoff, Paul. 1965. Advocacy and pluralism in planning. *Journal of the American Institute of Planners,* 31 (November): 331–338.

Dluhy, Milan. 1981. *Social Change: Assessing and Influencing the Policy Development Process at the State and Local Levels.* Washington: Aurora Associates.

Dyckman, John. 1983. Planning in a time of reaction. *Journal of Planning Education and Research,* 3 (Summer): 5–12.

Feshback, Dan and Takuya Nakamoto. 1981. Political strategies for health planning agencies. In Barry Checkoway, ed., *Citizens and Health Care: Participation and Planning for Social Change.* New York: Pergamon Press.

Foley, Donald. 1955. How many Berkeley residents know about their city's master plan? *Journal of the American Institute of Planners,* 21 (Fall): 138–144.

Forester, John. 1981. Planning in the face of power. *Journal of the American Planning Association,* 48 (Winter): 67–80.

Freire, Paulo. 1968. *Pedagogy of the Oppressed.* New York: Seabury Press.

Friedmann, John F. 1973. *Retracking America: A Theory of Transactive Planning.* Garden City, NY: Anchor.

Gil, Efraim and Enid Lucchesi. 1979. Citizen participation in planning. In *The Practice of Local Government Planning,* ed. Frank So. Washington: International City Managers' Association.

Glass, James J. 1979. Citizen participation in planning: The relationship between objectives and techniques. *Journal of the American Planning Association,* 45 (April): 180–189.

Glenn, John M., Lillian Brandt, and F. Emerson Andrews. 1947. *Russell Sage Foundation: 1907–1946.* New York: Russell Sage Foundation.

Glenn, Karen, Claire Lipschultz, and Susan Sherry. 1981. The consumer health advocacy project. In Barry Checkoway, ed., *Citizens and Health Care: Participation and Planning for Social Change.* New York: Pergamon Press.

Godschalk, David R., ed. 1974. *Planning in America: Learning from Turbulence.* Washington: American Institute of Planners.

Gordon, Robbie. 1978. *We Interrupt This Program . . . A Citizen's Guide to Using the Media for Social Change.* Amherst: Citizen Involvement Training Project.

Goulet, Denis. 1973. *The Cruel Choice: A New Concept in the Theory of Development.* New York: Atheneum.

Hemmens, George C., Edward M. Bergman, and Robert M. Moroney. 1978. The practitioner's view of social planning. *Journal of the American Institute of Planners,* 44 (April): 181–192.

Joslyn-Scherer, M.S. 1980. *Communication in the Human Services.* Beverly Hills: Sage.

Kahn, Si. 1980. *Organizing: A Guide for Grass-Roots Leaders.* New York: McGraw-Hill.

Kasperson, Roger E. and Myrna Breitbart. 1974. *Participation, Decentralization and Advocacy Planning.* Washington: Association of American Geographers.

Kimmey, James R. 1981. Technical assistance and consultation for consumers. In Barry Checkoway, ed., *Citizen and Health Care: Participation and Planning for Social Change,* New York: Pergamon Press.

Krueckeberg, Donald A. and Arthur L. Silvers. 1974. *Urban Planning Analysis: Methods and Models.* New York: John Wiley.

Krumholz, Norman. 1982. A retrospective view of equity planning: Cleveland 1969–1979. *Journal of American Planning Association,* 48 (Spring): 163–184.

Krumholz, Norman, Janice M. Cogger, and John H. Linner. 1975. The Cleveland policy planning report. *Journal of the American Institute of Planners,* 41 (September): 298–304.

Lancourt, Joan. 1979. *Developing Implementation Strategies: Community Organization Not Public Relations.* Boston: Boston University Center for Health Planning.

Lipschultz, Claire. 1980. *Political Action in Health Planning: Building a Consumer Constituency.* Bethesda: Alpha Center for Health Planning.

Lipsky, Michael and Morris Lounds. 1976. Citizen participation and health care: Problems of government induced participation. *Journal of Health Politics, Policy and Law,* 1 (1): 85–111.

Lynn, Laurence E. *The State and Human Services: Organizational Change in a Political Context.* Cambridge: MIT Press.

Marcuse, Peter. 1983. The feeble retreat of planning. *Journal of Planning Education and Research,* 3 (Summer): 52–53.

Marmor, Theodore R. and James A. Morone. 1980. Representing consumer interests: Imbalanced markets, health planning, and the HSAs. *Milbank Memorial Fund Quarterly/Health and Society,* 58 (Spring): 125–165.

Mazmanian, Daniel A. and Jeanne Nienaber. 1979. *Can Organizations Change? Environmental Protection, Citizen Participation, and the Corps of Engineers.* Washington: Brookings Institution.

Mazmanian, Daniel A. and Paul A. Sabatier, eds. 1981. *Effective Policy Implementation.* Lexington: Lexington Books.

Mueller, C. 1973. *The Politics of Communications.* New York: Oxford University Press.

O'Rourke, Thomas W. and Mohammed Forouzesh. 1981. Readability of HSAs' plans: Implications for public involvement. *Health Law Project Library Bulletin,* 6 (January): 23–26.

Peters, Thomas J. and Robert H. Waterman, Jr. *In Search of Excellence: Lessons from America's Best-Run Companies.* New York: Harper & Row.

Pines, Burton Yale. 1982. *Back to Basics: The Traditionalist Movement That Is Sweeping Grass-Roots America.* New York: William Morrow.

Riordan, William L. 1963. *Plunkitt of Tammany Hall: Very Plain Talk on Very Practical Politics.* New York: E. P. Dutton.

Riska, Eleanor and James A. Taylor. 1978. Consumer attitudes toward health policy and knowledge about legislation. *Journal of Health Politics, Policy and Law* 3: 112–123.

Roche, Joseph L. 1981. Community organization approach to health planning. In *Citizens and Health Care,* ed. B. Checkoway. New York: Pergamon Press.

Rosenbaum, Nelson, ed. 1983. *Citizen Participation: Models and Methods of Evaluation.* Washington: Center for Responsive Governance.

Schakowsky, Jan. n.d. *Coalition Building.* Chicago: Midwest Academy.

Schön, Donald A. 1982. *The Reflective Practitioner: How Professionals Think in Action.* New York: Harper & Row.

Schön, Donald A., Nancy Sheldon Cremer, Paul Osterman, and Charles Perry. 1976. Planners in transition: Report on a survey of alumni of MIT's department of urban studies, 1960–1971. *Journal of the American Institute of Planners* 42 (2): 193–202.

Scott, Mel. 1969. *American City Planning Since 1890.* Berkeley: University of California Press.

Spiegel, Allen D. and Herbert H. Hyman. 1978. *Basic Health Planning Methods.* Germantown, MD: Aspen Systems Corporation.

Staples, Lee. 1984. *Roots to Power: A Manual for Grassroots Organizing.* New York: Praeger.

Steiner, George A. 1979. *Strategic Planning.* New York: Free Press.

Strauss, Marvin, C.J. Harten, and M.A. Kempner. 1976. Training of planning personnel for local and state agencies. *Public Health Reports* 91 (January-February): 51–53.

Tait, John L., Janet Bokemeir, and Janet Bohlen. n.d. *Identifying the Community Power Actors: A Guide for Change Agents.* Ames: Iowa Cooperative Extension Service.

Texas Municipal League. 1975. *Building Citizen Support in Texas Cities.* Austin: Texas Municipal League.

Thompson, Frank J. 1981. *Health Policy and the Bureaucracy: Politics and Implementation.* Cambridge: MIT Press.

Twain, Mark. 1916. *The Mysterious Stranger and Other Stories.* New York: Harper and Brothers.

U.S. Department of Transportation. 1976. *Effective Citizen Participation in Transportation Planning.* Washington: Government Printing Office.

U.S. House Subcommittee on Health and the Environment. 1978. *Hearings on H. R. 10460.* Washington: U.S. Government Printing Office.

Welsh, Joyce C. 1977. Coalition formation and development. In Fred M. Cox et al., *Tactics and Techniques of Community Practice.* Itasca, IL: F. E. Peacock.

Winholz, William G. 1968. Planning and the public. In *Principles and Practice of Urban Planning,* eds., William I. Goodman and Eric Freund. Washington: International City Manager's Association.

Part IV

Interdisciplinary Planning

9

The Structural Approach to Planning and Policy Making

Moving Beyond Problem Solving

Kenan Patrick Jarboe

Introduction

Writing an essay on the theory of planning and policy making is, at best, a hazardous pursuit. The field is in turbulence. Consensus over how one should do "planning" and "policy making" is nonexistent. Debates rage over normative versus comprehensive planning, analytical versus transactive planning, professionalism versus participation, etc. There is not even agreement over what substantive fields the term "planning and policy making" covers. There are urban planning, regional planning, city planning, transportation planning, health planning, land-use planning, economic planning, strategic planning, corporate planning, social planning, policy analysis, systems analysis, etc. Picking up any of a number of recent books on planning theory is apt to leave the reader more confused than when he or she began.

The purpose of this essay is to explore one little corner of this theoretical debate. No grand synthesis of the issues facing the practice of planning and policy making is proposed. However, I hope to shed some light on the nature of the planning and policy-making process. My subject is an interesting piece of this confusion. On the one hand, planning and policy making are referred to as the process of setting and seeking to attain certain goals or objectives. On the other hand, planning and policy making are often referred to as applied problem solving. As we will see later, this is really a false dichotomy. However, as an orientation for the practitioner, it is important. Each orientation leads to different ways of viewing the world, and to different actions. Let us begin our exploration with the problem-solving approach to planning and policy making.

155

Planning as Problem Solving

The problem-solving approach to planning and policy making is a specific mode of inquiry and decision making. As a process of inquiry and decision, problem solving starts with a problematic situation. Young, Becker, and Pike define a problematic situation as a felt difficulty stemming from an inconsistency in a person's image of the world: "when a person becomes aware that two beliefs to which he is deeply committed are incompatible, when he notices that his acts or the acts of others clash with his values, when he discovers something in the nature of the world that doesn't 'fit' his conception of it, when he has a desire or a need that he finds he cannot fulfill, and so on."[1] In other words, a problematic situation is that vague feeling we have when we know that something is not quite right.

Of course, this does not mean that a person normally has a perfectly consistent image of the world, and that problematic situations are rare. Quite the opposite. Human beings manage to operate, even thrive, in complex situations with inconsistent images. The wag's definition of a genius is someone who can hold two opposing ideas simultaneously. However, when this problematic situation becomes too great, we look for ways to resolve it. We switch into a problem-solving mode.

Awareness of the existence of a problematic situation and the desire to resolve the situation are the entry point to the process of problem solving. As a process of inquiry and decision, problem solving follows a sequence of steps. First come the identification, exploration, and clarification of the problem. In this stage, the problematic situation is analyzed and the specific problem defined. The next stage is the search for alternative solutions to the problem as defined. The final stage is the choice of solution (the decision) and its implementation.

Of course, the process is not always as linear as the above description portrays it to be. There is often a great deal of interaction between the problem-definition stage and the solution identification and choice stages. The definition of the problem points the direction toward the class of solutions required, and the unfeasibility or unacceptability of a solution may require a redefinition of the problem.

Nor does the problem-solving mode necessarily follow a strict rational approach. As Allison has shown, decision making in a problem-solving mode can be explained in many ways.[2] Besides the rational model, there are at least two others: the organizational process and the government (bureaucratic) process. Allison's example, the Cuban missile crisis, was a problem to be solved. All three models proved to be useful in explaining the decision-making process that occurred in solving that problem.

Problematic situations and problem definitions need not be shared among members of a group or organization when problem solving occurs. In fact, one of the first steps to effective problem solving where more than one individual or interest is involved is the creation of a shared definition of the problem.[3] Problem solving can incorporate diverse values, interests, and world views. It can be highly political, involving intense bargaining and strong clashes of values. But it still remains problem solving, focusing on one problem at a time.

One of the most important critiques of the problem-solving approach deals with the nature of the problems themselves. According to Rittel and Webber, planning problems are "wicked" problems—not wicked in the sense of evil, but wicked in the sense of tricky or difficult.[4] Wicked problems have a number of specific characteristics. There is no definitive formulation of a wicked problem; the formulation of a wicked problem is the problem. There is no immediate and often no ultimate test of a solution to a wicked problem. Wicked problems do not have an enumerable (or an exhaustively describable) set of potential solutions, nor is there a well-described set of permissible operations that may be incorporated into the plan. Every wicked problem is essentially unique and every wicked problem can be considered to be a symptom of another problem.

The inherent "wickedness" of planning and policy-making problems severely limits the usefulness of the problem-solving approach in complex real-world situations. As Ackoff stated, organizations do not face problems but dynamic systems of problems, which he refers to as "messes."[5] Unfortunately, the problem-solving approach does not work well with messes.

Key to the problem-solving approach is the analysis and definition of the problem. In order to be able to analyze a problem, we often break it down into smaller discrete components, each of which can be solved individually. March and Simon refer to this breaking down of problems into manageable components as factoring.[6] The process of factoring creates isolatable, individual parts to the problem which, supposedly, can be solved for individually. While this may work well for highly structured problems, such as those in mathematics, it fails in the complex world facing planning and policy making.

Messes are not amenable to being resolved by the problem-solving approach. But dealing with messes of problems is only part of the answer to the failures of the problem-solving approach. Another approach is required, one which goes beyond individual, isolatable problems. The other approach must also shift its view away from problems and toward the nature of the system under study. It must focus on the structure of the system, not on its parts. I refer to this approach as the "structural approach" to planning and policy making.

The Structural Approach to Planning

Whereas the problem-solving approach is discrete and compartmentalized, the structural approach is systemic. In the structural approach, the focus of attention is on the structure of the system, and the workings of that structure—not on individual, isolated problems within the system. The goal of the structural approach is to ensure the smooth workings of the system and the attainment of system goals.

This does not mean to say that problems are not important in the structural approach. They are. But they are treated as symptoms, as clues to the health of the entire system, not as the focus of attention. When we go to see a physician, the standard question is, "So what seems to be the problem?" We then go on to describe our symptoms. Does that mean that the physician is concerned only with our symptoms? Of course not. He or she is using our symptoms as a starting point. The physician is concerned with the health of the body, not just the symptoms. The point of the process is not the solving of the problems, but to reach a state of health. Once that occurs, the problems will take care of themselves.

I opened this chapter with the distinction between the goal-oriented and the problem-oriented modes of planning and policy making. In a crude fashion, the structural approach may be said to be goal driven, whereas the problem-solving approach is problem driven. Of course, this is an oversimplification. Goals and problems are interrelated. A problem can be defined as the existence of a gap between the current state of affairs (reality) and a desired state of affairs (goals). Problems exist because reality does not match the goals. A traffic jam is a problem because the reality of the situation—a slow, congested flow of traffic—clashes with the desired situation—an uninterrupted, free flow of traffic. If we did not desire a free flow of traffic, a traffic jam would not be a problem.

Thus, problem-driven planning and goal-driven planning are similar. The difference is one of emphasis rather than of substance. In goal-driven planning, the goals are explicit, with the focus on the goals to be attained by closing the gap between the current and the desired state. In problem-driven planning, the goals are implicit. The focus is not on the goals but on the gap between reality and the goals.

While problem-driven and goal-driven planning are similar, the latter has certain advantages over the former. Because goals are explicit in the structural approach (goal-driven planning), they are more readily attained. Problem solving does lead to the desired state, but only through a roundabout process. Goals are identified only by their absence in the current situation. Thus, problem solving is always focused on the present, reacting to the current situation. Since it focuses on goals, the structural approach is proactive, focusing on where the system should be rather than where it is currently.

One point must be made perfectly clear at this point. The structural approach to planning is not the same as either the classical rational approach or the comprehensive mode of planning. The classical rational model of planning is a goal-driven approach where the planner (decision maker) chooses from a set of alternatives that option which maximizes his goals and objectives. First, goals and objectives are to be optimized; only the best alternative is selected. Second, all alternatives are known to the decision maker. Third, the consequences of the alternatives are known to the decision maker. Fourth, there is no cost associated with the decision making process.

As the work of Herbert Simon, James March, and others has shown, the assumptions inherent in the classical rational model of decision making are routinely violated, and, in some cases, theoretically impossible.[7] These critiques of the rational model have given rise to numerous features of the problem-solving approach, especially the decomposition of problems into discrete and individually solvable subparts (problem factoring).

The structural approach borrows a number of concepts from Simon's "bounded rationality." The structural approach does not, unlike the classical rational model, seek to maximize goals and objectives. Because of the complex and interrelated nature of systemic goals, optimization is not possible, especially if one considers a dynamic system where the goals themselves are in constant flux. Nor does the structural approach seek perfect information concerning the alternatives available and the consequences of those alternatives. Again, the complexity and dynamic nature of any system make such perfect information impossible to obtain. Goals are satisficed and actions are taken with the dynamic nature of the system in mind. No one action is expected to be final. The system is constantly managed, rather than fixed for all times.

While accepting some parts of bounded rationality, the structural approach explicitly rejects others. Specifically, the structural approach rejects the fragmentation of the system into discrete, isolatable parts. While actions can be taken in discrete steps, and a certain amount of analysis carried out on specific subparts, the entire effort is directed toward the works of the system as a whole, not at the problems of particular components in isolation of all others.

While concerned with the works of the system as a whole, the structural approach is not a form of comprehensive planning. Comprehensive planning is often associated with the rational model of decision making, and does, in fact, share certain characteristics. In comprehensive planning, a decision maker (planner) uses the rational model while viewing the situation as an interrelated system. In addition, it attempts to analyze and plan for every component in the system. This is why it is called comprehensive. Every factor—every element—is included in the plan, along with how each element fits together with every other element.

As one can readily understand, comprehensive planning is an extremely vast undertaking. Comprehensive planning was what I call the "brute power method" of dealing with uncertainty. It attempts to create certainty out of uncertainty by controlling every aspect of the situation. As the complexity of the system grows, and as the situation becomes less and less controllable in the finer details, comprehensive planning becomes less and less achievable.

The structural approach to planning takes a different tack toward uncertainty. It builds upon the flexibility of the system to absorb uncertainty. Rather than attempt to control and plan for every element in the system, it is strategically selective in its intervention. The purpose of the structural approach is to guide the system, not to chart out its every move.

In seeking to guide the system, the structural approach looks for key intervention points in the system—leverage points—by which it can change the system's direction. Constant control of the system is not required. Strategic guidance, or management, is the aim.

In operating as the system's strategic guidance process, the structural approach must be a learning approach. Since flexibility and the absorption of uncertainty are the mode of operation, constant feedback from the environment is mandatory. The system must learn from its past behavior and design its actions so as to elicit information from the environment.

Thus, the structural approach to planning is a constant guidance process concerned with shaping and reshaping the structure of the system. Planning is done continuously as new information is received and new actions taken. Planning as a process is the key to the structural approach, not plans. The structure of the system and its dynamics are its target, not the problems of separate components.

The Approaches Illustrated

To illustrate the differences between the problem-solving and the structural approaches to planning, let us examine the issue of economic development. At the national level, economic development takes on the title of industrial policy. In general, industrial policy is that set of government actions taken to aid or assist industry. Exactly what "aid" or "assistance" means is defined differently in the two approaches.

In the problem-solving approach, industrial policy concentrates on a single target. The target may be a specific firm or industry. Industrial policy consists of those actions taken by the government to solve the problems of that firm or industry. The target of the policy is viewed in isolation of all other components of the economy; the problems of the specific firm or industry are to be solved without regard to problems in other economic areas. Aid or assistance is defined as whatever solves the problems of the targeted industry.

A degenerative variation of the problem-solving approach also exists: the instrument-specific approach. Whereas functional problem solving targets numerous policy instruments on a chosen industry or firm, the instrument-specific variation uses one instrument at a time. No coordination among instruments exists; each is employed in isolation from all others. America's current de facto industrial policy is generally the problem-solving approach with a large, and often overwhelming, dose of the instrument-specific variation thrown in.

Problem solving need not be confined to the level of the industry or firm. The current fascination with reindustrialization is actually a larger version of the problem-solving approach. Whereas problem solving focuses on specific firms or industries, reindustrialization focuses on the entire manufacturing sector. It attempts to solve the problems of manufacturing as a whole.

Unlike problem solving, the structural approach views the national economy as a system, with certain systemic needs, rather than focusing in on particular industries or categories of industries. Structural industrial policy has as its goal and focus the creation and maintenance of a balanced structure of production. It seeks to simultaneously meet a number of important goals such as long- and short-run growth and wealth creation, continued gains in productivity, total employment, the mix of skill levels employed, balance of trade, national security, and energy and resource utilization. Aid or assistance is defined as whatever contributes to the goals of the entire system.

The structural approach is not without degenerative versions of its own. One such version, applied to industrial policy, I label as the "reallocation approach." Under this view, the purpose of industrial policy is to help the process of investment/disinvestment. In other words, industrial policy should channel resources away from areas of "poor" investment to areas of "good" investment. Poor and good investments are defined simply in terms of productivity or economic performance. No other criteria are used. Thus the reallocation approach is actually an incomplete formulation of the structural approach—a near miss. It looks at the structure of the economy, but drastically narrows the goals.

Let us now look more closely at the problems associated with each approach.

The Failure of Problem Solving

The failure of the problem-solving approach is the failure to view the firms, industries, and sectors that make up the economy as a system. The problem-solving approach separates and isolates segments of the economy, reducing the system to merely a set of components. It neglects the interrelationship among the various components of the economy. Thus, it attacks the "problems of the auto industry" or the "plight of steel" or "the energy problem" rather than the larger problem of the structure of the economy.

But, the components of the economy are not isolated components. For example, in order to understand the changes in the forest products industry, it is necessary to understand the changes in the construction industry; in turn, understanding the changes in home construction requires an understanding of changes in the financial sector. Industries are linked together in a chain of input and output.

Cyclical changes in one area of the economy may result in structural changes in other portions of the system. An example of this phenomenon can be found in the relationship between the agriculture sector and the farm implement industry. The agriculture sector is traditionally a volatile one; crop prices and, consequently, farm incomes fluctuate wildly. The farm implement industry, by definition, is closely tied to the highly cyclical movement of farm incomes. As farm incomes rise, expenditures on equipment also rise. Since 1980, farm incomes have been low while interest rates have been high. Both translate into a depression for the farm implement industry. As of early 1982, the industry operated at about 50 percent capacity. The depth of the economic slowdown in farm implements is so great as to force a restructuring of the industry. Some companies may not survive. Companies that do make it through will most likely be smaller with fewer products.

Clearly, the farm implement industry of the post-agricultural slump will be different than it was before. The agriculture sector may come out of the slump relatively unchanged; the farm implement industry won't. Cyclical change in one area produces structural change in another. What is the problem to be solved? Which areas should be targeted, or can they be targeted separately?

Likewise, structural change reverberates throughout the entire economy. Structural change in one industry, e.g., the oil industry's restructuring due, in part, to OPEC—may result in structural change in a second industry: the rise of the Japanese-produced small car and the restructuring of the auto industry. Which cause should be attacked, the oil "problem" or the auto "problem"? The problem-solving approach would attack both problems, in isolation of one another. With such a disjointed approach, the separate policies could easily work at cross purposes. For example, one solution to the "oil shortage" was to let the price of oil rise so as to increase the incentive for exploration. Prices would then decrease as new supplies of oil became available. However, rising oil prices decreased the market competitiveness of the large American automobiles and allowed the more fuel-efficient Japanese automobiles to gain a larger share of the market. Unstable oil prices would make the auto problem that much worse as the demand for automobiles fluctuated between large and small cars.

The actions taken under the guidance of the problem-solving approach may, in fact, alleviate an isolated problem. However, by concentrating on an isolated target area, it runs the risk of treating the symptoms while missing the disease. Unless one looks at the entire environment in which an industry operates, including that industry's relationship with the rest of the economy, one is likely to use the wrong policy instruments.

Margaret Dewar's examination of the New England fisheries industry illustrates the problem of choosing the appropriate policy instruments. Dewar found that the problems of the groundfish industry were consistently misdiagnosed and mistreated.

> The core of the groundfish industry's problem of very low prices was not that imports were too high but that demand was very low. Imports were only one of the factors that contributed to the fall in demand and were not the most important one. After World War II, demand for groundfish fell and became more elastic as government purchases declined and meat, rationed during the war, again competed with fish for the consumer's dollars.[8]

Yet, the policy instruments used to "solve" this problem were subsidies and import restrictions. These policy instruments did not have the desired effect. What the industry really needed was help in adapting to a changed market, such as finding alternative markets or decreasing the size of the industry. By failing to view the industry in the context of the structure of the economy, incorrect conclusions were drawn as to the nature of the problem and inappropriate remedies applied.

In summary, the problem-solving approach does not know which problem to "solve." Nor does it possess the necessary tools to always do the job. By focusing on the narrow concerns of a specific industry, the problem-solving approach "can't see the forest for the trees." It lacks the ability to go beyond the view of a particular industry to see how that industry fits into the economy as a whole. Thus, it is often unable to see how to solve the problems of an industry or, more importantly, if one should.

Shifting the focus from the individual firms or industries, as is the case in reindustrialization, does not overcome the failures associated with the problem-solving approach. Although reindustrialization seeks to overcome the myopic failings of the problem-solving approach, its failures are the same. Reindustrialization broadens problem solving's vision to include the entire manufacturing sector. Problems are no longer viewed in isolation; the problems of the entire sector are looked at in a comprehensive manner.

But not comprehensively enough. While comprehensive analysis and problem solving may be the aim of the reindustrialization school of thought, it fails in precisely that test. Just as the problems of industries can not be analyzed and solved in isolation, the problems of sectors of the economy are not isolatable but intertwined.

Manufacturing is not the only sector of the economy, nor does the economy necessarily revolve around the manufacturing sector. Various scholars have described the U.S. economy as becoming more information based. We have been labelled the post-industrial or the knowledge society. Information is overtaking manufacturing as the basis for our economic system.

Information is not merely an adjunct to the manufacturing process. Information-rich sectors, such as education, research, government, communications, and health care, make up the fastest-growing parts of the economy. For example, Marc Porat has estimated that over half of all workers are employed in information activities.[9]

Nor are information and manufacture the only important parts of the economy. Although small in absolute size, both agriculture and construction are vital to the health and well-being of the economy. Likewise, finance, which supplies the life blood of our economic system, is a critical sector. An economy with an unhealthy agricultural, construction, or financial sector cannot function properly.

Thus, an approach to policy that concentrates only on the manufacturing sector runs the risk of missing the point entirely. Manufacturing is tied into a web of other sectors. To concentrate on one, to the exclusion of all others, is not a way of broadening one's vision. It is merely a new form of myopia.

Flaws in the Reallocation Approach

Let us approach the description of the structural approach through the back door by starting with its near miss—the reallocation approach. Reallocation industrial policy is, in part, a reaction to the problem-solving approach. The reallocation approach appears, at first glance, to be a more systematic view of industrial policy. Yet, the reallocation approach is only somewhat more systematic than the problem-solving approach. The reallocation approach also divides the economy into components. The components are essentially separable; the only difference between the components is whether or not they are worthy of investment. The relationship between winners and losers is not analyzed, except those linkages concerned with the flow of resources out of losers and into winners. Likewise, the relationships among the industries within the separate sets of winners and losers are not analyzed. The system, as an interrelated working whole, is not at issue. The issue is the transfer of resources from one set of system components to another set of system components. Once again, the strategy is to divide and analyze.

The reallocation approach to industrial policy has other problems as well. In reallocation industrial policy, systemic considerations are at least acknowledged. However, limited and often unitary characteristics are used to decompose the system. The criterion of economic performance, however measured, is the sole means of determining the priorities for resource reallocation.

The limitedness of the decision criteria is the major drawback of the reallocation approach. The reallocation approach fails to recognize the multiform nature of the economy. Because it concentrates on one criterion, this approach seeks to optimize the system on that one criterion. Optimization on one criterion leads to suboptimization on all other criteria and, more importantly, suboptimization on the system-wide level.

Even trying to pick isolated winners based on optimizing over multiple criteria fails to provide for a balanced economy. An industry designated a loser on many criteria and a winner on only one may be so important on that one criterion that the industry's demise leads to an unbalanced economic structure. The importance of the industry on that one criterion might well be overwhelmed by all the other criteria in the optimization calculus.

An example of the failure of the reallocation approach is the housing industry. One of the most popular conceptions of "winners" in the realloca-tion approach is those industries with high value-added (low labor intensity), high productivity growth, and where the United States can enjoy a competi-tive advantage in world markets. Under no stretch of the imagination can housing construction be considered a high value-added industry. Nor can housing be thought of as an export-oriented industry in which the U.S. can dominate world markets through comparative advantage. Housing, with the exceptions of mobile homes and prefabricated housing, is a labor intensive, locally based, nonexportable industry. Yet housing is a vital component of the economy. Home ownership remains an important part of the American Dream. An economy that does not provide adequate housing for its populace is rightfully characterized as a failure.

In the reallocation approach, based upon the criterion of high value-added growth, housing would be characterized as a "loser" and targeted for disinvestment. Such a disinvestment process would lead to an imbalanced, failing economy. Clearly, criteria other than high valued-added and interna-tional comparative advantage need to be included in the investment/ disinvestment calculus.

Not only does the reallocation approach limit the goals to be achieved, but it also limits the policy instruments used to achieve that goal. Control over resource allocations, specifically of capital, is the only policy instrument used. The reallocation approach fails to consider other factors affecting industries. It fails to consider how indirect subsidies, such as infrastructure development, are needed by industries. It fails to consider organizational fac-tors within the industry, such as whether or not the firms are capable of util-izing all the resources directed their way. By placing its emphasis on capital, it also fails to consider the availability or nonavailability of other resources, such as labor and raw materials. The reallocation approach follows the for-mula of throwing money at a problem.

In essence, the reallocation approach misses the point of industrial pol-icy. As defined earlier, industrial policy in a market economy is best described as an attempt by government to influence the firms' decision mak-ers, to induce certain behaviors on the part of private sector managers. In essence, industrial policy attempts to shape the environment around the firm so as to control the firm's choice of strategic option. This does not describe the reallocation approach. The reallocation approach concentrates on the use of limited policy instruments to achieve narrow goals. It is not industrial pol-icy; it is merely one component of industrial policy.

Benefits and Difficulties of the Structural Approach

The major benefit of the structural approach to industrial policy is that it overcomes the flaws of the problem-solving and reallocation approaches. It is, however, not without difficulties of its own. From both a planning and a political perspective, the structural approach is difficult to operationalize.

The benefits of the structural approach derive from the fact that it takes a systemic view of the economy and utilizes multiple policy instruments. By taking a systemic view of the economy, the structural approach overcomes the failures associated with the myopic vision of the problem-solving approach. The structural approach is able to evaluate an industry's problems in the context of its relations with other industries and the economy as a whole. It is able to recognize the interrelationship among industrial problems and formulate a coordinated rather than a piecemeal attack.

More importantly, the structural approach is able to evaluate the importance of each industry in the context of the entire economy. System-wide performance is the goal, not the performance or survival of one subsection of the system. Therefore, the structural approach avoids the trap of aiding one industry to the detriment of the economy as a whole.

Not only does the structural approach evaluate industries in the context of the entire economy, it also uses multiple criteria in that evaluation. An economic structure must perform a number of tasks simultaneously, such as the creation of wealth, provision of employment, protection of national security, and wise use of resources. The failure of the reallocation approach was its inability to look beyond the narrow goals of economic efficiency and productivity. The structural approach overcomes this failure by utilizing multiple criteria based upon the goal of a balanced economic structure.

The difficulties of the structural approach stem from the same characteristics that make it preferable to the problem-solving and reallocation approaches. Taking a systemic view of the economy and utilizing multiple policy instruments, one is conceptually better equipped to confront industrial problems. However, the systemic view of the economy, with its complex interrelationships, its multiple goals, and its multiple policy instruments, is more difficult to operationalize.

One major difficulty in operationalizing the structural approach arises from its needs for an agreement in principle as to the desired structure of the economy. The political problem of reaching such an agreement within the body economic is enormous. One way of overcoming this impediment is by utilizing a policy-making configuration known as *corporatism*.

In a corporatist configuration, all interest groups are organized in a centralized, hierarchically controlled manner. Because each interest is centralized, corporatism allows for agreements concerning the desired structure of the economy to be arrived at in manageable manner. However, there are political dangers to individual freedom inherent in adopting the corporatist configuration. And, as we will discuss later, corporatism is not necessarily the only way of overcoming the political impediment.

Another major difficulty with the operationalization of the structural approach is its broad analytical requirements. The structure of the economy is a complex, ever-changing system. To be able to specify a desired structure that satisfies multiple goals is a huge analytical undertaking. The data requirements are immense and the analytic capabilities needed to synthesize the data and competing goals into an optimal solution are gigantic. To then translate this desired structure into the day-to-day operations of multiple policy instruments is an even larger task.

Yet, the analytical tasks of the structural approach are not as overwhelming as they may seem. Development of a vision of the desired and economic structure is as much a process of bargaining and interaction among members of the body economic as it is an analytical exercise. Lindblom refers to this as the strategic, rather than comprehensive, mode of planning.[10] Under strategic planning, analysis is used to inform the interaction and bargaining rather than substitute for it. Analysis provides information but does not attempt a comprehensive synthesis. Using strategic planning, the task of creating a structural vision for industry/policy becomes analytically manageable.

In other words, the structural vision is a constantly evolving synthesis of goals and objectives resulting from the analytically informed interaction of interested parties. It is a political process that may well be conducted through existing political channels. Rather than attempting to create a new process that is new, orderly, and rational, a complex, interactive process is used.

Translation of the vision into reality via the use of policy instruments can also follow the strategic planning process. Responsibility for implementation of the vision is divided among various bureaus. Each bureau designs its own set of industry-specific policies, based upon the overall vision. Conflicting use of the policy instruments is coordinated and mediated, not rigidly controlled, by a supervising body. Overlapping problems are attacked through interaction among bureaus responsible for the parts. Nonstrategic industries are ignored. In this manner, the analytic burden is spread among many analysts. Thus, the analytic task is again made manageable without loss of the structural characteristics.

Throughout the process, there is an acknowledgement of uncertainty, incomplete information, and changing environments. Policies are subject to revision as new information is obtained or as the situation changes. Feedback mechanisms are established to draw out information about the effects of the policies and the usefulness of the policy instruments. Actions are taken with the uncertain nature of the environment in mind. Problems are not solved, once and forever, but continuously managed.

Conclusion

While I have used them for purposes of illustration, industrial policy and economic development are not the only areas of planning where the structural approach applies. The structural approach is equally applicable to environmental planning, transportation planning, land-use planning, and so on. In environmental planning, the differences between the problem-solving and the structural approach are readily apparent. Under the problem-solving approach, one might be concerned with the question of reducing the emissions of a particular power plant, or the health effects of a particular substance, or the development of a particular piece of land. Planning would be reactive, constantly shifting to cope with the latest threat. Under a structural approach, environmental planning would concern itself with what the overall state of the environment should look like (or at least the direction in which one might wish to go) and how best to reach that state. According to many, the reactive problem-solving mode describes the current state of environmental planning in the United States, especially in the government.

To sum up, the problem-solving approach to planning and policy making takes a myopic view of the system in question, and fails to take into account the interrelationship among components. It is thus unable to determine the actual causes of a specific problem or to take actions that will benefit the system as a whole. By concentrating on each individual problem, or even on a mess of problems, this approach may optimize the component while suboptimizing the system.

On the other hand, the structural approach to planning and policy making takes a system-wide view, concentrating on multiple goals. The structural approach thereby creates both political and analytical difficulties in its operationalization. Both can be overcome by adopting a strategic planning model, which emphasizes interaction and bargaining as well as analysis.

Problem solving describes much of what really happens in the planning and policy-making process. While useful in certain limited circumstances, problem solving cannot live up to its promises—it cannot solve the problems facing our complex society. We must switch our view from problems to structures. Only by concentrating on the system and strategically intervening in its operations can we making planning and policy-making a useful exercise.

Notes

The author would like to thank Ernest Wilson, Kan Chen and Milan Dluhy for the comments and suggestions on earlier versions of this paper.

1. Richard E. Young, Alton L. Becker, and Kenneth L. Pike, *Rhetoric: Discovery and Change.* New York: Harcourt, Brace & World, Inc., 1970, p. 90.
2. Graham T. Allison, *Essence of Decision: Explaining the Cuban Missile Crisis.* Boston: Little, Brown and Company, 1971.
3. See Kan Chen, J.C. Mathes, Kenan Jarboe, and Janet Wolfe, "Value-Oriented Social Decision Analysis: Enhancing Mutual Understanding to Resolve Public Policy Issues." *IEEE Transactions on Systems, Man and Cybernetics,* September 1979.
4. Horst W.J. Rittel and Melvin W. Webber, "Dilemmas in a General Theory of Planning," *Policy Science* 4 (1973), 155–169.
5. Russell L. Ackoff, "On the Use of Models in Corporate Planning," in McCarthy, Minichiello and Curran, *Business Policy and Strategy: Concepts and Readings,* Third Ed. Homewood, IL: Richard D. Irwin, Inc., 1983.
6. James G. March and Herbert A. Simon, *Organizations.* New York: John Wiley & Sons, Inc., 1958.
7. See Herbert A. Simon, *Administrative Behavior.* New York: The Free Press, 1945; James G. March and Herbert A. Simon, *Organizations.* New York: John Wiley & Sons, Inc., 1958; and Richard Cyert and James G. March, *A Behavioral Theory of the Firm.* Englewood Cliffs, NJ: Prentice-Hall, 1963.
8. Margaret Dewar, "Government Intervention in Troubled Industry: Lessons from the New England Fisheries." Paper prepared for the Annual Meeting of the American Association for the Advancement of Science, January 6, 1982, pp. 6–7.
9. Marc Porat, *The Information Economy.* Stanford: Stanford University, 1976.
10. Charles E. Lindblom, "The Sociology of Planning: Thought and Social Interaction," in Morris Bornstein, ed., *Economic Planning East and West.* Cambridge: Ballinger Publishing Company, 1975, pp. 23–67.

10

Technological Planning in Industry: Increasing Emphasis on Human Resource Considerations

Kan Chen

The traditional concern of technological planning in industry, as discussed in the last chapter, has focused on the integration of technological plans into business plans. While new issues and new approaches continue to evolve with respect to this integration, the major disciplines applied to strengthen this integration are restricted to engineering and business administration. This is especially the case when *product* technology is considered. Recently there has been an increasing emphasis on human resource considerations as an integral part of technological planning in order to meet industrial needs of the coming decades. This emphasis has resulted not only from the desire to minimize human costs while maximizing economic benefits, but also from the recognition of the importance of the human element in the implementation of technological plans and in the functioning of the total production system. Thus, the underlying principles for technological planning are no longer restricted only to engineering and management sciences. Other disciplines, especially those of the social sciences, need to be added and integrated to the planning approach. This is particularly true when *process* technology is planned by industry. In this chapter, we will examine the recent trends in this new dimension of technological planning in industry, the findings from a set of case studies related to automation technologies in the automobile industry,[1] and the interdisciplinary nature of some work proposed or being done in this planning arena.

Recent Trends

There are several converging forces behind the increasing emphasis on human resource considerations in technological planning. The national priorities accorded to U.S. industry's productivity and international competitiveness have sharpened the focus of technological planning issues on automation process technology. However, the utilization of high technology for manufacturing is only a part of the equation for quality and productivity improvement. Another and perhaps the more important part is the human aspect: the manager, the engineer, as well as the worker, who control, operate, and maintain the manufacturing process. Unless the people involved are capable, willing, and motivated to work well with one another and with the new process technology in the total production system, the potential of the new technology will not be realized.

The last statement, of course, applies only to the people who remain involved after the new process technology is introduced. To those whose jobs are displaced or are potentially displaced by automation, the technological change exerts a negative impact or poses a threat that needs to be dealt with in technological planning. True, automation is nothing new and has been a long-term trend for almost forty years. However, until about five years ago the major use of computers in plant production had been for process control—continuous and batch processes for making chemicals and steel, for example. The impact of automation on employment had been less obvious because these processes employed relatively few workers originally and because the widespread implementation of computer process control took place mainly during a period of economic expansion. By contrast, the recent plant and office automation hit hard by impacting relatively labor intensive areas during a period of economic stagnation. This effect was coupled with increased foreign competition in the manufactured goods market in the United States.

The increased foreign competition is but one of several manifestations of yet another driving force, the changing global business environment. With the increasingly homogeneous world market, the consideration of global production and distribution of products at the planning stage is becoming the norm rather than the exception. The choice of process technology is often coupled with the choice of the country (or region) in which to locate new manufacturing facilities. The characteristics of the work force and the labor climate in the candidate country (or region)—worker's culture, education, trainability, wages, union organization, etc.—must be considered in the process of such technological planning.

The importance of considering human resources in technological planning has prompted some automobile companies to recognize four distinct types of technology: product, equipment, process, and managerial.[2] Product technology is embodied in the product itself, e.g., the automobile and its many parts produced by the auto industry. The major forces pushing for product technology changes are primarily customer demands (for comfort, reliability, performance, etc.) and secondarily government regulations (for safety, emission control, fuel economy, etc.). Both equipment and process technologies are used in manufacturing. A distinction between the two is made to emphasize the system aspect of process technology, as distinguished from the technology embodied in a piece of equipment that may stand alone or operate in concert with other equipment in a manufacturing process. Thus, the moving assembly line was a classical example of process technology, and the numerical control of machine tools was a later innovation in equipment technology.

In recent years, major innovations in automobile process technology have been advanced by the Japanese. The two basic concepts are the "just-in-time" production process, and "human-like automation."[3] The extensive and successful practice in Japan of the just-in-time production, including the organization of automobile suppliers into a tightly scheduled process, has led to substantial reduction of in-process inventory and in equipment set-up time. Human-like automation refers to automatic production systems that have human-like intelligence, and implies a wiser use of the worker–machine production system in the planning of process technology. Instead of being compartmentalized into narrow functions as in Taylor's scientific management, by plan the worker makes maximum use of his time and of his potential ability for the production process. This concept is supposed to be the basis for the work design that encourages teamwork by multifunctional workers.[4]

Finally, managerial technology refers to the philosophy, techniques, and organization through which humans are utilized for production. It is sometimes difficult to draw a sharp demarcation line between process technology and managerial technology, as both of them deal with the human element. However, it is understood that managerial technology puts even more emphasis on the human side of the production system and includes the organization of employees in the various line and staff positions in the company hierarchy as well as the workers on the shop floor. Although there seems to be a diversity of managerial technology in the automobile industry in various countries, the general trend is toward increased worker participation in production decision making, such as through the quality circle approach.

While the concept of the four distinct types of technology is interesting, for the remainder of this chapter we will revert to the conventional distinction of product technology and process technology, the latter being understood to include equipment technology and managerial technology. The point to keep in mind is that human resource considerations are more important in process technology planning.

Case Studies in the Automobile Industry

How human resource considerations have (or have not) actually been included in technological planning may be deduced from a set of case studies completed recently under the auspices of the Organisation for Economic Cooperation and Development (OECD).[5] The case studies on automation and human resource development were conducted in 1983–84 at five major automobile companies around the world (U.S.: Ford; Japan: Toyota; Germany: Volkswagen; France: Renault; and Sweden: Volvo). Certain findings from the case study· of the Ford Motor Company's Dearborn Engine Plant (DEP) are particularly relevant to the topic of this chapter.[6]

First, it was found that process technology introduction in the company is a dynamic but evolutionary process. It emerges from existing technology and continues to change and advance rather than remain fixed between major renovations or expansions. In a large company such as Ford, one can use a model of a spiral to visualize the process of technological change: technology within the company ascends the spiral gradually, moving from plant to plant increments. However, viewed from the perspective of a single plant, change may seem revolutionary—as in a jump from one level in the spiral to another.

The renovation of DEP in 1978–79 made it the most automated automobile engine plant in the world at the time, but its furthest advances have since been surpassed by other plants. The most important manufacturing technologies introduced at DEP include: the profile lathes that make the elliptical cross-section barrel-shaped pistons, the automatic hot and cold engine test systems, the fastener assurance system that monitors and controls the torque applied to fastening bolts, the optical gauge for cylinder head measurements, and the black light tests to check oil leaks. The more important plant engineering technologies include infrared detection of loose electrical connections and the use of liquid nitrogen sleeves to freeze water to isolate pipe segments for repair. Also new at the plant are a variety of processing procedures—on-line receiving, a carousel system rather than conventional storage bins, computer inputs to keep everything up-to-date, on-line shipping, and computer-automated highbay warehouses—making for, among other things, more stringent inventory requirements for the number of engine parts produced each day.

The crankshaft area has been highly automated as a result of the renovation. In the crankshaft area, one worker can now handle several grinding stations instead of having one or more workers per station, as was the previous case. As compared to former operations, tolerances are about 60 percent tighter. Consequently, automatic gauging, by electronic contact and noncontact types of gauges, is used extensively to monitor 138 characteristics (compared to 42 previously) to minimize defects in the crankshaft. Another manufacturing technology introduced to DEP that was new to Ford (but not to the industry) is the crankshaft mass centering system. In the more conventional geometric centering system, the rotational axis is established by drilling the centers at selected locations. In mass centering, the crankshaft is spun and the location of the mass center-line is calculated. The centers are drilled in relation to mass on each crankshaft, thus minimizing casting variations and increasing efficiencies at the crankshaft balancing operations. As in the rest of the manufacturing process, the crankshaft area uses programmable controllers (PC) extensively to perform logical decision making for control applications that formerly required relays. With PCs, changes in machine control can be accomplished quickly without hard wiring revisions. The PCs also provide the potential capability to communicate directly with a control computer to record production rates, downtime, and scrap counts.

The decision leading to the seemingly revolutionary technological changes in the DEP's major renovation in 1978–79 was largely market-driven and involved complex planning on an international scale. In other words, changes in both product technology and process technology were not the major driving force for change, but rather were keyed to a long-term (6–7 year), multiphased, and multilevel planning procedure. The five phases in Ford's car and truck planning process are: (1) business strategy, (2) strategies for marketing, manufacturing, and product development, the last to be followed by (3) concept development, (4) advanced program development, and (5) production program execution.

In the early stages of business and product development strategies, planning considerations were focused on such questions as whether and what kind of small cars should be produced and sold in which market segments in the world. Human resource considerations were not prominent, but entered only in a subtle way. Product technology planning became active in the third and fourth stages—concept development, and especially in advanced program development. Process technology planning became important in the last two stages, about the same time when location choice for production was considered. When alternative sites were compared, the consideration would include labor relations climate, labor quality, as well as labor cost. For example, it was noted that Dearborn had an experienced labor force. In 1977, three years before "Job 1" (the time for the first product to be produced for the new engine), a 10- to 12-month planning process for site selection and engineering design was initiated. The new engine program implemented at DEP marked the *first time* at Ford that human skills were considered during this early planning phase, for two reasons: (1) technology complexity (tight tolerance), and (2) changing management philosophy (managerial technology). This consideration of human skill requirements led to the allocation of a training budget of about $7 million even before the site was selected.

Given the "evolutionary" nature of technological change in the company, and the unprecedented emphasis on training during the DEP renovation, some managers argued that the most innovative aspects of the DEP renovation, with subsequent performance that met or exceeded original expectations in quality and productivity improvements, were not technological, but organizational in character. They pointed to a mangement style that increasingly emphasized participation and the establishment of a new learning center through which many workers have received training. Increasing emphasis on human resource considerations in technological planning, especially for process technology, seems to have become a widely accepted goal.

A range of technological innovations, including flexible robots, are being considered for future introduction at DEP. These innovations are considered necessary to improve the company's competitive position in terms of product quality, production cost, and efficiency in the manufacturing process. Improvements in the technological innovation process *per se* are also being considered. Such improvements fall under such themes as: consensus and commitment at the beginning of the process, sensitivity to external forces, flexibility and risk taking, integration among all parts of the organization, incremental change, participation, and better use of human resources. Of course, people at different levels of the company have different perspectives in this regard. In general, as one moves down the levels of the company, human (or social) considerations, particularly participation and training, become more prominently considered as vital elements of the innovation process.

On the other hand, while the people at Ford involved in the case study recognize the importance of combining the social and the technological innovations in order to compete internationally, not everyone is satisfied with what has been done to date. Nor does everyone know how to make concrete progress in this direction from his own purview. From what has been observed, Ford's product planning, in both technological and human resource dimensions, has been global in its perspective. The company's planning decision rationale with respect to technology has shifted from principally short-term financial approaches to increased consideration of long-term company goals and qualitative judgments (e.g., more weight is given to less tangible contribution of technology to product quality). With respect to human resources—especially the emphasis on training and employee involvement—both Ford and the United Automobile Workers Union (UAW) have made policy statements that are clear and have been heard by all concerned parties. However, strategic plans for implementing these policies appear only now to be emerging and will probably be expanded and operationalized as time goes on.

Admittedly, the case studies under the auspices of OECD have been focused only on limited parts of the automobile companies. Generalization from these case studies would be hazardous to be applied to the entire industry. It would be especially problematical if one tried to apply the findings from a mature industry, like automobiles, to a growing industry, like semiconductors. However, the findings that have been discussed can be used either as indicators of how human resource considerations are being integrated into technological planning in part of the automobile industry, or as hypotheses for larger and more rigorous studies.

The role of case studies is often to complement broad studies and statistical analyses. All these studies are necessary in a sound and comprehensive methodology for interdisciplinary planning research. Thus, case studies emphasize depth whereas broad studies by definition emphasize breadth. Case studies provide the richness in certain qualitative and structural changes that statistical data alone cannot reveal, especially if multiple disciplines, multiple perspectives, and multiple case studies are used in the case study approach.[7] For example, the Ford DEP case study[8] was conducted by five faculty researchers from the disciplines of engineering, sociology, and social work. The 87 persons who were interviewed at Ford provided the perspectives of both salaried and hourly employees at the plant, division, and corporate levels. The Ford study shared a common research grid with the other studies at Toyota, Volkswagen, Renault, and Volvo for the purpose of comparative analysis. In the next section, we will explore the interdisciplinary nature of some of the work being conducted or proposed for the planning of integrated manufacturing technology, e.g., integration of computer-aided design (CAD) and computer-aided manufacturing (CAM).

Technological Planning for Integrated Manufacturing

Computer-integrated manufacturing is an important and active part of contemporary high technology. The "integration" performed by the computer is not only in terms of the different levels of manufacturing production (e.g., coordination between plant-level and cell-level production), but also in terms of functions beyond direct production. The latter is typified by the closer linkage between product design and manufacturing process. Through CAD/CAM integration and facilitation, the CAD data base can be used directly to produce commands for robots and other CAM equipment. "Design for manufacturability" has become a feasible and high-priority goal for engineering design. This closer linkage between product design and the manufacturing process is likely to bring human resource considerations, which have hitherto affected mainly process technology planning, closer than before to product technology planning as well. Training as well as job displacement issues are of increasing concern to white-collar workers (draftsmen, engineers, managers) as well as blue-collar workers. The technological decision by one firm may also have tangible ripple effects on other firms. For example, the CAD/CAM system set up by a major automobile manufacturer will require its principal suppliers to set up compatible systems with all the accompanying human resource implications.

The result of high technology applied to automobiles, and especially to the operations by which they are designed and manufactured, is bringing a "fourth transformation" to the automobile industry—the first three being Ford's moving assembly and Model T at the beginning of the century, Europeans' diversity of automobile models after World War II, and the Japanese process technology innovations discussed earlier in this chapter.[9,10] Human resource considerations will be an integral part of the planning for the flexible automation in this fourth transformation. For example, the UAW has a 99-person team working with General Motors on new approaches to work organization that will be combined with the new design and manufacturing technologies in the Saturn Project, and efforts to develop a new small car for North American production toward the end of the 1980s.[11] In Answer to Saturn, the Ford Motor Company has launched its own Alpha Project.[12] It is not clear at this point whether the work organization in these projects will be keyed to the new technologies as given, or if human resource considerations will actually modify the initial plans for the technologies. However, these exercises do signify the continuing trend toward an increasing emphasis on human resource considerations based on multiple perspectives in industrial technological planning.

More recently, on the research side of activities, the Center for Research on Integrated Manufacturing (CRIM) at the University of Michigan is expanding its research program to include a component on the strategic management of integrated manufacturing technology, of which human resource consideration is an inherent part. The purpose of this component is to link technical research in this area to the industrial needs for productivity and quality improvement. In order to translate manufacturing technological advances to industrial competitiveness, the strategic management component will consist of four simultaneous and interrelated tasks:

1. assessment (of the present technology)
2. vision (of the future technology)
3. planning (to get from the present to the future)
4. implementation (and continued adaptation of the plan)

Assessment of the present technology will be conducted for both the core work (e.g., crankshaft production) and the support work (e.g., engineering design for the crankshaft) in terms of either the directly measurable productivity or, especially in the case of white-collar work, the discrepancies between ideal and actual conditions for productive work.[13] Remedies to be suggested may be both technological and work-organizational innovations. The major disciplines to be used for this task are industrial engineering and industrial sociology.

Technological forecasting in the second task will combine several forecasting methods. Preliminary results will be obtained initially by reviewing pertinent literature, interviewing knowledgeable researchers, checking against basic engineering and scientific principles, and applying the concept of generation dynamics.[14] The preliminary forecasts will be used as inputs to two Delphi panels.[15] The first is to consist of scientists and engineers who will revise and refine the technological forecasts and the second is to consist of a wide range of users who will identify the strategic management implications of the future technology. The major disciplines to be used are many branches of engineering, business administration, and social sciences.

The third task, strategic planning, will examine the present corporate planning process and methodology that deal with integrated manufacturing technology,[16] e.g., how information about future technology flows in the planning process, how decision makers in industry assess the strategic utility of manufacturing technology in terms of the instrumental goals of shorter lead time, fewer mistakes in design and manufacturing, etc., and how they make economic and human resource trade-offs in comparing technological alternatives. The leading disciplines for this task are business and engineering.

Finally, the fourth task of plan implementation will focus on sociotechnical innovations.[17] By identifying work design changes associated with the adoption of integrated manufacturing technology, one can systematically consider cross-functional interchanges, multiskill capabilities, participative work practices, changing career lines, reward systems, and training requirements. The results of this task will show tangible possibilities for modification of technology to meet the needs of the social environment as well as enhancing the company's economic benefits—the ultimate goal of including human resource considerations in technological planning. The leading disciplines for this task are sociology and engineering.

Conclusions: The Need for Integrative and Interdisciplinary Planning

The recent trends, corroborated by in-depth case studies, and some of the most significant work being done in industry, indicate an increasing emphasis on human resource considerations in technological planning. The high technology of integrated manufacturing has brought product technology and process technology closer to each other at the planning stage, thus making human resource considerations, which are traditionally close to process technology, increasingly linked to product technology as well. It has been pointed out that, with increasing complexities of technology, corporate strategic planning has evolved from a focus on financial issues (in the 1960s) to marketing (in the 1970s) and now to technology (in the 1980s).[18] This would suggest a much closer link between business administration and engineering disciplines at the strategic level. However, with the increasing emphasis on human resource considerations in technological planning, and all the complexities in future global competition, we suggest that there is a real and increasing need for integrative corporate planning.

We have seen many fallacies of planning based on narrow disciplines. Some electric utilities have gotten close to the brink of backruptcy for having failed to anticipate the environmental concern about nuclear energy. Many American companies have lost their international competitiveness for having neglected to upgrade their manufacturing technologies. Financial wizards successful in the corporate mergers in the short run sometimes ignore the need for keeping and developing critical human resources for the company in the long run. When single disciplines are used in corporate planning, narrow perspectives are used in the formulation of pivotal corporate policies and strategic plans, bringing other disciplines in only when unforeseen problems emerge at the implementation stage. By that time, some of these problems may be unsolvable or can be solved only with great inefficiency. With integrative corporate planning, the diverse disciplines of social sciences, law, etc., as well as management and engineering, will be combined eclectically in the formulation as well as implementation of corporate planning and policy.[19] Only in such an interdisciplinary planning approach can a proper balance be maintained among financial, marketing, technological, and human resource considerations; between private and public sector considerations; and between domestic and international considerations.

Notes

1. Organisation for Economic Cooperation and Development (OECD). "The Development and Utilization of Human Resources in the Context of Technological Change and Industrial Restructuring." *CERI/CW/*84.11, September 1984.
2. Ford Motor Company. "Human Resource Development and New Technology in the Automobile Industry: A Case Study Framework." Report prepared for OECD, May 1984.
3. Monden, Y. "What Makes the Toyota System Really Tick." *Industrial Engineering,* January 1981.
4. Tsuda, M. "Human Resource Development and New Technology in the Automobile Industry—The Japanese Case." Report prepared for OECD, October 1984.
5. OECD, "The Development and Utilization of Human Resources."
6. Chen, K. et al. "Human Resource Development and New Technology in the Automobile Industry: A Case Study of Ford Motor Company's Dearborn Engine Plant." Report prepared for OECD, University of Michigan, 1984.
7. Chen, K. "Delineation of a Case Study Approach to Assess the Impact of Automation Technologies on Employment." Report prepared for U.S. Department of Labor, University of Michigan, 1984.
8. See Note 2.
9. Altshuler, A. et al. *The Future of the Automobile.* Cambridge: MIT Press, 1984.
10. Womack, J. and Jones, D. "The Fourth Transformation in Autos." *Technology Review,* vol. 87, no. 7, October 1984.
11. Ephlin, D. "The UAW-GM Agreement: New Dimensions to Job Security." Speech at a Labor and Industrial Relations luncheon, University of Michigan, December 4, 1984.
12. United Press International. "Ford Stepping Up Its Alpha Project." *Ann Arbor News,* April 2, 1985.
13. Hancock, W.M. and Liker, J.K. "Improving the Productivity of the White Collar Workforce." *Proceedings of the 1983 Conference of the Institute of Industrial Engineers,* 1983.

14. Chen, K. and Chang, N. "Technology Forecast of Space Robots to the Year 2000." *Technological Forecasting and Social Change,* vol. 26, no. 1, 1984.
15. Linstone, H.A. and Murray, T. (eds.) *The Delphi Method: Techniques and Applications.* Boston: Addison-Wesley, 1975.
16. Hayes, R.H. and Wheelwright, S.C. *Restoring Our Competitive Edge: Competing Through Manufacturing.* New York: John Wiley and Sons, 1984.
17. Majchrzak, A. and Nieva, V. "CAD/CAM Adoption and Training in Three Manufacturing Industries." Report for National Science Foundation's Division of Industrial Science and Technology Innovation, 1984.
18. Roberts, E.G. "Strategic Management of Technology." Management of Technology Program, Massachusetts Institute of Technology, 1983.
19. University of Michigan, Ph.D. Program in Urban, Technological and Environmental Planning, "The Integrative Corporate Planning Program (ICP)," Prospectus, April 1983.

11

Shifting Demands on Interdisciplinary Planning: An Educational Response

Kan Chen

The commonalities of the diverse chapters in this book are that they are all related to planning yet they all go beyond traditional urban planning. This reflects the working of large social forces since the urban unheavals of the late 1960s, a period during which physical planning and social planning had to be combined across multiple disciplines to deal with the national crisis of the United States at that time. Planning has remained broadly interdisciplinary as the substantive issues of highest U.S. national priorities shifted successively, about every three to six years, from urban development to environmental protection, to energy sufficiency, to industrial competitiveness, and recently to high-technology development. The result is the spawning of many planning enterprises that require different basic knowledge and skills and attract undergraduate students from different schools and colleges into interdisciplinary planning programs at the graduate level. The question arose as to which educational response to the shifting demands on interdisciplinary planning would make the best sense. In this concluding chapter, we will discuss the generic goals and defining characteristics of such interdisciplinary planning programs at the graduate level, and describe a specific Ph.D. program at the University of Michigan that has been structured as such an educational response.

Generic Goals and Defining Characteristics

Broadly speaking, the graduate of an interdisciplinary planning program at the graduate level should have the core knowledge about planning that is basically invariable over time and application areas, should possess the expertise for marshalling the necessary knowledge and resources across multiple disciplines to do effective planning in the substantive area of his current and near-term interest, and should be adaptive to highly uncertain and shifting priorities of planning programs in the future. The risks of any interdisciplinary program are superficiality and a lack of focus. The shifting national priorities are such that new problems emerge that cannot be solved by readily applying existing knowledge. For these reasons, the graduate of the interdisciplinary planning program should have sufficient depth of knowledge in several disciplines and the capability of combining these disciplines to do planning research as well as practice in diverse application areas.

The above-stated generic goals may be converted to a number of instrumental goals. Thus, the student in the interdisciplinary planning program should have a set of core knowledge and skills, including planning theory and practice (as described by Rothman and Hugentobler), research methodology, and analytic skills. Planning theory and practice should eventually include both fundamental theory from the cognitive perspective (as described by Kochen and Barr) and real-world practice from the process perspective (as described by Dluhy). Implementation (as described by Checkoway) should clearly be a part of the core knowledge as good plans must be implementable.

Research methodology and analytic skills should include both qualitative and quantitative methods, with an emphasis on the latter, as never before has the use of sophisticated quantitative analysis for planning research and practice been so apparent. The synergism between social planning and physical planning in the last two decades has led to a convergence of social research tools and engineering research tools for planning. For example, social planning and decision making have benefited from such "hard" engineering tools as microcomputers and remote sensing, and such "soft" engineering tools as R&D models and VOSDA (as described by Chen and Mathes). On the other hand, technological innovation is planned along with work organization, participative management, corporate strategy (as described by Bitondo), and human resource considerations (as described by Chen). The learning, application, and further development of these cross-disciplinary, as well as the more traditional, analytic methods for planning and integrative problem solving (as described by Hart) should be important instrumental goals for interdisciplinary planning programs.

The generic goal to train an "adaptive" planning student may be served by two instrumental goals: to teach him the core knowledge and skills that are applicable to a wide range of application areas as described above, and to expose him to a range of planning problems approached by the same core set of theory and methods. This latter approach is partly illustrated by the collection of chapters dealing with diverse application areas in this book, ranging from environmental planning (as described by Bulkley) to industrial policy (as described by Jarboe). For the sake of adaptability, still another instrumental goal is to expose the student to the basic approaches to a set of relatively broad planning issues, such as planning at the interface between public and private sectors, and international and cross-cultural dimensions in planning.

These goals may be restated as a set of defining characteristics for an effective interdisciplinary planning educational program:

1. Core knowledge in planning theory and practice
2. Basic and interdisciplinary research methodology and analytic methods
3. In-depth knowledge in selected disciplines and capability for combining these disciplines for planning research and practice
4. Expertise and experience in interdisciplinary planning in a concentrated area
5. Exposure to broad planning issues and planning enterprises outside one's concentrated area

A Sample Interdisciplinary Planning Program: The Structure of UTEP

There are many ways to design an interdisciplinary planning program to satisfy the above-stated defining characteristics. The optimum response may depend critically on the particular history and situation of a university. The specific example to be described is the Ph.D. Program in Urban, Technological, and Environmental Planning (UTEP) at the University of Michigan, which was restructured in 1982 with the above defining characteristics. The experience in the past three years has seemed to prove its viability, although improvements are expected to continue indefinitely.

The predecessor of the UTEP program was the Ph.D program in Urban and Regional Planning (URP), which was established in the late 1960s as an interdisciplinary and intercollegiate program on a university-wide basis to help convert knowledge into action in response to significant urban and related problems. The program does not have its own tenured faculty, nor its own courses except for a set of core seminars which all students in the program are required to take. At present, participating faculty come from nine schools and colleges in the university—Architecture and Urban Planning, Business Administration, Education, Engineering, Medicine, Natural

Resources, Public Health, Social Work, as well as Literature, Science, and the Arts (LSA), the core of the university. The program is administratively under the graduate school. The flexibility of the program has allowed it to adapt fairly easily and rapidly to shifting national priorities and student and faculty interests. The Ph.D. level of the program makes it complementary to the master-level planning programs in many of the participating schools, and provides sufficient time for the students in the program to gain depth as well as breadth of knowledge and to do planning research—thus satisfying some of the tough program requirements discussed previously.

In 1982, the program was restructured in accordance with the defining characteristics stated above, and the name of the program was changed to reflect the broadening of student and faculty interests beyond traditional urban planning. Three major thrusts were initiated simultaneously: technology planning, planning at the interface between the private and public sectors, and an increased emphasis in the international dimension.

The UTEP program is structured around five areas of study:

    I. Planning Theory and Analytic Methods (Core)
   II. Interdisciplinary Studies
  III. Substantive Concentrations:
      a. Urban and Regional Planning
      b. Sociotechnological Systems
      c. Environmental Analysis and Design

The first area (Planning Theory and Analytic Methods) constitutes the core of the program and is required of all students. The second area (Interdisciplinary Studies) is designed to ensure that students will have the ability to view problems from various theoretical approaches and to solve problems in an individualized, interdisciplinary way. All students are expected to design an appropriate sequence in this area. The remaining three areas are substantive concentrations: clusters of faculty and students around each particular substantive or research interest. Overall, the student must take and achieve certification in three of the five areas (Areas I, II, and one of the options in Area III). Typically, a well-prepared student with a master's degree will arrive with substantial accomplishment in several of the areas; the individualized program is designed to exploit previous accomplishment while broadening considerably the knowledge and skills of the student in other areas.

The Core area (Area I) is designed to provide the student with proficiency in methods of inquiry and the organization of research effort (analytic methods), and with knowledge of planning's intellectual and ethical heritage, approaches to the major issues of public policy, and the relationship of planning to the larger social, political, economic, and industrial systems (planning theory). Specifically, the major components of the Core area include:

1. *Planning Procedure:* Rational approaches to decision making and planning
2. *Planning Perspectives:* The context in which planning takes place
3. *Research on Planning:* Research design and methodology
4. *Statistics:* Quantitative analysis
5. *Core Seminar:* Introductory and advanced seminars

Since all students are required to take the core seminars, a great deal of cross-fertilization across planning areas is achieved through mutual learning among faculty and students engaged in a variety of research projects.

The Interdisciplinary Studies area (Area II) is designed to provide the student with the ability to integrate approaches in an interdisciplinary way. The program is concerned that students acquire ample baseline knowledge from several different disciplines relevant to their professional objectives, and that students acquire and demonstrate the capability of *integrating* this knowledge rigorously and creatively in planning solutions to applied problems. Interdisciplinary studies refer to the foundation sciences and professions that buttress the field of planning and contribute to its theoretical base, including the social sciences (sociology, political science, economics, psychology, and anthropology), the natural sciences (physics, biology, chemistry), and the professions (urban planning, natural resources, public health, education, engineering, business administration, social work, architecture, etc.).

Students are required to complete two, three-hour graduate level courses in each of three disciplines. Preferably two of the three disciplines are in the sciences, with the third discipline in an applied or professional area. Certification in the interdisciplinary studies area involves successful completion of the coursework and an evaluation of the interdisciplinary project mentioned above. Such evaluation is by a review panel composed of faculty from each of the three disciplines in the project. Typically, the project is completed in the second year of study—preferably in the third term of the program.

The three concentration areas (Areas IIIa, IIIb, and IIIc) are designed to focus clusters of program faculty and students around substantive areas of planning and application, creating an effective environment for specialized study and research. Additional concentrations may be added in the future in response to changing societal needs.

Urban and Regional Planning (Area IIIa) covers direct interventions in the social system by local, state, or national governments. While sometimes producing results quite different from those originally intended, such interventions usually reflect some of public policy established by an appropriate governing body. The policies are usually carried out through other administrative agencies such as planning offices; social service, health, or educational agencies; parks, recreation, and environmental agencies; or other operating arms of government. Specific topics that might be addressed within the Urban and Regional Planning concentration include, but are not limited to, the following: housing, planning law, social services, transportation planning, public health, education, conservation and recreation, community development, public works and services, population and labor force planning, land use planning, and so on.

The Sociotechnological Systems area (Area IIIb) is concerned with the planning that deals with physical, industrial, and technological systems in both the private and public sectors meant to serve societal needs. Among the more prominent systems are transportation, communication, automation, utilities, housing, medical, and consumer products. Emphasis is on planning for technology in a societal as well as corporate context. Students in this area will combine an understanding of technological systems with analytical and problem-solving skills in planning.

The Environmental Analysis and Design area (Area IIIc) concentrates upon the interrelationships between the environment and individuals and groups. It is intended to cover the dynamics of change in the environment and its impact upon the attitudes and actions of society, as well as the nature of society's need to utilize the natural elements of the physical environment and how such demands impact upon the environment. Toward a fuller understanding of these interrelated dynamics, course work is aimed at understanding natural systems in the context of urbanization and change, environmental perception and behavior, and the planning and design methodologies that attempt to arrange the most beneficial fit between people and a sustainable environment.

The requirements for the concentrations vary somewhat, but include the equivalent of three graduate level courses from an approved list of courses, plus an advanced level concentration seminar. Substantive matter and advanced analytical skills are covered by the coursework: the seminar includes the preparation of a dissertation prospectus.

Initial Experience of UTEP

By the summer of 1985, the UTEP program had gone through two full years of operation, the year 1982–83 being a transitional period. In the past three years the program experienced a surge of applications for admissions by students with increasing quality and experience. Quite a few entering students, for example, have law degrees or master's degrees in engineering. The amount of interdisciplinary planning research has increased substantially, with funding from both public and private sectors. In spite of the relatively stringent requirements, about half of the students have been able to achieve Ph.D. candidacies, ready to embark upon dissertation research, after two years of full-time study, following the representation timetable given in Table 11.1. The range and thrust of interdisciplinary planning activities are represented by the research programs and projects listed in Table 11.2. Graduates from the program have followed the traditional job patterns set prior to the program restructure: one-third to college teaching and research; one-third to government agencies, including foreign and international organizations; and one-third to the private sector, including consulting and private foundations.

It may be said that the UTEP program has been quite successful in meeting its restructured goals by assuming the defining characteristics discussed previously for interdisciplinary planning programs. On the other hand, the program has its share of difficulties, most of which are administrative in nature—internal budget retrenchment, uneven enthusiasm among participating schools and colleges, etc. Another uneasiness lies in the program's relative uniqueness. As there are few equivalent programs in peer universities, it is hard to gauge the success and progress of the program in comparative terms. It is hoped that the publication of this book will serve to share with our colleagues in the "invisible college of planning" what UTEP has been doing and to invite constructive criticisms and suggestions for better education to meet shifting demands on interdisciplinary planning.

TABLE 11.1

Representative Timetable for Students to Satisfy UTEP Requirements in Two Years (or Four Terms)

Areas	1st Term	2nd Term	3rd Term	4th Term	Certification
I. Core	Introductory Seminar (3)** Statistics I (3)	Research Design (3) Statistics II (3)	Planning Perspectives (3) Planning Procedures (3)	Advanced Seminar (3)	Exam on Planning Exam in Analytics Evaluation of Research Design
II. Interdisciplinary Studies*	Discipline (3) Discipline (3)	Discipline (3) Discipline (3)	Qualifying Project (3)		Successful Coursework Qualifying Project
III. Substantive Concentration			Concentration (3)	Concentration (3) Concentration (3) Seminar (3)	Exam Dissertation Prospectus

*One disciplinary requirement is assumed to have been accomplished prior to entrance to UTEP.

**Numbers in parentheses are credit hours; full load is 12–15 credit hours per term.

TABLE 11.2

Representative Research Programs/Projects in
UTEP's Nontraditional Planning Areas

- Urban security systems planning
  Interdisciplinary planning for major cities to deter and combat crime and
  terrorism, combining both social and technological approaches.

- Integrative corporate planning
  Simultaneous consideration of legal, technical, financial, marketing, and human
  resources development factors in the formulation as well as implementation of
  corporate strategies.

- Motor vehicle transportation planning and policy
  Pitfalls and appropriate use of mathematical models for motor vehicle regulations;
  demonstration planning for electric vehicles.

- System planning in different social settings
  Comparative study of system planning methodologies – computer models, cost
  optimization, cost-benefit analysis, and decision analysis – in different countries,
  such as the United States and China.

- High technology development planning
  Determination of factors affecting the locational choices of high technology
  firms; employment effects of computer integrated manufacturing; environmental
  impacts of biotechnology.

Appendices

Interdisciplinary planning has a vast and growing literature. Professionals from diverse disciplines frequently contribute and it can be difficult to keep abreast of current works. As a companion aid we have added Appendices A and B for the readers' convenience. In addition, Appendix C provides brief biographical summaries of the contributors.

Appendix A offers a listing of journals and periodicals which may be useful for the interdisciplinary planner. It was compiled from many sources.

Appendix B contains 129 contemporary journal citations that are, in the main, relevant to this book. Some of these articles are heuristic, others are theoretical, and some are illustrative. This list was created by reviewing a subset of the journals in the first appendix. Criteria for inclusion were made from the thematic headings used to organize this book. Approximately 8,000 titles were manually reviewed and several electronic searches were made. A ten-year timeframe for inclusion was chosen.

While these appendices are not intended to be comprehensive, and we certainly must have omitted favorite journals and articles from unmet colleagues, we extend it as a resource for people interested in further exploring interdisciplinary planning theories, methodologies, and techniques.

Robert F. Vernon
UTEP Ph.D. Program

Appendix A: Planning Journals

Academy of Management Journal
Academy of Management Review
Administration Law Review
Administration in Social Work
Administration and Society
Administrative Science Quarterly
Advances in Applied Social Psychology
Advances in the Economics of Energy and Resources
Advances in Environmental Psychology
Advances in Environmental Science and Engineering
Advances in Environmental Science and Technology
Advances in Transport Processes
American Academy of Political and Social Science Monographs
American Journal of Political Science
American Journal of Sociology
American Political Science Review
American Sociological Review
Annals of the American Academy of Political and Social Science
Annals of the Association of American Geographers
Annals of Public and Cooperative Economy
Annals of Regional Science
Applications of Management Science
Applied Economics
Applied Energy
Artificial Intelligence
Automatica

Behavioral Sciences and Community Development
Behavioral Sciences and Rural Development
Berkeley Planning Journal
Bulletin of Science, Technology, and Society

Coastal Zone Management Journal
Community Development Journal

Community Work Series
Computers and Automation
Computers and Industrial Engineering
Current Contents/Engineering Technology and Applied Sciences

Education and Urban Society
Energy Policy
Environmental Impact Assessment Review
Environmental Science and Technology
Environmental Technology Letters

Futures
Futurist

Group and Organizational Studies

Harvard Business Review
Human Relations
Human Systems Management

Impact Assessment Bulletin
Information Society (The)
Institute of Electrical and Electronic Engineering Transactions on Systems,
    Man, and Cybernetics
Institution of Environmental Sciences Series
International Journal for Housing Science and its Applications
International Journal of Man-Machine Studies
International Journal of Public Administration
International Journal of Vehicle Design

Journal of the American Institute of Planners
Journal of the American Planning Association
Journal of the American Society for Information Science
Journal of Applied Behavioral Studies
Journal of Environmental Economics and Management
Journal of Environmental Management
Journal of Environmental Quality
Journal of Environmental Sciences
Journal of Environmental Systems
Journal of Interdisciplinary Modeling and Simulation
Journal of the Operational Research Society
Journal of Planning Education and Research
Journal of Policy Analysis and Management
Journal of Policy Modeling

Journal of Regional Science
Journal of Rural Economics and Development
Journal of Science and Technology
Journal of Social Policy
Journal of Social, Political, and Economic Studies
Journal of Systems Management
Journal of Transport Economics and Policy
Journal of Urban Analysis
Journal of Urban Economics
Journal of Urban History
Journal of Urban Law
Journal of Urban Planning and Development
Journal of Water Planning and Management Division, American Society of
    Civil Engineers

Knowledge: Creation, Diffusion, Utilization

Land Economics
Landscape Planning
Local Government Studies
Local Government Studies—New Series
Long Range Planning

Management Science
Marine Policy

Operational Research Quarterly
Operations Research
Organization Studies
Organizational Behavior and Human Decision Processes
Organizational Dynamics

Philips Technical Review
Planning and Administration
Policy Review
Policy Sciences
Policy Studies Journal
Progress in Planning
Public Administration Review
Public Affairs Bulletin
Public Choice
Public Finance
Public Opinion Quarterly
Public Policy

Regional Sciences and Urban Economics
Regional Studies
Research in Corporate Social Performance and Policy
Research Policy
Resources Policy
Rochester Studies in Economics and Policy Issues

Sage Research Papers in the Social Sciences
Science, Technology, and Human Values
Sloan Management Review
Social Policy
Social Policy and Administration
Social Strategies: Monographs on Sociology and Social Policy
Socio-Economic Planning Sciences
SRA—Journal of the Society of Research Administrators
Strategic Management Journal
Studies in Regional Science and Urban Economics
Studies in Comparative International Development
Studies in Management Science and Systems
Systems Review

Technological Forecasting and Social Change
Technology and Culture
Technology Review
Technology in Society

Urban Affairs Annual Reviews
Urban Affairs Quarterly
Urban Ecology
Urban Law and Policy
Urban and Social Change Review
Urban Studies

Water Resources Bulletin
Water Resources Research
Wiley Series on Studies on Environmental Management and Resource
    Development
World Development
World Futures

Appendix B: Selected Bibliography

Arnopoulos, Paris. "Towards a Model Procedure for Social Forecasting." *Technological Forecasting and Social Change,* vol. 13, no. 1 (January 1979): 31–42.

Aujac, H. "Towards a New Social Input-Output Table: The Dynamics of Social Groups and Institutions." *Technological Forecasting and Social Change,* vol. 10, no. 1 (1977): 89–101.

Backoff, Robert W. and Hal G. Rainey. "Technology, Professionalization, Affirmative Action, and the Merit System." *Urban Affairs Annual Review,* vol. 13 (1977): 113–39.

Barnekov, Timothy K. and Daniel Rich. "Privatism and Urban Development." *Urban Affairs Quarterly,* vol. 12, no. 4 (June 1977): 431–60.

Baum, Howell S. "Towards a Post-Industrial Planning Theory." *Policy Sciences,* vol. 8, no. 4 (December 1977): 401–21.

Bella, D.A. and K.J. Williamson. "Conflicts in Interdisciplinary Research." *Journal of Environmental Systems,* vol. 6, no 2 (1976–1977): 105–24.

Beyer, Janice, ed. "The Utilization of Organizational Research," *Administrative Science Quarterly,* Special Issue. Part I, vol. 27, no. 4 (December 1982): 588–695.

Blau, Peter, Cecelia McHugh Falbe, William McKinley, and Phelps K. Tracy. "Technology and Organization in Manufacturing." *Administrative Science Quarterly,* vol. 21 (March 1976): 20–40.

Bozeman, Barry, and L. Vaughn Blankenship. "Science Information and Governmental Decision Making: The Case of the National Science Foundation." *Public Administration Review,* vol. 39, no. 1 (January/February 1979): 53–57.

Bozeman, Barry, and Ian Mitroff, symposium editors. "Managing National Science Policy." *Public Administration Review,* vol. 39, no. 2 (March/April 1979): 103–47.

Branch, Melville C. "Critical Unresolved Problems in Urban Planning Analysis." *American Institute of Planners Journal,* vol. 44, no. 1 (January 1978): 47–59.

Burrows, B.C. "Urban and Regional Planning: A Systems View." *Long Range Planning*, vol. 13 (April 1980): 67–81.

Carroll, Archie B. "Setting Operational Goals for Corporate Social Responsibility." *Long Range Planning*, vol. 11 (April 1978): 35–38.

Chen, Kan. "An Analysis of Research Institutional Roles in Developing Countries." *Proceedings of the International Conference on Systems, Man and Cybernetics* (1983): 1019–23, and *IEEE Transactions on Systems, Man and Cybernetics*, vol. SCM-14, no. 3 (1984): 470–73.

Chen, Kan. "Systems Analysis in Different Social Settings." *Proceedings of the International Conference on Systems, Man and Cybernetics* (1983): 1181–85, and in *Systems Research*, vol. 1, no. 2 (1984): 117–26.

Chen, Kan, and Paul Appasamy. "Anticipating Environmental Problems—A Systems Approach." *Journal of Environmental Systems*, vol. 15, no. 1 (1985–1986): pp. 45–55.

Chen, Kan, J.C. Mathes, and Kenan Jarboe. "Value Oriented Social Decision Analysis: Enhancing Mutual Understanding to Resolve Public Policy Issues." *IEEE Transactions on Systems, Man and Cybernetics*, vol. SMC-9, no. 9 (1979): 567–80.

Chen, Kan, and Diane Sablc. "Environmental Impacts on U.S. Coal Exports." *Environmental Impact Assessment Review*, vol. 3, no. 1 (1982): 8–26.

Choldin, Harvey M. "Electronic Community Fact Books." *Urban Affairs Quarterly*, vol. 15, No. 3 (March 1980): 269–89.

Clifford W. "The Long Range Planning of Criminal Justice Systems." *Long Range Planning*, vol. 12 (August 1979): 42–50.

Coates, Joseph F. "New Technologies and Their Urban Impact." *Urban Affairs Annual Review*, vol. 23 (1982): 177–95.

Coates, Joseph F. "Technological Change and Future Growth: Issues and Opportunities." *Technological Forecasting and Social Change*, vol. 11, no. 1 (1977): 49–74.

Collins, Martin R. and John M. MacGregor. "Designing Computer Models that Work." *Long Range Planning*, vol. 13 (December 1980): 60–69.

Coulter, Philip B. "Measuring the Inequality of Urban Public Services: A Methodological Discussion with Applications." *Policy Studies Journal*, vol. 8 (Spring 1980): 683–716.

Craig, G.D. "A Simulation System for Corporate Planning." *Long Range Planning*, vol. 13 (October 1980): 43–56.

Cramer, James C., Thomas Dietz, and Robert Johnston. "Social Impact Assessment of Regional Plans: A Review of Methods and Issues and a Recommended Process." *Policy Sciences,* vol. 12, no. 1 (June 1980): 61–82.

Crickman, Robin, and Manfred Kochen. "Citizen Participation Through Computer Conferencing." *Technological Forecasting and Social Change,* vol. 14, no. 1 (June 1979): 47–64.

Danziger, James. "Computers, Local Government, and the Litany to Electronic Data Processing." *Public Administration Review,* vol. 37, no 1 (January/February 1977): 28–37.

Davos, Climis A. "Environmental Policy Evaluation Within a Social Context: The Necessity of Synthesis." *Journal of Environmental Systems,* vol. 7, no. 3 (1977–1978): 201–14.

Dewar, Robert, and Jerald Hage. "Size, Technology, Complexity and Structural Differentiation: Towards a Theoretical Synthesis." *Administrative Science Quarterly,* vol. 23, no. 1 (March 1978): 111–36.

Duda, Frank T., Marlin M. Mickle, and William G. Vogt. "A Model for Occupational Dynamics." *Journal of Interdisciplinary Modeling and Simulation,* vol. 3, no. 2 (1980): 193–226.

Dudek, R.A. and W.M. Marcy. "Public Policy and Social Responsibility With Regard to Rehabilitation and Maintenance of Disabled Persons." *Technological Forecasting and Social Change,* vol. 17, no'. 1 (May 1980): 61–72.

Dunn, L.F. "Measuring the Value of Community." *Journal of Urban Economics,* vol. 6, no. 3 (July 1979): 371–82.

Ebel, Roland H., William Wagoner, and Henry F. Hrubecky. "Getting Ready for the L-Bomb: A Preliminary Assessment of Longevity Technology." *Technological Forecasting and Social Change,* vol. 13, no. 2 (February 1979): 131–48.

Egelhoff, William G. "Strategy and Structure in Multinational Corporations: An Information Processing Approach." *Administrative Science Quarterly,* vol. 27, no. 3 (September 1982): 435–58.

Enk, G., and S. Hart. "An Eight Step Approach to Strategic Problem Solving." *Human System Management,* vol. 5, no. 3 (in press).

Elizur, Dov, and Louis Guttman. "The Structure of Attitudes Towards Work and Technological Change Within an Organization." *Administrative Science Quarterly,* vol. 21 (December 1976): 611–22.

Evans, Mark, and Jeffrey Baxter. "Recognizing National Projections with a Multi-Regional Input-Output Model Linked to a Demographic Model." *Annals of Regional Science,* vol. XIV, no. 1 (March 1980): 57–71.

Fisher, Ann, and Robert L. Greene. "Do Public and Private Interests in Pollution Control Always Conflict?" *Journal of Environmental Systems,* vol. 11, no. 2 (1981–1982): 113–23.

Fleming, John E. "The Future of U.S. Government–Corporate Relations." *Long Range Planning,* Vol. 12 (August 1979): 20–26.

Follain, J., Jr. "Local Government Response and the Reliability of OLS Analysis of Pooled Data." *Annals of Regional Science,* vol. XIV, no. 1 (March 1980): 31–42.

Foxall, G.R. "Forecasting Developments in Consumerism and Consumer Protection." *Long Range Planning,* vol. 13 (February 1980): 29–33.

Fried, Jacob and Paul Molnar. "A General Model for Culture and Technology." *Technological Forecasting and Social Change,* vol. 8, no. 2 (1975): 175–88.

Frohman, Alan L., and Domenic Bitondo. "Coordinating Business Strategy and Technology Planning." *Long Range Planning,* vol. 14, no. 6 (1981): 58–67.

Fujii, Edwin T., and James Mak. "Forecasting Tourism Demand: Some Methodological Issues." *Annals of Regional Science,* vol. XV, no. 2 (July 1981): 72–82.

Garg, Devendra P., A Ray Roberts, and Robert Pittillo. "Educational Decision Making Through Electronic Participatory Technology: A Model-Systems Approach." *Journal of Interdisciplinary Modeling and Simulation,* vol. 1, no. 4 (1978): 295–314.

Geurts, J., S. Hart, and N. Caplan. "Decision Techniques and Social Research: A Contingency Framework for Problem Solving." *Human Systems Management,* vol. 5, no. 4 (in press).

Goldsmith, Marlene Herbert. "Technology and Teleology: Social Engineering." *Technological Forecasting and Social Change,* vol. 19, no. 4 (June 1981): 307–11.

Greenhut, M.L., and C.C. Mai. "Towards a General Theory of Public and Private Facility Location." *Annals of Regional Science,* vol. XIV, no. 2 (July 1980): 1–11.

Griffith, Carl R. "Assessing Community Cohesion Impact Through Network Analysis." *Journal of Environmental Systems,* vol. 9, no. 2 (1979–1980): 161–67.

Halal, William E. "Beyond the Profit Motive: The Post-Industrial Corporation." *Technological Forecasting and Social Change,* vol. 12. no. 1 (June 1978): 13–29.

Harman, Alvin Jay. "Industrial Innovation and Government Policy: A Review and

Proposal Based on Observation of the U.S. Electronics Sector." *Technological Forecasting and Social Change,* vol. 18, no. 1 (September 1980): 15–37.

Hart, S., M. Boroush, G. Enk and W. Hornick. "Managing Complexity Through Consensus Mapping: Technology for the Structuring of Group Decisions." *Academy of Management Review,* vol. 10 (1984): 587–600.

Hawkins, Kevin, and Robert J. Tarr. "Corporate Planning in Local Government, A Case Study." *Long Range Planning,* vol. 13 (April 1984): 43–51.

Henry, Mark S. "On the Value of Economic-Demographic Forecasts to Local Government." *Annals of Regional Science,* vol. XIV, no. 1 (March 1980): 12–20.

Hetman, Francoise. "Social Assessment of Technology and Some of Its International Aspects." *Technological Forecasting and Social Change,* vol. 11, no. 4 (April 1978): 303–13.

Higgins, J.C. and D. Romano. "Social Forecasting: An Integral Part of Corporate Planning?" *Long Range Planning,* vol. 13 (April 1980): 82–86.

Hill, Gerald E., and David W. Cravens. "A Conceptual Approach for Analyzing Social/External Information Forces." *Technological Forecasting and Social Change,* vol. 8, no. 2 (1975): 131–45.

Hillman, Harold. "Keeping People Alive—The Implications of Planning." *Long Range Planning,* vol. 10 (February 1977): 48–53.

Hiltz, Starr R. "Computer Conferencing: Assessing the Social Impact of a New Communications Medium." *Technological Forecasting and Social Change,* vol. 10, no. 3 (1977): 225–38.

Hirschhorn, Larry, and Tom Gilmore. "The Application of Family Therapy Concepts to Influencing Organizational Behavior." *Administrative Science Quarterly,* vol. 25, no. 1 (March 1980): 18–37.

Holloway, Clark, and John A. Pearce II. "Computer Assessed Strategic Planning." *Long Range Planning,* vol. 15, no. 4 (August 1982): 56–63.

Holroyd, Philip. "Is There a Future for Social Forecasting?" *Long Range Planning,* vol. 13 (October 1980): 29–35.

Houlden, B.T. "Data and Effective Corporate Planning." *Long Range Planning,* vol. 13 (October 1980): 106–111.

Hrebiniak, Lawrence. "Job Technology, Supervision, and Work-Group Structure." *Administrative Science Quarterly,* vol. 19, no. 3 (September 1974): 395–410.

Huber, Joseph. "Limiting the System and Reshaping Lifestyles: Solving Unemployment by Social and Technical Innovations." *Technological Forecasting and Social Change,* vol. 15, no. 1 (September 1979): 37–54.

Ishikawa, M., M. Toda, S. Mori, and Y. Kaya. "An Application of the Extended Cross Impact Method to Generating Scenarios of Social Change in Japan." *Technological Forecasting and Social Change,* vol. 18. no. 2 (October 1980); 217–33.

James, Barrie G. "Social Impact: The Pharmaceutical Industry." *Long Range Planning,* vol. 11 (February 1978): 2–9.

Jansen, Torben Bo. "Information Technology: The Need for Social Experiments." *Technological Forecasting and Social Change,* vol. 23, no. 4 (August 1983): 325–352.

Jensen, R.C., and S. Macdonald. "Technique and Technology in Regional Input-Output." *Annals of Regional Science,* vol. XVI, no. 2 (July 1982): 27–45.

Karunaratne, Neil. "Multiplier Analysis in Multi-Regional Planning." *Journal of Urban Analysis,* vol. 7 (1982): 57–69.

Kasprzak, Waclaw, and Karol Pelc. "Analysis of Human Needs as a Basis for Research Policy." *Technological Forecasting and Social Change,* vol. 12., no. 2/3 (August 1978): 135–43.

Keim, Gerald D., Roger E. Meiners, and Louis W. Fry. "On The Evaluation of Corporate Contributions." *Public Choice,* vol. 35, no. 2 (1980): 129–36.

King, John L. "Local Government Use of Information Technology: The Next Decade." *Public Administration Review,* vol. 42, no. 1 (January/February 1982): 25–36.

King, Stephen. "Conflicts Between Public and Private Opinion." *Long Range Planning,* vol. 4 (August 1981): 90–105.

Knight, Kenneth E., and Helen R. Baca. "The Role of Government in Industrial Innovation." *Long Range Planning,* vol. 11 (December 1978): 79–88.

Lambright, W. Henry, and Paul J. Flynn. "Bureaucratic Policies and Technological Change in Local Government." *Journal of Urban Analysis,* vol. 4 (1977): 93–118.

Lambright, W. Henry. "Preparing Public Managers for the Technological Issues of the 1980's." *Public Administration Review,* vol. 41, no. 4 (July/August 1981): 410–17.

Lenz, R.T., and Marjorie A. Lyles. "Tackling the Human Problems in Planning." *Long Range Planning,* vol. 14, no. 2 (April 1981): 72–77.

Lientz, Bennet P., and Myles Chin. "Long Range Planning for Information Services." *Long Range Planning,* vol. 13 (February 1980): 55–61.

Lientz, Bennet, and Myles Chin. "Assessing the Impact of New Technology in

Information Systems." *Long Range Planning,* vol. 14, no. 6 (December 1981): 44–50.

Linstone, H. "The Multiple Perspective Concept." *Technological Forecasting and Social Change,* vol. 20 (1981): 275–325.

Linneman, Robert E., and Harold E. Klein. "The Use of Multiple Scenarios by U.S. Industrial Companies." *Long Range Planning,* vol. 12 (February 1979): 83–90.

Mackintosh, I.M. "Integrated Circuits: The Coming Battle." *Long Range Planning,* vol. 12 (June 1979): 28–37.

Mandelbaum, Seymour J. "A Complete General Theory of Planning Is Impossible." *Policy Sciences,* vol. 11, no. 1 (1979): 59–71.

Marsh, Robert M., and Hiroshi Mannari. "Technology and Size as Determinants of Organizational Structure of Japanese Factories." *Administrative Science Quarterly,* vol. 26, no. 1 (March 1981): 33–57.

Maruyama, Magoroh. "New Mindscapes for Future Business Policy and Management." *Technological Forecasting and Social Change,* vol. 21, no. 1 (March 1982): 53–76.

McGowan, Robert P., and Stephen Loveless. "Strategies for Informative Management: The Administrator's Perspective." *Public Administration Review,* vol. 41, no. 3 (May/June 1981): 331–39.

Miller, David K. "Simulation as a Tool for Developing Explanations of Aggregate Social Behavior." *Journal of Interdisciplinary Modeling and Simulation,* vol. 1, no. 2 (1978): 179–95.

Mitchell, Arnold, and Christine MacNulty. "Changing Values and Lifestyles." *Long Range Planning,* vol. 14, no. 2 (April 1981): 37–41.

Mitroff, I., J. Emshoff, and R. Kilmann. "Assumption Analysis: A Method for Strategic Problem Solving." *Management Science,* vol. 25 (1979): 583–93.

Morris, G.K. "The Use of Futures Research in Product Planning." *Long Range Planning,* vol. 15, no. 6 (December 1982): 67–73.

Morris, G.K. "The Use of Futures Research in Product Planning." *Long Range Planning,* vol. 8, no. 3 (June 1975): 64–71.

Moss, Allan. "Developing a Manpower Strategy for an Industry." *Long Range Planning,* vol. 13 (June 1980): 69–90.

Naylor, Thomas H., and M. James Mansfield. "The Design of Computer Based Planning and Modeling Systems." *Long Range Planning,* vol. 10 (February 1977): 16–25.

Nelkin, Dorothy. "Some Social and Political Dimensions of Nuclear Power: Examples from Three Mile Island." *American Political Science Review,* vol. 75, no. 1 (March 1981): 132–42.

Newgren, Kenneth E., and Archie B. Carroll. "Social Forecasting in U.S. Corporations—A Survey." *Long Range Planning,* vol. 12 (August 1979): 59–64.

Nutt, A.B., and R.C. Lenz, Jr., H.W. Lanford, and M.J. Cleary. "Data Sources for Trend Exploration in Technological Forecasting." *Long Range Planning,* vol. 9, no. 1 (February 1976): 72–76.

Nutt, P. "Hybrid Planning Methods." *Academy of Management Review,* vol. 7 (1982): 442–54.

Oral, Muhittin, Nuknet Yetis, and Riza Uygur. "Participatory Planning of Industrial R&D Activities." *Technological Forecasting and Social Change,* vol. 19, no. 3 (May 1981): 265–77.

Orishimo, I. "On Systems of Cities—An Approach to Central Place Theory." *Annals of Regional Science,* vol. X, no. 1 (March 1976): 16–28.

Otway, Harry J., and Detlof von Winterfeldt. "Beyond Acceptable Risk: On the Social Acceptability of Technologies." *Policy Sciences,* vol. 14, no. 3 (June 1982): 247–56.

Perry, James L. "Cooperation in Intergovernmental Networks and the Diffusion and Transfer of Computer Applications." *Journal of Urban Analysis,* vol. 5 (1978): 111–29.

Perry, James, and Kenneth Kraemer. "Innovation Attributes, Policy Intervention, and Diffusion of Computer Applications Among Local Governments." *Policy Sciences,* vol. 9, no. 2 (April 1978): 179–205.

Post, James E., Edwin A. Murray, Jr., Robert B. Dickie, and John F. Mahon. "The Public Affairs Function in American Corporations: Development and Relations with Corporate Planning." *Long Range Planning:* vol. 15, no. 2 (1982): 12–21.

Preble, John F. "Future Forecasting with LEAP." *Long Range Planning,* vol. 15, no. 4 (1982): 64–69.

Punt, Tom. "Social Trends and Corporate Plans." *Long Range Planning:* vol. 9, no. 5 (October 1976): 7–11.

Renas, Stephen, and Rishi Kumar. "The Cost of Living, Labor Market Opportunities, and the Migratory Decision: A Case of Misspecification?" *Annals of Regional Science,* vol. XII, no. 2 (July 1978): 95–104.

Rescher, Nicholas. "Methodological Issues in Science and Technological Forecasting: Uses and Limitations in Public Policy Deliberations." *Technological Forecasting and Social Change,* vol. 20, no. 2 (September 1981): 101–12.

Rondinelli, Dennis A. "Public Planning and Political Strategy." *Long Range Planning,* vol. 9, no. 2 (April 1976): 75–82.

Rowan, Brian. "Organizational Structure and the Institutional Environment: The Case of Public Schools." *Administrative Science Quarterly,* vol. 27, no. 2 (June 1982): 259–79.

Savas, E.S. "Municipal Monopolies vs. Competition in Delivering Urban Services." *Journal of Urban Analysis,* vol. 2 (1974): 93–116.

Schooler, Dean. "Political Directions and the Non-Profit Sector: Elements of an Integrated Comprehensive Agenda." *Policy Studies Journal,* vol. 11, no. 3 (March 1983): 436–44.

Sebenius, J.K. "The Computer as Mediator: Law of the Sea and Beyond." *Journal of Policy Analysis and Management,* vol. 1, no. 1 (1981): 77–95.

Skolimowski, Henry K. "Technology Assessment in a Sharp Social Focus." *Technological Forecasting and Social Change,* vol. 8, no. 4 (1976): 421–25.

Slatter, Stewart St. P. "Strategic Planning for Public Relations." *Long Range Planning,* vol. 13 (June 1980): 57–60.

Smit, Jan de and N.L. Rade. "Rational and Non-Rational Planning." *Long Range Planning,* vol. 13 (April 1980): 87–101.

Sproule-Jones, Mark. "Public Choice Theory and Natural Resources: Methodological Explication and Critique." *American Political Science Review,* vol. 76, no. 4 (December 1982): 790–804.

Thomas, D.W., and C.D. Johnson. "Application of Disturbance-Accommodation Control to Some Economic Problems." *Journal of Interdisciplinary Modeling and Simulation,* vol. 3, no. 1 (1980): 83–118.

Vargish, Thomas. "Why the Person Sitting Next to You Hates Limits to Growth." *Technological Forecasting and Social Change,* vol. 16, no. 3 (March 1980): 179–89.

Vichas, Robert P., and Kimon Constas. "Public Planners and Business Investors: Why Can't They Collaborate?" *Long Range Planning,* vol. 14, no. 3 (June 1981): 77–84.

Wagner, G.R. "Strategic Thinking Supported by Risk Analysis." *Long Range Planning,* vol. 13 (June 1980): 61–68.

Ward, E. Peter. "Organization for Technological Change." *Long Range Planning,* vol. 14, no. 4 (August 1981): 121–28.

Ward, E. Peter. "Planning for Technological Innovation—Developing the Necessary Nerve." *Long Range Planning,* vol. 14, no. 2 (April 1981): 59–71.

Ward, E. Peter. "Focusing Innovation Effort Through a Convergent Dialog." *Long Range Planning,* vol. 13 (December 1980): 32–41.

Weihrich, Heinz. "The TOWS Matrix—A Tool for Situational Analysis." *Long Range Planning,* vol. 15, no. 2 (April 1982): 54–66.

White, Irvin L. "An Interdisciplinary Approach to Applied Policy Analysis." *Technological Forecasting and Social Change,* vol. 15, no. 2 (October 1979): 95–106.

White, Irvin L., Steven C. Ballard, and Timothy A. Hall. "Technology Assessment as an Energy Policy Tool." *Policy Studies Journal,* vol. 7, no. 1 (Autumn 1978): 76–83.

Williams, D. Glyn, and D. John Harris. "Corporate Management and Planning in Local Government." *Long Range Planning,* vol. 9, no. 4 (August 1976): 45–51.

Appendix C: Contributors' Biographical Summaries

Charles Barr is research associate with the Information Science Program and the Mental Health Research Institute of the University of Michigan. He has done graduate study in natural resource planning and policy analysis and has worked for nonprofit environmental organizations and in management science research with an emphasis on information systems development. He is participating in the development of the sociotechnical systems area of the Urban, Technological, and Environmental Planning program at the University of Michigan.

Domenic Bitondo was associated with the Bendix Corporation for eighteen years, including duties as the executive Director of Corporate Research and Development. He developed the methodology and process for the strategic planning of research and development, first at the laboratory and then for the corporation. He is currently president of Bitondo Associates and also teaches technological planning at the University of Michigan. In addition, he has conducted numerous workshops in technological planning at several universities.

Jonathan William Bulkley is professor of natural resources in the School of Natural Resources and also a professor of Civil Engineering within the College of Engineering at the University of Michigan. In addition, he was appointed both as vice-chairman of the Michigan Environmental Review Board and special master and monitor in Civil Action 77-1100 (the Detroit Waterwaste Treatment Plant Case). His research and teaching activities are in the areas of water policy, multiobjective planning and programming, and risk–benefit assessment.

Barry Checkoway is associate professor of social work at the University of Michigan. He previously taught urban and regional planning at the University of Illinois at Urbana-Champaign and the University of California

209

at Berkeley. His work on urban social policy planning, citizen participation, and community organization has been published in national and international journals. His edited works include books on citizen participation in health care, policy problems in the metropolitan Midwest, and strategic perspectives on planning practice.

Kan Chen is professor of electrical engineering and computer science, and also the director of the Ph.D. program in Urban, Technological, and Environmental Planning at the University of Michigan. Dr. Chen directed systems research programs at Westinghouse Electric Corporation and at the Stanford Research Institute before joining the faculty at Michigan in 1971. Professor Chen is currently teaching and conducting interdisciplinary research in technology planning and assessment, social decision making, and computer integrated manufacturing systems. He is a fellow of IEEE and AAAS.

Milan J. Dluhy is associate professor of social work and adjunct associate professor of political science at the University of Michigan. Professor Dluhy has held various policy and administrative positions with the United States Department of Health, Education and Welfare, and in the states of Michigan and Illinois. He is the author of a number of books and numerous articles in the areas of social policy, aging, and housing.

Stuart L. Hart is currently project director at the Institute for Social Research at the University of Michigan. He is also adjunct assistant professor in the Department of Industrial and Operations Engineering and lecturer in psychology. His research in the areas of impact assessment, group decision making, strategic problem solving, and technological innovation have been published widely in both books and journal articles. His current interests include studies of how new technology-based organizations and industry-university relationships can serve to facilitate regional economic development. He is also working with The Netherlands government in establishing a national program in technology planning.

Margrit Hugentobler is a doctoral student in the Ph.D. program in Urban, Technological, and Environmental Planning at the University of Michigan. Her dissertation explores the dynamics of recent technological changes in the printing industry in Switzerland, reflecting her current interest in the quality of worklife in the manufacturing and printing industry. Her previous work experience is in action-research and participatory planning with senior citizens, including a variety of community organization projects with parent groups, adolescents, and consumer advocacy groups.

Kenan Patrick Jarboe is an industrial policy and strategic planning consultant in Washington, D.C. He received his doctorate from the University of Michigan's Ph.D. program in Urban, Technological, and Environmental Planning, with speciality in sociotechnical planning. Dr. Jarboe has consulted for numerous groups including the Congressional Office of Technological Assessment. In addition he has taught business at the University of Maryland and at George Washington University.

Manfred Kochen joined the IBM Research Center where he was manager of the Information Retrieval Project. He has been with the University of Michigan since 1965 and is now a professor of information science. He is affiliated with the university's medical school as a scientist in the Mental Health Research Institute and is also a professor in the Department of Psychiatry. He is also an adjunct professor of computer and information systems in the Graduate School of Business Administration and an affiliate with the Ph.D. program in Urban, Technological, and Environmental Planning. He has authored over 250 publications including eight books, 160 technical articles, and numerous reviews.

J. C. Mathes is a specialist in technical and management communications, and also is active in social systems research. He is a professor of technical communication in the College of Engineering at the University of Michigan and a member of the Ph.D. Program in Urban, Technological, and Environmental Planning. His numerous articles include several on social decision analysis with Kan Chen and Kenan Jarboe, and he is the author of six books. He has participated in research projects on the Mekong River Basin and the Gambia River Basin. He heads a program to certify Japanese managers, engineers, and technical writers in technical communication in English, in cooperation with the Japanese Association for Technical Communication.

Jack Rothman is professor at the School of Social Welfare, UCLA, where he heads the Macro Practice Program. He previously served on the faculty at the University of Michigan for 22 years. He has been a researcher, teacher, and practitioner in the human services for over 30 years. A continuing theme in his work has been the systematic application of social science knowledge to contemporary issues of policy and practice. He is the author of

13 books. His main areas of writing have included community organization, organizational innovation and change, and race and ethnic relations. He has been a recipient of the Gunnar Myrdal Award for Distinguished Research in Human Services of the Evaluation Research Society.

Index